WOMEN'S WORK AND WAGES

BIRMINGHAM WOOD CHOPPERS.

Frontispiece.]

A GARLAND SERIES

THE ENGLISH
WORKING CLASS

A Collection of
Thirty Important Titles
That Document and Analyze
Working-Class Life before
the First World War

Edited by
STANDISH MEACHAM
University of Texas

Women's Work and Wages

Edward Cadbury
M. Cécile Matheson
George Shann

Garland Publishing, Inc.
New York & London
1980

For a complete list of the titles in this series,
see the final pages of this volume.

The volumes in this series are printed on acid-free,
250-year-life paper.

This facsimile has been made from a copy in
the Yale University Library.

Library of Congress Cataloging in Publication Data

Cadbury, Edward.
Women's work and wages.

(The English working class)
Reprint of the 1906 ed. published by T. Fisher Unwin, London.
1. Women—Employment—England—Birmingham.
2. Wages—Women—England—Birmingham.   3. Labor and
laboring classes—England—Birmingham.   I. Matheson,
Marie Cécile, joint author.   II. Shann, George, 1846—
joint author.   III. Title.   IV. Series: English
working class.
HD6136.Z6B573   1980   331.4'09424'96   79-56954
ISBN 0-8240-0108-7

Printed in the United States of America

WOMEN'S WORK AND WAGES

A PHASE OF LIFE IN AN INDUSTRIAL CITY

EDWARD CADBURY

M. CÉCILE MATHESON

AND

GEORGE SHANN, M.A.

LONDON: T. FISHER UNWIN
ADELPHI TERRACE · MCMVI

THIS WORK

IS DEDICATED TO

MRS. EDWARD CADBURY,

WHOSE SYMPATHY, HELP, AND CRITICISM

THE AUTHORS GRATEFULLY

ACKNOWLEDGE

BIRMINGHAM

Thou mighty city! stretching toil-worn hands
To grasp the sweet green pastures at thy sides;
Defiling with thy breath the pleasant lands,
Building great factories, filled with surging tides
Of men and women, toiling for their bread;
What dost thou gain by all this strife for gold?
Spite of thy wealth, the grey and skull-like head
Of Poverty is seen within thy fold:
The "Workshop of the World" men call thy name,
And thou art proud to own thy title great;
Be heedful lest thy wealth become thy shame,
Scarr'd by the sin and misery in thy gate.
Though "Forward" be the watchword of thy town,
"Upward" would be its Glory and its Crown.

ALICE D. BRAHAM.

CONTENTS

———◆◆———

IMPROVEMENTS—PRESENT AND POSSIBLE

APPENDICES

ILLUSTRATIONS.

INTRODUCTION

———❦———

THERE is a growing demand at the present time for a scientific method by which we may attack what is called, more or less vaguely, the Social Problem, and more and more reformers and philanthropists see that before any lasting advance on the lines of "What ought to be" can be made, we must have a clear and systematised knowledge of "What is." Amongst the regions that are being explored is the field of Women's Work and Wages. Till the last few years, in their attempt to formulate a scientific explanation of the economic position of working women and the attendant complex problems, and also in their attempt to point out in what direction reformers and philanthropists could best work toward the amelioration of the many undoubted abuses connected with women's work, economists have felt hampered because so little has been done by investigators in this important branch of our industrial system, and therefore accurate knowledge of the actual facts has largely been absent.

The present inquiry has aimed at systematising

and offering in a comprehensive form, for the purposes of the general reader and the social worker amongst women, the valuable work done recently by various writers and associations, and to this end the present writers have taken full and free advantage of the work done by others in this field.

At the same time a great deal of original investigation, extending over a period of three and a half years, has been done, and we offer no conclusions except those which our own inquiry bears out. We have also entered fields never before explored as far as we know, and some old phases of the question are looked at from a new point of view.

As will be seen in the following pages, the investigators have endeavoured—

1. In one large city to give a complete survey of the conditions under which women are earning their livelihood at the beginning of the twentieth century;

2. To provide some definite standard of comparison so that future investigators may be able to ascertain what progress has been made toward the improvement of these conditions;

3. To ascertain to what extent the present industrial and social conditions are helping forward or retarding the physical, mental, and moral condition of the workers; and

4. To indicate upon what lines they think reformers will obtain the best results in their attempt to raise and brighten the lives of those who are the future mothers of our race.

The method of work has been "intensive," an attempt being made to investigate the conditions holding in the one city of Birmingham. This city has peculiar difficulties as well as special interest owing to the fact that it has a large number of trades divided as a rule amongst very many small firms, and so is different from a textile town with a staple trade in the hands of a limited number of large firms.

The writers have taken every precaution to make the results offered accurate, and above all impartial, and are not concerned to support any particular theory. The training and outlook of the three investigators told for an impartial treatment. One writer has been for several years in the position of a managing director of a firm employing between two and three thousand girls, this position giving him exceptional opportunities of becoming intimately associated with every phase of their work, and of experimenting with some of the practical problems which are discussed in the following pages. He has also become acquainted with the workers' point of view by being directly associated with several movements for the social betterment of working men. Another writer worked as a factory hand from ten years of age until he went to Glasgow University for six years' training, at the end of which time he graduated with First Class Honours in Economic Science. This writer was also Warden of Glasgow University Settlement, and has had a long experience in practical social work amongst working men and women. The third writer has been intimately associated with Girls' Clubs, has acted as a school manager in London, and has conducted for the

Board of Education inquiries into the provision of technical education for girls at home and abroad.

We have obtained information chiefly from four sources :—

1. Personal interviews with upwards of six thousand working women ;

2. Interviews with upwards of four hundred Trade Union secretaries, managers, and foremen of works employing women ;

3. Interviews with employers ; and

4. Interviews and correspondence with the members and officers of girls' clubs and Girls' Friendly Society branches, and interviews with clergymen, school attendance officers, and with the members of various philanthropic agencies ; also by the help of some well-known social workers in Birmingham.

The evidence thus collected has been carefully sifted and checked.

The first stage of the work was beset with difficulties, and as far as we know this is the first time that information has been so largely gained from the workers themselves. The girls are naturally averse to revealing their private affairs, and often even a girl's mother has no definite knowledge of the exact wages earned by the girl. The girls were also nervous lest through giving information they should get into trouble with their employers. They were often suspicious as to the motives of the inquirer. After a most careful explanation of the aim of the investigator one would hear such remarks as, " What cheek to ask us what we earn." " They are going to take our answers to the masters to get our wages lowered."

If reserve and suspicion could be broken down there was no further trouble. It was generally found that the girls could not be induced to answer questions on the ground of any possible advantage to themselves, as the almost invariable answer was, if too polite to refuse abruptly, " I am quite satisfied, thank you." When it was made clear that a knowledge of these satisfactory conditions might benefit other poorer and less fortunate girls they were often ready to give information.

Of course there is often the risk of deception or inaccuracy, but if the inquiry be made on a sufficiently broad basis the answers given by different girls and at different times check each other, and we find that our cards show very little variation. Then we had the further check of information got from the other sources.

The work is not so complete as we hoped to make it, but it was thought advisable to issue the results without further delay. If it helps to systematise the ideas of a few readers, and indicates the problems arising from the present conditions of women's work and wages, the writers will consider their time well spent.

WOMEN'S WORK

CHAPTER I

LEGISLATION

DURING the last few years considerable attention has been given to the consideration of the
economic effect of factory legislation, particularly in
regard to women's work and wages. It had long
been evident to serious economic students and
social reformers that careful and detailed investigation into the actual facts and conditions of women's
work was necessary before the various problems
peculiar to women's work and wages could be discussed in any satisfactory manner. The lack of
detailed and accurate information with regard to
actual conditions allowed much loose reasoning, and
facts were made to suit any particular theory.

About the year 1874 two diverse points of view
in regard to legislation and women's work were
evident, and the upholders of both professed themselves concerned for the welfare of the women
workers. When the Act of 1874 was before Parliament an amendment was moved to exclude women
altogether from the operations of the Act, and the
Women's Rights party asserted that the aim of

the men's unions in advocating the further extension
of factory legislation in regard to women, was to
restrict by law the conditions of women's work,
so that they would be excluded from employment
altogether.

Since that time a great deal has been written
and said on both sides of the question. But it is
evident that such problems cannot be settled by any
a priori method, and therefore, the object of this
inquiry has been to collaborate with the recent efforts
to gain the necessary precise information from all
possible sources, and thereby amass a collection
of accurate statements of fact. A position may then
be gained from which to consider proposed legislation
affecting women's work.

The law relating to Factories and Workshops was
consolidated in the Factories and Workshops Act
1901, and now not only are the con-
History.   ditions of the employment of women
and children regulated by law, but the regulations
also extend in many ways to the employment
of men. Even at the start of State interference,
factory legislation was not devised specially for
women. From the beginning of the nineteenth
century numerous statutes have been passed—the
first, in 1802, aiming at the preservation of the health
and morals of apprentices and others. The demoralising conditions out of which the demand for
this Act sprang are too well known to need repeti-
tion here, but it is interesting to note that the Birmingham justices anticipated the Act and refused to
apprentice children to cotton mills, thus showing the

beginning of that enlightened sympathy which has never been altogether wanting in Birmingham in the years that have followed since.[1]

In 1819 another Act was necessary to regulate the long hours of children's work, and the employment of children under nine years of age was prohibited in cotton mills, and the long hours of children above this age were limited to twelve.

In 1825 young persons up to the age of sixteen were included under the scope of the Act, and were not allowed to work more than twelve hours a day. The Act of 1831 extended these restrictions to all persons under eighteen, and no girls under twenty-one were allowed to do night work. The next step taken extended the Factory Acts to all textile industries, and children under thirteen were not to be employed more than eight hours a day, and those from thirteen to eighteen years of age not more than twelve hours a day.

Up to this time the women above eighteen could work any number of hours, and so the manufacturers, restricted as to the employment of girls under eighteen, turned to the labour of women and girls above eighteen; and many under eighteen were illegally worked more than twelve hours a day. Some factories were systematically run more than twelve hours a day. The resulting evils led to the Act of 1844, which included women in textile factories in regard to hours under those restrictions that had previously been applied only to young persons.

[1] See Report of Peel's Committee, H. C., 1816, III.

The motives that led different people to urge the passing of this Act were various. Some looked at the matter from a humanitarian and sentimental point of view, for they felt that the weakness of women called for protection. On the other hand, many of the working men knew that the division of labour which resulted in men and women working at different processes in the same shop, and even on the same articles, of necessity would mean that any limitations of the hours of women would also affect, directly or indirectly, the hours of the men.

The results of this pressure from different sources was the Ten Hours' Act of 1847, with Acts completing and amending it in 1850 and 1853. These amending Acts lengthened the day to ten and a half hours, but stipulated for a "normal" day. This rendered the enforcement of the Act much easier.

Another series of Acts resulted in the Factory Acts' Extension Act and the Workshops' Regulation Act, which made the Acts apply practically to all manufacturing processes carried on for purposes of trade and gain, whether in factories or workshops.

It is interesting at this point to note the attitude of certain manufacturers in Birmingham towards legislation. An earthenware manufacturer states in 1867 that, although the great majority of the earthenware manufacturers had been opposed to the last Act when it was introduced, after their experience of the Act nineteen-twentieths would be unwilling for it to become obsolete.[1] In some cases manufacturers voluntarily anticipated the regulations of the Act in

[1] *Birmingham Daily Post*, March 19, 1867.

regard to hours, &c.[1]   Of course there was opposition
on the part of small masters, and certain differences
which the Act made between small and large shops
were attacked by large employers, who asserted that
the regulations pressed more heavily upon them
than upon small masters.   Thus a meeting of manufacturers was held at the Birmingham Chamber of
Commerce, March 18, 1867, opposing the division of
workplaces into factories and workshops, and asking
for a uniform system.[2]

Again, in the Report of the British Association
Meeting at Birmingham, 1865, Ephraim Bull, reporting on the Nail and Chain Trades, said: " In several
districts around Dudley, Halesowen, Cradley, &c., a
large number of men, women, and children are engaged in the manufacture of chains of every description ; large quantities of cheap American traces, &c.,
are made by women and children at very low wages,
hence of inferior quality.   Also large quantities of
other chains of very inferior quality have been manu-
factured, which the new Act of Parliament relating
to chain cables will no doubt remedy, and a more
healthy trade be established for first-class goods."[3]
In another place in the same Report another writer,
speaking of the Brass Trade, said: "Thus the
system of female labour and juvenile employment,
fostered by ignorance and competition, has grown

---

[1] " History of Factory Legislation," p. 159.

[2] *Birmingham Daily Post*, March 15, 1867, and March 19,
1867.

[3] Birmingham and Midland Hardware District (1865),
p. 116.

and is increasing, resulting in the neglect of the preparation for household duties and the attractions of
a home. 'Many of the children die, the mothers
become familiarised with the fact, and speak of the
deaths of their children with a degree of *nonchalance*
rarely met with among women who devote themselves mainly to the care of their offspring'; and
these are the mothers who deliver over the child of
six or seven years to the foreman or other operatives
for a paltry sum of 1s. 6d. to 2s. per week—the price
of childhood neglected and natural affection lost.
Liberty not infrequently means licence, and legisla-
tive interference is frequently uncalled for; but in
the wholesale employment of female and juvenile
labour, it is surely justifiable to place some limits on
such degrading work. Legislation has borne good
fruit as regards other industries, and a little wholesome interference would be productive of much
good. . . ." [1] These extracts show an enlightened
interest in, and understanding of, factory legislation.

But certain sections of the people took an entirely
opposite view, for in 1874, when an Act was passed
which restricted the hours of women and children in
textile industries to ten hours a day, as we have
noted above, the Women's Rights' movement became
prominent, and in the House of Commons an amendment was moved to altogether exclude women from
the operations of the Act. The idea behind this
movement was that any special restrictions on
women's work would handicap them in competition

[1] Birmingham and Midland Hardware District (1865),
p. 366.

for a place in the industrial world, and that the men were fully aware of this probable result when they pressed for the limitation of the hours of women and young persons to ten a day. As a matter of fact the object of the men was to secure the limitation of their own hours of work by limiting through Act of Parliament the hours of the women.

Thus the Commission of 1876 had no excuse if they failed to see both sides of the question. " Mr. Joseph Chamberlain and Mr. Arthur Chamberlain, both Birmingham manufacturers in a large way of business, gave evidence, the one in favour of, the other against, the regulation of women's labour by law, the one demonstrating that the economic position of women was thereby improved and the demand for their labour increased ; the other that their wages had risen little if at all, and that ' if there were no restrictions women now getting their 8s. or 9s. would get 30s.' " [1]

This opposition movement was even stronger in 1878, and amendments were moved to omit women from the scope of the clauses of the Consolidation Bill. This movement was so far successful that, although these amendments were not admitted as far as factories and ordinary workshops were concerned, where both women and young persons were employed, yet in places where no young persons were employed less restricted arrangements were

[1] " History of Factory Legislation," p. 190 (H. C., 1876, XXIX.). Minutes of Evidence, Mr. J. Chamberlain's evidence, Q. 5,249, &c. Mr. A. Chamberlain's evidence, Q. 4,954, &c.

permitted. A woman might work for ten and half hours per day, and these hours could be taken between the hours of 6 a.m. and 9 p.m. In the case of domestic workshops—that is, private houses, places, or rooms where no power was used, and in which the only persons employed were members of the same family dwelling there—the word woman was omitted altogether, with results that are now evident. As Miss Amy Hutchinson points out in her valuable report on women's work in Liverpool, "the Report of the Select Committee on the Sweating System showed that all the evils characteristic of that system, namely, long hours, low wages, and insanitary conditions, were to be found in their most aggravated form in those classes of workshop to which special exemptions had been granted in 1878 —namely, in women's workshops and domestic workshops."

This statement applies especially to Birmingham, the characteristic of which is the great number of small employers, and although attention was paid to the matter by the City Council and Factory Inspectors, the greatest difficulty was found in locating the small workshops, dwelling rooms, and garrets in which work was carried on.[1]

Having now briefly traced the history of factory

[1] " History of Factory Legislation," p. 237. Also see Fourth Report, Sweating System. Evidence given by Alderman Cook, Chairman of the Health Committee of the Birmingham City Council (Q. 27,547, &c.), and by Mr. Knyvett, Factory Inspector (Q. 27,602, &c.), before Select Committee of the House of Lords, 1889.

legislation, we may go on to consider the facts
revealed by our inquiry as to the economic effects of
this legislation on women's work in Birmingham.
In closing this section we may with advantage give
the summary of the principal regulations in force at
the present time, which is given in the Report of the
British Association, 1903 : " In *textile* factories the
hours of women were limited in 1850 to a period of
12 hours, less 1½ hours for mealtimes on the first
5 working days, and to 7½ hours on Saturday,
amounting to 60 hours per week. In 1874, ½ hour
was cut off each of the 5 days and 1 hour off Saturday, making the total hours per week 56½ ; on
January 1, 1902, another hour was cut off Saturday,
making the total hours 55½. Regulations of women's
hours, resulting by 1878 in a uniform 60 hours' week
as legal maximum (viz., not more than 10½ hours on
5 days, to be taken in the 12 hours beginning either
at 6 or 7 or 8 a.m., and 7½ hours on the sixth day),
were extended in 1864, 1867, 1870, and 1878 succes-
sively, to all *non-textile* factories in which mechanical
power is used, and *workshops* where manual labour is
employed in making, repairing, or altering any
article for sale. In addition to these hours, overtime is allowed under certain restrictions in certain
industries (notably bookbinding and the making of
wearing apparel), where there is a seasonal or sudden
occasional pressure, or where the materials are liable
to spoil, *e.g.*, fruit preserving and fish curing ; before
1895 overtime might be worked for 48 evenings in
the year, 2 hours an evening, less ½ hour for meals,
not more than 5 evenings being in any one week ; in

1895 the number of evenings permissible was reduced to 30, not more than 3 in 1 week.

" As each industry came under the Act night work by women in it was prohibited, except in the case of *laundries.*

" There are many modifications to suit special circumstances, and some important exceptions."

The Commission on Children's Employment, 1862–1866, gives valuable information as to the conditions

General Conditions of Work in Birmingham prior to 1860.

of work in Birmingham at that time. Abuses of all kinds were prevalent, and even where legislation had been introduced it was often violated. In the Report on Percussion Cap manufacture,[1] the Report said "That such provisions " (*i.e.*, general regulations for ameliorating the awful conditions of work) " are specially needed in Birmingham is clear from Mr. White's description of the buildings there in which these dangerous processes have been carried on, the defective arrangements of which have occasioned so much loss of life and no small amount of bodily injury and suffering. Mr. White (Assistant Commissioner) states that the four factories in Birmingham are merely adaptations of private houses, in crowded streets, and the necessary space is obtained only by throwing out small workshops and narrow galleries in the yards at the back. The result, also, in addition to the danger of explosions, is that the working rooms are nearly all cramped, low and ill-ventilated, and without other suitable

[1] Children's Employment Commission (1862), First Report of the Commissioners, p. lvii.

provision for the comfort of those employed." And
in regard to the condition of workplaces generally
the Report says, " This is very various.   Many workplaces, including some of the establishments of the
highest standing in Birmingham, are in one or more
parts very deficient in space, ventilation, light, and,
perhaps in consequence of this, in cleanliness.   The
passages are sometimes almost entirely dark, and the
ladder steps, by which the shops are reached, often
steep and dangerous.   This arises, no doubt, chiefly
from factories having grown from small beginnings
in crowded places, where adequate extension on the
spot is impossible or difficult, and removal may, for
several reasons, be inconvenient.   Many seem merely
adaptations of common street houses." [1]   Also the
following : " The gloominess of many of the workplaces is extreme.   In some, as casting and many
stamping shops, good light is not essential to the
work.   Where it is essential it is generally got by
working close in front of the windows.   Some of the
stamping shops, placed on the ground floor on
account probably of the shocks of the stamps, are
half cellars, and most are extremely dark and untidy,
and seem likely to be damp in winter, at least in the
pits which are often sunk for the workers to stand
in, as a means of gaining height for the fall of the
stamp; the soil, however, of Birmingham is dry, and
in a great measure drains itself.   Some places depend
for much of their light upon the furnaces, and after
dark the nailers have no light but that of their forge

[1] Children's Employment Commission (1862), Third Report
of the Commissioners, p. 53.

and the hot iron." [1] " A full account of the jewellers'
factories, usually spoken of as the closest workplaces
in Birmingham, with details as to cubic space, is
given in the Privy Council Report, which speaks of
some of them as amongst the very worst arranged
factories in Birmingham, and of several of the shops
in the best as close and very hot when visited early
in the forenoon, every aperture for the admission or
exit of air, though plentifully provided, being carefully closed, and nearly all the operatives burning
gas for the blowpipe ; though the most crowded of
these (best) shops, containing from 150 to 170 persons, chiefly women and girls, gave on the average
upwards of 300 cubical feet of space per head. In
another of like kind, and nearly as large, the atmosphere is described as oppressive and stifling, and the
operatives of pallid, unhealthy aspect, and the ample
means of ventilation practically useless, being all
closed. Indeed in most of the jewellers' factories
inspected the means of ventilation that existed are
described as for the most part closed up to prevent
draughts, and as a rule all insufficiently ventilated,
an evil greatly aggravated by the constant consumption of gas. No account is given of the temperature,
but in the Coventry watchmakers' shops, in which
gas is largely consumed after dusk, as each operative
requires a separate light, and though it is usual to
extinguish the fire in the stove as soon as the gas is
lit, the temperature of some is said to be as high as
80° on a winter's evening after the gas has been lit

[1] Children's Employment Commission (1862), Third Report
of the Commissioners, p. 54.

WORKSHOPS IN THE JEWELLERY DISTRICT, 1906.

To face page 30.]

for several hours. Jewellery workers require not only strong light but jets of gas for the blowpipe in addition, and are therefore exposed to a probably still higher temperature." [1] At the risk of wearying the reader we give another extract describing Percussion Cap manufacture. Public opinion has advanced a long way since such things were allowed. " The percussion cap manufacture, which is very limited in extent, there being but six manufactories in the kingdom, two in or near London, and four at Birmingham, is carried on mainly by female labour, including that of many young girls, and is perhaps the most dangerous of all general manufactures. The danger arises from the unavoidable use of highly explosive materials, in particular of fulminating mercury, one of the most violent substances known. It is, however, confined to the preparation and application of these materials, and ceases when they are distributed in single caps. The danger is plainly of a kind which reaches to all employed under the same roof, or in close neighbourhood, whether actually engaged in a process dangerous in itself or not. Five or six serious explosions have happened in Birmingham alone, one about three years since causing the loss of nineteen lives. The greater part of those who have suffered on these occasions have been young people." [2]

Hours of work were often excessive and night

---

[1] Children's Employment Commission (1862), Third Report of the Commissioners, p. 54.

[2] Ibid. (First Report) p. 105.

work was common. One girl stated [1] that she went
to work before she was eight years of
age, and that she worked from 8 a.m. to
7.30 p.m. At one place she stayed till
9.30. Another girl gave the following
evidence, which is corroborated by other girls from
the same shop: " Oh, my gracious ! we have been
here till 12 and 11 at night—till 10 and 11, and 12
usually, and I only wish the time would come again.
We have stayed till 10 and 11 for weeks and months
together. Can't get here before 8. Most in this
shop, viz., japanners and wrappers up, stayed, and
I'm compelled to stay to finish wrapping, &c. ; but in
other parts they would leave at 8 or 8½ or 9. It was
a great deal through so overworking himself that
master's illness was caused. We may work in
dinner-time once in a way. Lately, however, there
has not been full work, and there are only 30 or 40
now instead of near 80. Came here when I was 11
or 12, *i.e.*, 11 years ago. Most of those who stayed
late have left now." [2] Night work was adopted in
some works. The following is the evidence of Mary
Ann Stanley, age 14 : " Riddle screws in a sieve.
Have worked over 'most all the time I have been
here, six months till the last fortnight, but now a
girl comes at six and works through the night and I
leave. Was at Turner's steel pen factory in Birmingham. There were towards 200 girls, and the regular
hours from 7 a.m. to 8 p.m., with two hours for
meals ; never made any overtime." [3]

Hours previous to 1860. (margin)

[1] Children's Employment Commission (1862), Third Report,
p. 85.
[2] Ibid. (1862), p. 83.   [3] Ibid. p. 111.

The hours in some trades were comparatively short, viz., from 8 till 7. " In some cases the above stated hours of work " (8 to 7) " are scarcely ever exceeded ; in others not to any great extent, *i.e.*, to beyond 8 or 9 p.m. But an excess to this extent is by no means uncommon for the young of both sexes. Cases, however, of far longer hours, not isolated or accidental, but systematic and long continued, are shown to exist, amounting, in an extreme instance, to work by two boys regularly for six days and three nights weekly for six months, with no stoppage for sleep except what could be got in mealtimes. Other instances of systematic night, in addition to the ordinary amount of day, work are given. The trade in which there is said to be the greatest fluctuation of demand is naturally gun and sword work ; the latter, however, forming but a small trade in Birmingham. Some of the instances of longest night work of boys and girls were found in gun and sword making, metal rolling, edge tool making, iron works, tin-plate working, brassfoundry, painting and screw making." [1]

From the above account *re* hours of work prior to 1860, it is evident that the Acts of 1864 and 1867 introduced changes, and did not merely enforce what was customary before, although in one or two cases the Act was anticipated to some extent, as, *e.g.*, by Mr. Manton, a button manufacturer, who said : " We have for very many years employed from 400 to 500 people in the works. In 1865 we were so dissatisfied

[1] Children's Employment Commission (1862), Third Report of the Commissioners, p. 57.

with the general condition of our workpeople that we determined to apply voluntarily the conditions of the Factory Acts to our own manufacture. We did that two years before the law became applicable to Birmingham. The result was in every way beneficial to ourselves and to the workpeople." [1]

Under the Act of 1867 the maximum allowed was 60 hours per week, a period of 12 hours per day, less 1½ hours for mealtimes on the first 5 working days, and 7½ hours on Saturday. The great effect of this Act stipulating a normal day was to lessen irregularity rather than to lessen number of hours worked per week, for even before 1867 the hours of work in a week often would not exceed 60. The need for alteration was not so much due to the number of hours as to the irregularity of work. At times of pressure employers worked their employees any number of hours they pleased, and the irregular habits of the workpeople themselves often compelled employers to work long hours to make up for lost time.

On the whole, after experience of the working of the Act, little opposition on the part of masters or workpeople seems to have been offered to it, and in 1876 employers and employees, together with factory inspectors, admitted the benefit of the Act. The evidence given before the Commission of 1876 is instructive on this point. The evidence proves that generally the hours worked were less than the 56½ proposed by the new Act, though in many cases it

[1] Report of the Commissioners into the Working of the Factory and Workshop Acts, 1876, vol. ii. p. 240.

was suggested that it would be preferable to the employers if they could work an hour later in the evening, as the custom in Birmingham was to start late in the morning, and this could not be broken down. Women in some cases came to work as late as 9 a.m. Mr. Davis voices this opinion as a representative of the Brassworkers: "I should like to say that in our trade of brassworkers there are a very great many young people engaged, and also a great many females, but I suppose altogether in the trade there are about 20,000 hands employed. The lacquerers in our trade are in the habit of coming to work at 9 o'clock in the morning, or between half-past 8 and 9, and my opinion is that if we were to have a clause in the Act stating that they could work between 6 and 6, or 7 and 7, or 8 and 8, it would include everything that is desired. There are a great many married women engaged in that trade as lacquerers, and they find it very difficult for them to get to work before 9 o'clock in the morning, and if they cannot by law get to work before 8 o'clock, their situation is closed, and they cannot go to work at all. Therefore I think it would be better myself for a clause to be inserted giving power to the workpeople to work between the hours of 8 and 8, so that they could go at 9 o'clock in the morning and leave at 7 o'clock at night."[1] But in answer to the question as to whether Mr. Davis and the other representative, speaking for the people they represented, approved of the factory legislation generally, the

[1] Factory and Workshops Acts' Commission, Report of the Commissioners, vol. ii. p. 238.

answer was, "Yes, provided that it is kept within reasonable bounds." It was also elicited that those who worked in workshops and who did not come under the Act would gladly see the provisions of the Factory Act extended to them. Mr. Johnson, Sub-Inspector of Factories, corroborated [1] the above evidence as to hours being often less than the legal maximum for the week, though he had to prosecute for excessive hours being worked in large millinery establishments. He also pointed out that the tendency of the Acts was to shorten hours by making the people leave earlier than they would do.[2] But the manufacturers were quite satisfied with the shorter hours, as they found that they got just as much work done, and on the whole they did not consider themselves to be sufferers by legislation. Still Mr. Johnson considered that the legislation respecting hours was too vague, and should have the limits more sharply defined.

This witness did not think that the limitation of the hours of women would lead to the substitution of men for women, nor to any reduction of women's wages. He did not consider that there were many trades where men could be substituted for women, because of the nature of the work. This was an intelligent and true forecast of what has actually happened.

An opposite view was taken by some employers, notably in the button trade, that though in the past

[1] Factory and Workshops Acts' Commission, vol. ii. p. 205.
[2] See also evidence of Mr. Parker, Factory and Workshops Acts' Commission, vol. ii. p. 222, Q. 4,363–4,367.

no women had been displaced and the employers did not object to legislation so far as it had gone, yet any further restriction on the hours of women's labour would lead to their labour being displaced through loss of trade due to foreign competition.[1]

The conclusion seems to be that legislation has shortened hours by making women cease work earlier than they would have done, while they refused to start any earlier. Excessive irregularity of hours especially was stopped.

As regards the hours of men's work, legislation respecting women's work did not have much direct effect, since in most cases women's work is so well marked off from men's. They do not work together on the same job in the same way as in a textile factory. The evidence given before the Commission of 1876 shows that the men were more concerned about the hours of youths and boys than the hours of women and girls. As a matter of fact, however, where men and women are both employed they usually work the same hours, except of course in the case of overtime.

One effect of this restriction of hours was to increase outwork in the several trades which lent themselves to this form of work, and so far this tended to irregular work in another way.[2] Small factories especially adopted this way out of the difficulty in times of pressure. Large factories with more

[1] See also evidence of Mr. Parker, Factory and Workshops Acts' Commission, vol. ii. p. 224, Q. 4,395.

[2] Factory and Workshops Acts' Commission, vol. ii. p. 257, Q. 5,119–5,121.

space took on more girls in time of pressure and then
dismissed them when the press of the work was over.
This latter effect is seen at the present time, and now,
as then, such places as job printing firms complain
of the restrictions limiting overtime.   On the whole,
however, employers and employees are beginning to
recognise that overtime "does not pay."   "Loss of
overtime is not necessarily a loss of work, but a
redistribution (and an economical one, too) of the
times at which work is done, and does not therefore mean a loss of income, but a steadying and
regulation of income." [1]   And at the present time
outwork also is decreasing, but it must be remembered in this connection that we have had a long
depression in trade.   Still, apart from bad trade, the
larger employers dislike outwork.

Opposition to the limitation of hours comes from
some employers in the Cycle Trade, in which, during
the busy season, men and youths have to do the
women's work after the women have left.   One employer in the French Polishing Trade said the women
seldom worked beyond legal hours in his shop
because "it was not worth the risk"; he hinted,
however, that some employers in his line did evade
the law occasionally.

At the present time the hours seldom reach the
legal maximum, the majority of women working $52\frac{1}{2}$
hours or less per week.   In the Brass Trade, for
example, the hours vary with different shops from

[1] J. Ramsay Macdonald, "Women in the Printing Trades,"
p. 79.

48 to 54 ; in the Ammunition Trade from 47 to 54½ ;
Button making from 45 to 52½.

Legal overtime is worked in most trades when
occasion arises.

There is no doubt that the law in regard to hours
and overtime is sometimes evaded in small shops.

It is often stated by those who oppose regulation
of women's work by legislation that the effect of such
legislation is to displace women in favour
of men.   Our inquiry seems to prove,   **Men and**
                                          Women.
however, that this idea is erroneous, and
that in the large majority of cases, as we have pointed
out in the chapter on Wages, it is other questions
altogether that determine the division of labour
between men and women.   A great deal of light has
been thrown on the question of women's work and
wages generally by the elucidation of the fact that as
a rule men and women do different work, and the
relation between men and women workers is, on the
whole, that of two non-competing groups.   It is quite
true that that marginal division between the two
groups is continually shifting, but in the particular
trades where this is the case the questions considered
are the difference in wages [1] between the two groups,
their aptitude and physical fitness for certain work,
and the fact that women expect to leave work when
married.

In the following trades, through the introduction
of machinery for the most part, women have replaced
men :—

[1] Factory and Workshops Acts' Commission, vol. ii.   Evidence of J. Chamberlain, p. 267, Q. 5,310.

Brass Lathe Burnishing.
Chain Making.
Cycle Saddle Frame.
Enamel Saucepans, Piano Frames, &c.
Harness Stitching.
Gold and Silver Cheap Jewellery.
Spectacle and Eyeglass Grinding, &c.
Corset Fasteners.
Cycle Work.
Wood Box-making.
Wire Mattress Weaving.
Military Ornaments.
Layers-on in the Printing Trade.
Tailoring Trade.
Tin-plate, Press Stamping, &c.
Whip Trade.
Umbrella and Frame Building.
Bookbinding.
Brass Casters' Core Maker.

In the printing shops girls are taking the place of
boys as layers-on because boys refuse to do the work
that leads to nothing in the future.[1]

The effect of machinery with regard to the labour
of men and women seems to depend to some extent
on the heaviness and complexity or the simplicity
and lightness of the machine.   When the machine is
heavy men are minders, where the machine is light
women take charge.

Legislation, by restricting hours of work, in some

[1] The men in the trade welcome this development from a
Trade Union point of view. Previously lads would stay till
nineteen or twenty years of age, and some of them by moving
from shop to shop would at last "sneak" into the trade. The
presence of this half-skilled labour was a menace to the
Unions in times of dispute.

cases, led to the introduction of machinery, and thus indirectly displaced women at first. But the machine was bound to come, any way, and, as we have seen, the result of machinery on the whole has been to increase the field of women's work.

Legislation has little direct bearing on the question of women's wages, and the evidence gathered shows that it certainly does not depress them. **Wages.** Legislation has shortened hours, and as most of the work is done by piece-work, the total amount and quality of work done in shorter but more regular hours has actually increased. It was found very difficult to get any documentary evidence as to wages prior to 1860, but the following facts are interesting. In 1865 the wages of girls and women were :—

Trade.	1865.[1]		Present Wages.	
	Girls.	Women.	Girls.	Women.
Buttons.........	1s. to 1s. 6d.	7s. to 9s.	3s. 6d. to 10s.	6s. 6d. to 13s.
Saddlery	...	9s. and upwards.	4s. 6d. to 8s.	8s. to 20s.
Plated Wares	...	7s. to 20s.	4s. 6d. to 14s. 6d.	7s. to 18s.
Rope Making	...	6s. to 10s.	5s. 6d. to 6s.	6s. 6d. to 13s.
Hinges	...	5s. to 10s.	...	8s. to 10s. 6d.
Nails	...	6s. to 15s.	5s.	6s. to 12s.
Pens	...	5s. to 12s.	5s. to 10s.	7s. to 15s.
		Occasionally 20s.		
Fire-irons......	...	7s.	...	...
Leather Trade	...	7s.	4s. to 10s.	6s. to 20s.
Brass—				
Lacquerers	3s. to 5s.	8s. to 10s.	4s. to 9s.	6s. to 15s.
Wrappers up	...	8s. to 10s.	5s. 6d. to 7s.	7s. to 12s.
Piercers ...	3s. 6d. to 5s.	8s. to 12s.	4s. to 8s.	9s. to 13s.
Solderers ...	...	10s. to 12s.	4s. 6d. to 7s.	10s. to 12s.
Wirers	...	4s. to 8s.	...	...
Lamp Trade...	5s. to 7s. 6d.	10s. to 12s.	3s. 6d. to 9s.	6s. 6d. to 24s.

[1] Birmingham and District Hardware Trade, Hardwicke 1865.

The effect of legislation on general conditions of work is very marked in its good effects. Employers, foremen, and employees all agree almost without exception that sanitary arrangements and conveniences are much improved, though even yet further improvements are necessary, as in several shops separate sanitary convenience is not provided for men and women. In the Bedstead Trade there is now "more attention to ventilation, cleanliness, whitewashing," &c. But in the Cycle Saddle Trade it was suggested there was still much room for improvement. In the Harness Stitching Trade a committee of Trade Unionists who were interviewed said that in their trade "conditions were up to the average, but not very good." A foreman in the Iron-plate Trade said that twenty-five years ago conditions of work in his trade were very bad; there was no separate accommodation for men and women, and the shop used to be left in a very dirty condition; but changes for the better have now been made. A foreman in Tin-plate Works said, "Years ago the sanitary arrangements were an abomination, but everything now is up to date, and lavatories are provided where employees can get a wash."

General Conditions of Work.

Large employers in dangerous trades do not complain of these special rules, and in some instances take more precautions than the law compels; but small shops feel the restrictions very much, and evade them when possible. One girl who had worked at a large shop afterwards got work at a small shop, but stayed only

Special Rules for Dangerous Trades.

three weeks, as the conditions of work were so bad. The girl said it was a horrible place to work in, as there was nothing to protect the girls from inhaling the poisonous fumes arising from the burning of the enamel, which was done in the same room where the girls worked. The girls had to pass the material through a fine sieve, which filled the room with dust. This dust contained lead, which caused lead-poisoning, &c. The result upon the girls was to cause them to often fall down in a fainting condition. She felt her own health giving way, and so left after working there three weeks. No doctor or inspector visited the place while she was there.

The tendency of these Special Rules for Dangerous Trades is to displace small masters in favour of large firms. From the point of view of the community this is a distinct gain, as the standard of the conditions of the work thereby becomes better and more uniform. We were told of one or two cases where small shops had been closed altogether, while others had been able to build new and up-to-date premises. For information as to present conditions of work the reader is referred to Chapter II

CHAPTER II

GENERAL CONDITIONS OF WORK

Work regulated by the Factory Acts

IN the course of this inquiry more than one hundred trades and occupations have been investigated. Most of the trades are divided into a number of sub-divisions, each of which may rank as a separate trade in the eyes of the workers themselves.

Grouping.

It is obviously impossible to deal with every branch of work separately, but there are two ways of dividing the manual work of women into main groups.

The first is that adopted by the authorities of the Home Office in the Census returns. According to the Census of 1901 there are 62,370 women (above ten years of age) engaged in different manufacturing processes in Birmingham and district,[1] that is, about 20 per cent. of the total number of female inhabitants, and 53

Census Method.

[1] District—Birmingham, Aston Manor, Smethwick, Handsworth, and Kings Norton.

per cent. of the total number of occupied female inhabitants.[1]

Their work may be roughly grouped under the following main headings :—

1. Metal Workers (with Japanners)...	25,349	—about 22	
2. Jewellery Workers	5,961	„ 5	
3. Leather Workers (including boots)	2,889	„ 2	
4. Paper, Printing, &c., Workers ...	4,895	„ 4	
5. Clothing Workers	14,910	„ 13	
6. Food and Tobacco Workers ...	2,324	„ 2	
7. Wood (furniture) Workers ...	2,454	„ 2	
8. Miscellaneous Workers (including Chemicals)	3,588	„ 3	

[2] Per cent. of total No. of women occupied.

A second plan is to divide all kinds of work approximately into the two broad classes of skilled and unskilled labour, or, work that can be picked up within a month and work **Skilled and Unskilled.** that must be properly learnt, either under a teacher or by long experience; in other words, work in which only mechanical speed and accuracy are needed as contrasted with processes which demand thought and some power of adaptation. Detailed investigation of the main groups mentioned

[1] The remaining 47 per cent. are engaged in the professions, commercial work, domestic service, charing, laundries, the distributive trade, &c.

Total number of women (over 10 years of age ... 310,312
Total number unoccupied (18 per cent. under 15 years of age) 193,331
Total number occupied in work unregulated or partially regulated by Factory Acts 54,511
Total number occupied in work regulated by Factory Acts ... 62,370
116,981 = 38 per cent. of total female population.

[2] Percentages given to nearest unit.

above will show that the majority of women's trades must be reckoned as unskilled.

In metal work, for instance, hand lacquering and light hand burnishing and some of the lathe processes are the only departments requiring more than speed and accuracy. In the leather and clothing trades all machine work (sewing) may be classed as skilled ; and hand cigar and cigarette-making demand long years of apprenticeship. French polishing and also the finer work in cardboard box-making are other skilled occupations. But, when all are reckoned together, we shall find we have accounted for only a small minority of the many thousands of women workers.

Examples.

The reasons which determine an ordinary girl's choice of work have been so frequently discussed that we need only enter into one or two of them here. There is a very general complaint that girls will not learn a trade because, in the first place, they all hope to marry and thenceforth to be under no necessity of earning their own living. One would think that the existence of such a vast number of married women working in factories in a city like Birmingham would have a sobering effect on such speculations. It is difficult to gauge the relative determining influences in a working girl's choice of a career, but it is certain that the reason commonly given and quoted above is only one of many. Usually a girl drifts into the first work suggested to her because, through ignorance or the mental inertia of an ill-nourished physique, she has not the power to discriminate

Choice of Work.

or even to understand the existence of comparative advantages and disadvantages in different kinds of work.   Another cause is the economic one ; skilled work necessitates months or perhaps years of training for what is familiarly called a " pocket-money wage," *i.e.*, from 1s. 6d. to 3s. 6d. a week.   Very often the poverty of the home makes it imperative that the girl should look to present profit rather than to future prospects, or the greed or want of foresight of the parents will not permit an enterprising girl to sacrifice the small difference in initial wage for the sake of a more assured position later.   There is, however, one consideration which influences all girls who have been awakened to any sense of self-respect and all mothers who have any thought for their children's welfare.   This is the question of class distinction, and, as will be seen later, and as Mr. Charles Booth has also pointed out in deal-ing with Women's Work,[1] it has led to curious economic anomalies, which are generally beneficial to the employers.

As soon as a girl takes any thought for herself at all, her desire is to " keep herself respectable," and when one realises the environment in which many of these girls live, their familiarity from their earliest years with the surroundings of vice and crime, one can understand how this desire, once awakened, becomes a ruling power in a girl's life, and also why rigid class distinctions permeate the rank and file of manual workers.   These distinctions are

[1] " Life and Labour of the People," vol. iv. p. 317, &c.   See also "Women in the Printing Trades," pp. 67–68.

familiar to most social workers, but those who speak generally of the "working classes" or "the poor" can have no conception of their influence or their extent. For instance, a warehouse girl often knows very little or nothing about the work-girls in the factory, and many similar examples will be found in the work-rooms themselves.

The ordinary factory does little to break down these conventional barriers, though they sink into comparative insignificance wherever a factory as a whole gains a high reputation for respectability. There can be little interchange between skilled and unskilled work, but sometimes a girl whose ambition has been aroused through the refining influence of her evening club or Sunday class raises herself to a higher social level by changing her situation, either leaving heavy or dirty work for lighter duties of the same kind, or giving up ordinary factory work for a place in a warehouse, a small shop, or, more rarely, in domestic service. Generally speaking, one soon learns that most kinds of work are performed by distinct classes of girls. We must not imagine that this is always due to the refining influence of the better kinds of work. It is of course better for a girl to do work requiring skill and attention than to feed a power-driven machine ; to handle dainty material than to mend sacks ; but in most cases a girl's "class" is fixed before she starts work, and this is the determining influence in her choice of a trade. Even financial prospects have less importance in the eyes of the more refined girls than this great question of caste. The economic aspects of the problem are dealt with in Chapter III., but we may notice here that they are certainly influenced by this consideration. Because one trade is more respectable, or, as Mr. Charles Booth puts it, more fashionable than another, there will be great competition to enter it and consequently a depressing effect on the wages given. Of course there are many exceptions, but, to take an example, it is probable that warehouse girls would have better prospects were not that occupation the general refuge of the poorer girls who make some determined attempt at refinement, just as clerkships are sought by girls and boys alike who want to " rise " into the ranks of business as distinguished from manual work. Another economic influence, viz., that warehouse girls and clerks come from better-class families and are therefore more frequently subsidised by their parents, is discussed in the chapter on Wages.

However, it will be in studying social conditions that the division of work into skilled and unskilled will be most useful ; for our present purpose we will base on the Census division our attempt to give some idea of the work of the women in the chief groups of occupations mentioned above.

To enter into a description of every trade would be impossible in a work of this length, but a short description of some of the main groups will, it is hoped, serve as an introduction and guide both to more serious study of labour conditions, and to the study of investigations into separate trades which are being brought out by the Christian Social Union, the Women's Industrial Council, Glasgow

Council for Women's Trades, members of settlements, and others.[1]

I. *Women in the Metal Trades.*

According to the Census of 1901 more than 25,000 women in the Birmingham district are engaged in **Metal Trades.** various kinds of metal work. The subdivisions of labour are almost endless, to such an extent is differentiation of process now carried. Such branches of work as casting and charging employ only few women, but these are cases of women being employed for the lighter branches of men's work. Again, many processes are peculiar to the article in question ; for example, chandelier and other flat chains require a kind of linking which is done partly by hand and is not used in any other kind of chain or metal work. The brass knob on a bedstead may go through at least six processes before it reaches the manufacturer of bedsteads, and no two of these processes are done by the same girl, one might almost say by the same class of girl. When we come to a complicated article like a bicycle lamp, probably for the cleaning and the fitting of parts alone the article will pass through two or three hands.

Roughly speaking, the largest part of the work of women metal-workers falls under four heads :—

[1] Paper, Printing, &c. : See "Women in the Printing Trades" ; see Charles Booth, "Life and Labour of the People." Jewel-case Making, Embroidery, Machining : *Women's Industrial News,* Nos. March, 1903, June, 1904, September, 1904. "Laundry Work—Work in Laundries," by Margaret H. Irwin (Glasgow).

1. Press Work.
2. Lathe Work.
3. Soldering.
4. Various surface processes (excluding Machine Polishing and Burnishing).

Press work is regarded among girls themselves as a distinct trade, quite irrespective of the article that is made by their machine. Ask one of these girls at what she works, and the answer most frequently is, " I'm on the press." Further questioning elicits the fact that it is a power press, or a hand press, &c., but she is quite surprised that you want to know whether she makes knobs, studs, hinges, or spoons. She goes from one class of goods to another, only trying to get on a press in each new factory.

1. Press Work.

A press has been described as a machine that goes up and down, a lathe as one that goes round and round. The distinction is an elementary one, but it holds good for the present purpose. Presses differ chiefly in the amount of strength required to work them. A pen passes under five presses, and these are light machines worked generally by a hand lever. Others are worked by means of a treadle or stirrup. Heavier machines are generally driven by power ; they may work continuously with absolute regularity, or the power may be applied by means of a hand or foot lever. Ordinarily, there is a certain class differ-ence among the workers, the rougher girls drifting into the deafening press-shops where the big machines are at work ; but this rough classification has, of course, many exceptions. Taken as a whole, this class of work has certain characteristics.

In the first place, it is not skilled work, *i.e.*, in a week at the longest a girl has learnt all she ever will

Training. learn about her machine. She is taught by the foreman or the next girl, and soon falls into the monotonous regularity of movement which is all that is required for feeding a press. The correct placing of the metal may demand a certain amount of attention, but in many kinds of work it is almost impossible to make a mistake, and girls do not often learn more than they need about the machine itself.

Press work is not in itself necessarily dangerous to health. It does not create much dust, and, provided

Hygiene. a girl works in a properly arranged "shop," she may be as well off as in any kind of factory work. Much of the work is also clean, but some articles have to be taken out of suds or oil, and this is unpleasant for the hands and sometimes causes rheumatism. There is, moreover, nothing in the work to make proper ventilation a matter of difficulty. That many press shops are crowded, oppressively hot, and far from clean, points to need of hygienic education for both employers and employees. Shops are to be found where girls are working under fair conditions, particularly in the lighter branches of the work. The heavier machines undoubtedly in many cases unduly tax the strength of growing girls, but this objection could also be obviated by a more careful organisation of work and workshops. The chief element of danger lies in the nature of the machinery ; in greatly varying degree there is always some risk to the hands, and hundreds of Birmingham women show maimed and scarred fingers as the result of their service in the press shops. The visitor to a factory would remark at once that with ordinary care a worker can easily keep her hands clear, and there can be no doubt that many accidents are due to carelessness. "Familiarity breeds contempt," and girls get so accustomed to the presence of danger that they are apt to look away to talk with their companions, and in a moment of inattention the hand is caught under the machine. They have, however, some excuse. The incessant noise of the machinery, the excessive monotony of the work, and, above all, the long hours, which are too often spent in an ill-lighted and ill-ventilated atmosphere, all tend to produce a depressing and deadening effect which cannot fail to destroy alertness of attention and to create a craving for excitement which will catch at the least opening for distraction. A study of the hours at which press accidents occur would probably bring out some suggestive facts. The lady inspectors have already done something in this line of inquiry in laundries. If it could be proved that accidents occur most frequently during particular hours of work, say the fifth in the morning or towards the end of the afternoon, or even between dinner and tea, employers who have the welfare of their employees and the reputation of their factories at heart might devise plans to ensure greater immunity.[1] A working day of eight hours instead of nine or ten would obviously be better for the girls,

[1] " The incidence of accidents according to the time of day

and would probably lead to a decrease in the number of accidents.

Unlike press work, this group includes a great variety of distinct processes, requiring every degree of skill that machine work can demand of women. They are alike only in this, that they are executed by a machine whose distinctive work is performed by its revolutions; and the grouping here followed can only be described as a rough classification adopted in order to enable the onlooker to form some general idea of girls' work in

2. Lathe Work.

is somewhat surprising, the most dangerous hours apparently being between 11 a.m. to 12 noon, and 4 to 6 p.m.

MORNING.

	6–7	7–8	8–9	9–10	10–11	11–12
Accidents............	—	9	19	18	27	46

AFTERNOON.

	12–1	1–2	2–3	3–4	4–6	6–7	7–8	8–9	Hour unknown
Accidents	23	11	18	22	48	24	8	6	16

The hour 1–2 being frequently a dinner hour, the fall at that time is easily accounted for, and probably 11 a.m. to 12 noon is more generally than any other time the last tiring hour of a five hours' spell; 4–6 p.m. covers the time when most generally the transition is from daylight to artificial light. It is remarkable that there is no record of laundry accidents occurring after 9 p.m." (Annual Report of the Chief Inspector of Factories and Workshops for year 1903, p. 211).

the metal trades without getting lost in their endless intricacies and subdivisions. Cutting, worming (screws, &c.), forming, polishing, machine burnishing, and lacquering are a few only of the different kinds of lathe work.

It is very difficult to form a correct impression as regards the length of training required in this class of work. Not only does the skill required **Training.** vary with the machine, but in the different factories the regulations differ widely in respect to any one branch. Slackness in teaching arrangements seems to be a characteristic of the majority of branches of women's factory work, and consequently rate of progress depends very much on individual capacity, ambition, and standard. One girl will tell you that she learnt her work "at once," another that it took six months. In lathe work we find the time varying from a few hours to one or two years. This points to varieties of process, but also to different rules, chiefly relating to the time a girl must serve before she is allowed to "go piece-work." She is generally shown how to do her work either by the toolmaker, forewoman, or by a senior girl, but many girls give the answer that they "picked it up."

Grinding in the Pen Trade is an exception. This work is recognised as needing both skill and experience, and it consequently ranks as one of the better-class trades for women. One **Examples Grinding.** large firm pays a teacher to instruct the learners in this branch of work; in the others, the regulations vary, but the general consensus of opinion is that a girl requires some years of practice and experience before she becomes expert enough to earn the average wage, *i.e.*, 10s. to 12s.[1]

Polishing is another important subdivision. This is not distinctly women's work; in some places they only

Polishing.

do the lighter work, and the men's unions in some cases forbid women to polish at all. One woman, after forty years of factory life, writes that "There are lots of factory work that is too degrading for women who do it," and polishing was one of the things she condemned when further questioned. Here, again, no definite rule can be found as regards learners. Some are shown by toolmaker or shop-mate, some serve for a time on a small day wage, some "pick it up," earning what they can during the process, but one girl said, "You have never finished learning." This is probably the most truthful point of view, as the worker must adapt herself to every change of shape that fashion or progress may dictate, and there are few articles that are not influenced by one or other of these considerations. The process consists in holding the articles against a rapidly revolving mop or brush until a smooth bright surface is produced. It is only one of several processes through which a spoon or a brass knob must pass before the proper colour is obtained.

In machine burnishing, on the contrary, the article is placed on the machine and the rough,

Machine Burnishing.

discoloured surface is removed by an instrument resembling an ordinary screw-

---

[1] In a few cases the maximum wage is said to be from 13s. to 16s., but the average is as above. A machine has now been invented for this work, but has not been generally introduced.

driver, which is pressed against it as it revolves. This requires great skill and judgment, and is, in consequence, largely in the hands of men, though some employers consider that there is a tendency for women to displace the men in the light branches of the trade.

Forming is a much simpler matter, Let us take again our example of a bedstead knob. This comes to the girl from the press in the shape of a plain cup. The neck, rings, or other **Forming.** ornamentations are "formed" by holding the knob against the different revolving forms on the lathe.

Still another lathe does the threading, *i.e.*, forms the screw part inside the knob or handle and outside the ordinary screw. **Threading.**

If the skill and experience needed by lathe workers vary in almost every "shop," all kinds of lathe work have some characteristics in common. They are nearly always dirty, **Hygiene.** frequently dangerous, and generally more or less unhealthy.

As far as danger is concerned, what has been said about press work applies almost equally here. Most employers or foremen seem to consider the work safe if ordinary care is taken, **Danger.** and in the majority of cases this is the opinion of the girls themselves. With hair properly tied back, and no trimmings that are likely to be caught, above all with consistent alertness and attention, no one need be hurt by the power-driven lathe. How far it is fair to expect such attention under conditions of long hours, fatigue, noise, monotony, or want of proper nourishment is another question. It is also very difficult to train working girls to a sense of responsibility for their own lives, or indeed for anything. They are generally very reckless, and while it seems almost impossible to the average mind to keep up attention and speed to the necessary pitch for long regular hours, it must not be forgotten that the employers have much difficulty with the girls, who frequently object to the protections provided for them, especially in the matter of facilities for fresh air.

Dirt and disease are so closely associated that it is better to consider these conditions together. The unpleasantness of much of the work is due to the fact that it must "be done in suds, oil, or grease." This has one advantage, inasmuch as it checks the dust which is the most serious objection to many forms of lathe work. It will readily be seen that dust is inseparable from this occupation, and the danger is increased when emery or rouge are used, or when a mop is necessary. A mop is composed of a number of discs of cotton material, and is used for some kinds of polishing. The fluff and rouge[1] are bad for the lungs, as are also the emery and brass dust that fill the air in many shops. One girl remarked that her work was all right, as she "made no account of swallowing brass dust," but many complain of the choking feeling caused by the various kinds of dust. Polishing girls generally cover their hair and wear long pinafores,

[1] Rouge has been introduced in some trades as a substitute for putty powder, and therefore marks an advance on old methods, which were apt to cause lead-poisoning.

leaving the arms bare.   There are unfortunately still some factories where no facilities for washing are provided, and the girls have to go through the streets looking quite black from the fine powdery dust.

It is very difficult to suggest remedies to those who are in the midst of the work and know all its details.   So much also lies in the hands of the girls themselves, and too often they are absolutely careless.   However, good conditions always exercise some influence, and girls will endure much where they feel that consideration is shown for them.   In the first place, proper washing facilities should be made compulsory by law.[1]   A bucket is not enough, and where there is a rule that no one may wash at all, it is difficult to see how any self-respect or care can reasonably be expected.   Such a rule is, however, exceptional.   Respirators are sometimes provided, but they are unpopular, and their use is attended with many objections from the point of view of the wearers.   One wonders whether it would not be possible to provide a fine, cheap veil which would cover the hair and face, and which could be washed or renewed frequently.   It would be more comfortable (and more becoming) than a respirator, and would protect eyes, nose, and ears, as well as mouth, and if really fine in texture the sight need not be impeded.[2]   It is well known that proper ventilation

[1] Complaints have been made by employers of loitering, gossip, and waste of water where washing facilities are provided, but such abuses should be dealt with by other means than the refusal of such facilities.

[2] White Lead Commission.—Minutes of Evidence.—Appen-

is of great use, and exhaust fans, &c., are of great
utility for this end, although it is doubtful whether
any perfect arrangement has yet been devised to
carry off all the harmful dust. Also, although
exhaust fans are ordered by the " Special Rules," it
is very difficult to enforce their use as the workers
object to the draught caused by them.

Soldering must stand alone, because it is a distinct
process, although it is one which employs a comparatively small number of women. It is
another case in which men do the heavier
3. Soldering.
or more skilled kinds of work, and women attend to
a separate class of goods requiring less skill and less
strength. In some cases they use rather heavy

dix IV. Respirators (p. 375): " A perfect respirator should
have the following characteristics. It should prevent all
access of dust to the mouth and nose, and perhaps cover the
ears ; should not interfere with the breathing or work of the
wearer, and should touch the skin of the face as little as
possible, since the friction between the skin and the respirator,
particularly when the wearer perspires, as is almost invariably
the case, facilitates absorption, the perspiration tending to
catch and fix the dust to the face. The cambric bags above
described, when of sufficient size, nearly fulfil these requirements ; but it might be worth while to try whether a veil,
attached to the head, covering all round and falling some
distance below the chin, but gathered loosely round the
neck, particularly if the headgear had a projecting rim like
a hat, might not be an improvement. Such a veil would, at
the same time, serve as a cover for the hair and ears, which
are at present left in great part unprotected" (Signed)
A. Dupré.[1]

_____

[1] August Dupré, Ph.D., F.R.S., Lecturer on Chemistry in
the Westminster Hospital Medical School.

irons, *i.e.*, weighing about 3 lbs., but this seems to be exceptional. As to whether skill is needed the answers vary very much. Undoubtedly much of the work must be considered skilled, and some girls say that it takes years to learn thoroughly, but there seem to be no regular arrangements for teaching. Girls "pick it up" or show each other.

The work needs close attention, and is often trying to the eyes. The heat does not suit all girls, but, on the whole, it is not unhealthy or particu- **Hygiene.** larly dirty. However, it is not a "fashionable" trade among the girls themselves ; either there are not many openings, or the girls do not consider it particularly desirable. There are cases of bad disease [1] arising from the occupation, but these are generally due to faulty management and not to the work if executed under proper conditions. Several girls have said that it is very disheartening because there is no hope of progress or promotion, but many girls lament these facts when it is too late to learn a trade, while few will give them consideration when they first look for work.

The surface processes are almost as varied as the articles coloured and require as many degrees of

[1] We heard of a case of a girl in hospital suffering from lead-poisoning. Inquiry elicited the fact that she was a solderer, and that she had contracted the disease through using a pipe with a tinned mouthpiece, from which the tin had worn off. The Union forbids men solderers to use any pipe which has not a silvered mouthpiece ; the girls have no such protection, and consequently may have to be content with tin, which soon becomes defective.

skill. Many kinds of painting are quite unskilled and require no detailed description. In

4. Surface Processes.

the brass trade the actual colouring is done by men. The articles are dipped into various baths containing different acid solutions, both baths and exposure differing according to the colour desired. Plating is another process requiring care and judgment, and this also is not entrusted to women. They sometimes work in the plating shop, but as a rule they only help in the extra parts of the work, and in connection with dipping their chief duty is "wiring up," *i.e.*, stringing the small articles on loops of wire in order that a great number may be dipped at the same time. This is quite unskilled work and is chiefly done by young girls.

There is, however, one kind of dipping that is a distinct branch of women's work ; this is the colour-

Dipping.

ing of common black bedsteads.[1] They are simply dipped into a deep well of black paint and are then put into a heated room to dry. It is a rough and dirty trade, as the women have to dip their hands into the paint with the bed-steads, and the colour can be removed only by wash-ing in petroleum or turpentine. In addition, they must pass in and out of the hot drying-room, carry-ing the bedsteads to and fro, a duty that would seem more suitable for strong youths.

Japanning and blacking are closely allied to dip-ping, only the name is usually given to the blacking

---

[1] Coloured work and some of the best black work are still done by brush.

of smaller articles. The processes vary with the class of goods. The commonest are dipped once and then stoved ; better goods, such as best trouser buttons, for example, are blacked and dried twice and then varnished and dried again. Sometimes the "dead black" is brushed on, sometimes the colour is obtained by dipping. The varnish may be simply poured over the articles and the superfluous drops shaken off. It is obvious that this class of work is not particularly skilled. Some parts are very heavy ; japanning umbrella ribs was given as a very tiring occupation, but this was because so much work was handled at once. It is always dirty work, so dirty that it is mostly undertaken by a very rough class of women. However, much of the work is sent out from the factories to small domestic workshops, and here may be found a better class of girls who work at home or with neighbours and friends. It is a simple business to carry on in an ordinary shed, as no machinery is necessary, the only plant required being the annealing furnaces and ovens and the japanning fluid, the composition of which is a jealously guarded trade secret. These fluids are highly inflammable, and there is always great risk of fire. Naked lights are generally forbidden, and, as one little girl said, " if the blacking gets on your apron and you go near the fire you will catch light, and then there is no escape." Every good japanning shop is furnished with a sand heap, which is the only help if any one catches fire. In spite of dirt and danger, however, japanning is usually considered a healthy occupation on account of the fumes. The

(margin note: Japanning and Blacking.)

same girl said, when questioned on this point, " japanning makes you eat more." She had gone into the
trade for the sake of her health, which she declared to
be much improved, but probably some of the credit
was due to the kindness of her employers. Domestic
workshops may be so many opportunities for sweating evils, but, on the other hand, they also provide
opportunities for the display of much kindness and
neighbourly feeling, opportunities which seem to be
often used where employer and employee work
together almost as one family.

But we have wandered from our description of
"surface processes." Let us pass from the bedstead
Transferring. dippers to the transferring room. Here
we at once notice a different atmosphere.
The work still requires very little skill, but it is both
lighter and cleaner, and therefore sought by and
entrusted to a different set of women. Their duty
is to put on the gilt patterns and ornamentations
which are a usual feature of ordinary metal articles,
a simple process not altogether unlike transferring
into scrap-books of nursery days.

A great deal of public attention has been called
to enamelling, as this process is one of the dangerous
Enamelling trades, lead being a frequent constituent
(Tin and Iron of the colours used, though some firms
Plates for
Advertise- seem to have adopted leadless mixtures
ments, &c.). with good results.

Before the special rules for this trade came into
force there was a great deal of plumbism
Hygiene. among girls employed at enamelling.
These special rules require the provision of perforated

tables through which the dangerous dust can sink, washing conveniences with a sufficient supply of hot and cold water, soap, nail brushes and towels; regular medical inspection and attendance; the free provision of an approved acid drink; proper dining rooms; and overalls, which must be removed before meals. They also prohibit the employment of any girl under twenty years of age in a dangerous process, require stringent rules prohibiting any food in the work-room, and insist on washing before meals, &c. Lead, at all times a powerful and insidious poison, is especially dangerous to an ill-nourished physique. One of its first effects is to aggravate the early symptoms of anæmia, which are probably present in many of its victims before they are brought into contact with the poison. Hence an unusual rule has been included, viz., in order that no one shall start work hungry, that half a pint of milk and a biscuit be allowed to each woman. The wearing of respirators is a great difficulty, as most of those provided are found to be too hot and uncomfortable. The veil described on page 60 was suggested to the Royal Commission, which inquired into these industries, beginning May 11, 1893.

As a result of these precautions, it is gratifying to read in the Factory Inspectors' Report for 1903 that—" In the enamelled iron-plate trade the rules have been exceedingly well observed, and no cases of lead-poisoning have been reported where the rules are established." [1] That the rules must be

[1] Report of Chief Inspector of Factories and Workshops for 1903, p. 72.

difficult to enforce goes without saying, but if ignorant girls are employed in injurious processes the employer takes on himself the responsibility of protecting them.

The rough and dirty nature of the work has resulted in the employment of a poor class of girls who, through habit, malnutrition and home conditions are especially open to the influence of any poison with which they may be brought into contact. As women are more liable than men to the effects of lead poisoning, if they are to do this work at all, it is imperative that it should only be under the best conditions.

Enamelling is not at present a prominent industry in the Birmingham district, though there are several large factories on the outskirts where every precaution is now taken. The chief danger is found in the small enamelling shops in the centre of the town, where men and women alike suffer from working at a trade which can only be properly pursued on a scale large enough to compensate the employer for all the special conveniences required.

There are two surface processes which are regular trades, recognised as such and highly skilled. These **Burnishing.** are hand-burnishing and hand-lacquering. Although common work of both kinds can be done on a lathe, in neither trade does the machine seem likely to entirely supersede manual work.

Burnishing is still a large home industry. Young girls often learn from a relative or neighbour before they enter a factory. The process is a curious one;

the dull metal articles are polished to a brilliant silver or gold colour by scraping them with edged tools which are not unlike elongated or curved screw drivers. The tools are dipped in soap-suds, or sometimes in beer, and, after burnishing, the articles are laid in fine sawdust and dried in an oven or stove. The tools are expensive, costing from £3 to £5, but they are bought by degrees, and as they "last a lifetime," a good burnisher is always able to return to work, if necessary, either in a factory or at home.

When a girl learns the trade at a factory she is generally either apprenticed or put under a woman for two years, starting with a wage between 3s. and 6s. a week. After two **Training.** years she is put on piecework. The work requires great care and skill, as the tool must not be allowed to slip. Much of it is very fine, as both imitation and real jewellery is burnished by hand, and there is a great deal of work in some of the buckles, clasps, and brooches which are so cheaply bought. Embossed dull silver is only burnished in the parts where there is a smooth, bright surface, but this kind of ornamentation is a recent fashion. The old-fashioned electro-plate is all burnished in the old-fashioned way, and hand-burnishing is mostly a woman's trade.

As suds are necessary, the work is damp and cold to the hands, but this is a minor objection and otherwise the work is light and healthy. Socially, it is an excellent trade and is **Hygiene.** learned by a more refined class of girls. It is not overcrowded, as few can afford the long apprenticeship, and the conditions of work as regards the company, and the absence of men from the workshops make it one of the best trades which an intelligent girl can learn, especially as it offers a real "living wage," *i.e.*, from 12s. to 20s. per week for experienced workers.

In lacquering, cheap goods are sometimes dipped. Knobs and simple articles are placed on a lathe and **Lacquering.** a brush is used for colouring. This is women's work and demands some skill and judgment, but the hand-lacquering is the real trade. The articles which are to be coloured are placed on supports over a heated table; this is generally of metal and heated by gas. The colouring mixture is brushed on; in fact, lacquering is a process of painting. Curtain rods and the long tubes of brass bedsteads are among the most difficult things to lacquer. They must be gone over several times and the surface must be absolutely even. If any of our readers have ever tried to paint a door or a mantelpiece in their own homes they will know that it is not so easy as it looks to get a smooth surface and not to betray the fact that the work is that of an unaccustomed hand. It is more difficult to use lacquer, for much depends on the temperature, and the article must bear no suggestion of having been coloured; it must look as if it had simply received a brilliant polish.

When we come to the question of training, we find **Training.** again the same confusing contradictions that confronted us in respect to lathe work. This is a skilled trade, but different firms have different rules for teaching it. Sometimes the girls "teach each other," a phrase which carries different obligations in different factories. Very often the little learner is put under a woman for any period up to two years. Here, as in many other trades, the woman is on piecework, and she is paid for her pupil's work together with her own. Out of the combined earnings she pays the learner a fixed weekly sum, and the trouble of teaching is gradually rewarded by the extra earnings of the little girl which thus fall to her share, especially during the latter part of the "time." The average starting wage is a good index as to the estimation in which a particular trade is held; paradoxical as it may sound, the lower this wage the better the trade, *i.e.*, the trade is considered to be so well worth learning that some preliminary disadvantage may be endured. Of course there is also another consideration; the more difficult the work, the more material is the beginner apt to spoil; certainly the less will she produce. Lacquering girls begin with 2s. 6d. to 4s. a week, and their wages are slowly increased as their work improves. A large proportion of the experienced hands are on day work, a circumstance which is unusual and may possibly arise from the fact that the best work in lacquering demands a quiet, steady hand, and any suggestion of haste would spoil it. Taken as a whole lacquering is certainly the best paid branch of women's work in the metal trades, girls of twenty often earning 15s. a week, while many rise to 18s. or 20s. when trade is good. Girls who say they can learn in a week, a month, or "pick it up," are employed on small cheap articles, and unless especially gifted do not aspire to a curtain rod or long flat tube.

Lacquering is, on the whole, a good occupation, and as the work needs a good light the shops generally

Hygiene. have the advantage of brightness and the possibility of airiness. The work is clean, generally light,[1] and the chief disadvantage is the smell. Unless very perfect heating apparatus is provided the gas fumes will have a bad effect on the girls, but given good conditions—and these are easier to obtain in this department than in any of those previously considered—there is every reason to consider lacquering a good opening for any girl who can accustom herself to the heat and, in most cases, to the standing. There is a method of cold lacquering, but the ingredients of the mixture are apt to cause so much sickness that in most factories the process described here is preferred.

There is another reason for recommending lacquering ; it is one of the best metal trades from a social

Girls. point of view. One little press girl said in answer to a question, "Oh, the lacquering girls are ladies." Others tabooed a certain factory because they would not mix with the "hands," but made an exception in favour of the lacquerers, evidently considering them as quite apart from the rest. So marked is the distinction that in one factory the idea of providing a dining-room had to be abandoned because the lacquerers would not

[1] 24 per cent. of the cases interviewed said that their work needed strength.

eat in the same room with the dippers. This must not be put down to simple snobbishness. These girls know so well the lower strata of society, they are so well aware how easily a girl or family is dragged down by the pressure of want or ill-luck, that it is only natural that they should make what seems to the onlooker to be a hard or unnecessary distinction and protest against being classed in any way with the rougher women. The observant visitor who passes through the different rooms in a large factory will at once assume that in some the sound of the "bull" will be the signal for an unrestrained display of animal spirits, loud laughter, shouting, and rough movements. In the same way he would know where to expect with certainty more decorum of manner, pleasure and freedom taken with an obvious attempt at refinement, and a care for appearances that may strike him as exaggerated. Better manners may not denote better characters in all respects, but such girls are undoubtedly more civilised, and to this class lacquerers almost always belong. In evening clubs, &c., they may meet press girls and others, but they generally keep together and very often exercise a most helpful influence in quieting and refining the general tone of the place. The younger girls look up to them and desire to emulate them when they would not think it conceivable that they should ever try to emulate their teachers. Unless the girls meet in this way they will not mix at all, and the club will be composed of unskilled workers and the lacquering girls will be found with girls who are in the clothing trades or other skilled occupations.

In conclusion, we may perhaps ask : What is the opinion of women themselves about their working conditions as distinct from conditions in and outside the factory which affect their lives in the more human aspect? The majority tell you that " the work is all right and they have no complaints to make." They accept it as a kind of fate, never think of trying to understand their legal safeguards, and when an accident happens, rarely of their own initiative claim compensation. They are afraid of any new teaching or suggestion that could by any possibility offend the master. There seems to be a general vague idea that the work must be as it is, that " what is to be will be," be it accident or infection or any other misfortune ; in fact, that it is better to

*Summary :
Metal Work.*

> "rather bear those ills we have
> Than fly to others that we know not of."

On the other hand, this acquiescence in monotony or danger or disease breeds an enviable freedom from worry and anxiety. The one dread is to be out of work or on short time. Otherwise they are careless and happy as soon as released from work, though it must not be forgotten that they are immensely proud of any consideration on the part of their employers, and will often accept slightly lower wages where the place is clean or the language controlled. The fact that they do not grumble more must not be taken as a proof that their lot does not need improvement, and the reader will hardly envy

the press or lathe girl, of whose duties we have
endeavoured to give some idea.

Though a division of the metal trades, the jewellery
trade is unique in some respects.   A great deal of the
work has already been described, as all
the main divisions given for women's   Jewellery.
work in the metal trades apply also to jewellery,
and in the manufacture of cheap or imitation
jewellery, fancy links, buckles, studs, &c., both class
of girls and class of work are the same as in the
lighter kinds of metal work.   As we gradually
ascend the scale in class of work the other conditions
improve, and we find a superior set of girls earning
at first the same wages as the rougher girls, but
giving more thought to their work and finding their
recompense in the more refined surroundings.   Ascend
higher still, and we find girls doing work which
requires a high degree of skill, and earning an
average of 12s. to 14s. a week, and at last, in a few
cases, earning from 15s. to 20s.

In the jewellery trade, ordinary press work, polishing (on a mop), soldering and burnishing are as
important as in other metal manufactures, and the
average wage is about 2s. per week higher.   The
best jewellery is polished with rouge, and this work
is often done by girls and is as unhealthy as in other
polishing shops.   However, there are compensations,
for the work is light and wages up to £1 per week
are paid for best work.   Among these workers, too,
rules seem to be less rigid, as befits a higher class of
girls who must be intelligent and trustworthy if they
are to handle the valuable materials.

There remain several special processes, each of which employs a very small number of women. Some of these trades are gold-cutting, gold-frosting, jewel-turning and polishing, pearl-stringing, and allied trades such as lens-polishing and various kinds of pearl work—the last being one of the old domestic industries which is being killed by modern industrial conditions.

Gold-leaf cutting is a skilled occupation which is generally done in the factory, though occasionally a trusted man is allowed to take it home to his wife. The gold-leaf comes to the worker in a " mould," *i.e.*, a book of gold-beater's skin. One square inch of gold-leaf as thick as ordinary writing paper is beaten out by hand into sixteen sheets, each five inches square and one-millionth of an inch thick. The leaves are then equalised with a cane " cutter," and each one is lifted with a cane forceps and blown between two of the leaves of thin paper in a " book."

Polishing precious stones is another very small trade, but one in which there is not much competition. Men always facet the gems, but girls polish the flat stones for inlaying and do " carbuncle cutting," *i.e.*, they cut the jewels which have round tops and flat backs. The average wage in this work seems to be about 14s. for experienced workers. Girls begin at 4s. 6d., but in most of these sub-divisions the initial wage is lower.

The jewellery trade is still largely in the hands of small employers, and there are numbers of small factories or workshops where master and man work together on friendly terms, and where no rigid discipline is necessary. This state of things has lingered longer in this trade than in most, but it will probably soon pass, and there are many large factories employing several hundred workers. In these the rules are sometimes very strict, and the workpeople may not enter any shop but their own. Jewellers and silversmiths have regular slight seasonal fluctuations which are shared by allied trades such as electro-plating. They are all quickly affected by any general trade depression, and the busy time comes in the autumn and early winter, though where the trade is largely colonial it naturally comes rather earlier.

Taken as a whole good jewellery (including silver work) is one of the best kinds of metal work for a girl. It certainly shares many of the ordinary disadvantages of metal work, but these disadvantages are often lessened by the better conditions necessitated by the quality of the work, perhaps also by the higher standard of intelligence both in employer and employed.

There is one important branch in factory work, of it and yet not of it, which is the link between the manual and the clerical occupations open to girls. This is warehouse work, a **Warehouse Work.** general term which includes every possible kind of wrapping-up, sorting, boxing, weighing, and packing. The warehouse is a department of the factory, and the warehouse girls are therefore subject to the regulations of the Factory Acts, though they are often exempt from the chief discomforts of factory life.

Most kinds of warehouse work are distinctly unskilled, and can be learned within a week, though
Training. sorting and looking over in their many
forms demand a speed which only comes
with practice. Occasionally six months is stated as a
learner's time, but the variations in the answers depend
more on the girls than on the work, some considering
that they have learnt when they understand the
movement required, others naming the time needed
to attain average speed. The work does not offer
good prospects, as far as wages are concerned, and
though the maximum wage works out at 15s., the
average attained by girls over eighteen is barely 10s.
They usually begin with about 4s., and are paid a
time-wage. In jewellery and one or two trades
where valuable materials are used, higher wages
are naturally paid, and women can earn from 16s.
to £1.

Notwithstanding the low wages, warehouse work is
very popular and eagerly sought after by the best
class of working girls. As work, it has
Hygiene and Workers. much in its favour ; it is generally light
and clean ; it is chiefly women's work,
they usually have the warehouse to themselves,
and it need not be unhealthy. A few of the cases
investigated (10 per cent.) said that their work was
not healthy, but as more than half of these girls
worked in one large warehouse at a trade which is
usually perfectly harmless, it is obvious that their
complaints were due to the place, and not to the
nature of their work.

The warehouse girls rarely mix with the factory

girls, they generally profess to know nothing about them in all factories where the women do "unskilled" work. Naturally, in better-class work the distinction gradually fades away, and the girls are often drawn from the same class. With all these social advantages it is not surprising that there is an over-supply of applicants for warehouse posts, and this popularity is probably one of the factors which depress the wages. In the case of warehouse girls the influence of home support and subsidy undoubtedly has its share. Indeed, the only disadvantage in the majority of factories is the want of prospects, and if a girl is likely to be thrown entirely on her own resources it is unwise for her to attempt to enter a line of work which is already overcrowded. However, very few girls do look forward at this early stage of their career, the scarcity of the really good posts does not trouble them, and the advantages of cleanliness, easy work, and, above all, of nice company are all important in their eyes.

Of the 2,454 women included in the Wood, Furniture, Fittings, and Decorations' division, by far the largest number are French Polishers. Theirs is a skilled occupation, and the difference between men's and women's work consists only in the kind of articles **Wood: French Polishing.** polished. As a rule men do the largest furniture, but there are factories where women only are employed in the polishing room.

The term French Polishing includes both staining and varnishing. Some kinds of wood require no colouring matter. Satin wood, for example, is only

Process. treated with oil and varnish to bring out
the beautiful colour and grain of the
wood. Mahogany is frequently treated with colour,
while deal is stained to any shade of red or green,
often to imitate other and more fashionable woods.
The process is apparently straightforward. The
colouring mixture and varnish are applied and
vigorously rubbed in with a soft rag. The ingredients used are simple, and contain a great deal
of shellac and methylated spirit. The women say,
"You must work until it has a body on it," and they
take two or three pieces of wood, or parts of a piece
of furniture, and rub first one and then another
until the desired surface is obtained. The same
forewoman said, "It takes a lot of learning and
judgment, and you want three or four years to learn
properly." This is partly because each different kind
of wood has more or less grain which must be filled
in, or it will not wear well, and the smooth, polished
surface and colour will become uneven. Oak and
birch are said to be the most difficult to manage, but
the common "red" work is both the dirtiest and the
hardest.

The time of learning varies from six months to
four years, but generally it is fixed at two years and
after that time the worker is no longer a learner,
though she does not yet rank as an experienced
hand. The first year's wage varies between 2s. 6d.
and 5s. a week, occasionally it is even lower, and
there are places at which the girls work at first for
nothing. The second year they may have "a shilling

rise," and the general wage varies between 3s. 6d. and 6s. Sometimes there is a regular apprenticeship. One enterprising girl had been in the trade eight years and had been in seven or eight places. This was not the result of mere restlessness. She said, " They do not trouble to teach you properly at any one place ; you must move about so as to get experience in every branch if you want to learn the trade thoroughly." Here we see the effect on the masters of the general disinclination of girls to learn a trade thoroughly, against which the energetic exception had to make way.

Unlike the metal trades, where the amount of work depends chiefly on the state of the market, French Polishing is regularly affected by times and seasons. There are usually a few Seasons. short weeks in the course of the year, but these are compensated by the rush before public holidays. Going away into the country does not seem consistent with buying new furniture, but holiday weeks are the great times for weddings among the poorer people— furnishing immediately precedes such an event, and though the large and fashionable firms are superior to these considerations, it must not be forgotten that Birmingham is still largely the home of individual enterprise and the small employer, and it is these smaller masters who between them employ the majority of workers in this trade.

The trade is, in common with all others, undergoing some modifications at the present time. Machinery has been introduced for polishing knobs, &c., but, as in the cases of lacquering and burnishing, it is obvious that it is not likely to supersede all manual work—at any rate for some time to come.

The average wage in this trade is not very high, *i.e.*, it is about 13s. for women over eighteen. There are, however, many exceptions, and it must be borne in mind that the work is fairly regular. It is generally sought by a respectable class of women, as one would expect in the case of work that takes two or more years to learn.

It must, however, have a good reputation among girls, for it is generally dirty and is always very hard.

Hygienic Condition. To stand all day, too often to stoop, and incessantly to rub or polish is hardly a tempting outlook. Added to this, the smell of the polish makes it very trying to beginners. However, they consider it rather a healthy trade, and there is nothing harmful in the smell of the materials. To our modern ideas the chief disadvantage arises from want of ventilation. To obtain satisfactory results the atmosphere must be warm and dry and free from dust. Naturally, when the goods are not thoroughly dry, dust must not be allowed to settle, but it is not so obvious that damp cold "chills the work," *i.e.*, gives it a bluish-white sheen, to remove which much additional rubbing and much additional time are required. On a cold, damp day, such as all England knows only too well, the average polisher has no idea beyond shutting the windows and lighting the gas. The result can be better imagined than described. If there is any comfort in the reflection, we may remember that the workers have not yet got to the stage of regarding fresh air as a necessity, hardly as a luxury of life.

It has often been stated that French Polishing is a great temptation to drunkenness ; in fact, it has been said in London, " The trade that drinks most is that of the French Polishers." [1] Whether there is any truth in this assertion or not, it can be certainly contradicted on behalf of the women in the trade in Birmingham. The hard work, the smell, and the state of the atmosphere must be very thirst-producing, but the women as a class are above those who are without a sense of shame in this matter, nor does the terrible vice of drinking the methylated spirit, occasionally found among London workmen, appear to be known among women here. Of course there must be many degrees and many exceptions, but the occupation does not seem to work much harm to the cause of temperance in Birmingham, thanks largely to the fact that it is followed chiefly by a class of women who start with some self-respect, so that they are exempt from the initial temptations into which many young girls fall in low-class unskilled work. In conclusion, it may be noted that a large number of married women follow this occupation.

Upholstery is a good skilled trade for a limited number of unmarried women. Much of the work is heavy, but experienced workers earn from 12s. to 15s. a week, and there are better prospects for the exceptional few. **Upholstery.**

Girls are generally apprenticed for one year, during which they earn from 2s. to 3s. 6d. a week, but they

[1] Charles Booth, "Life and Labour in London," final volume, p. 73.

have slightly increased " day wages " for some time longer, and promotion is slow. On the other hand, there is not much short time, so the trade is a fairly good one for a girl who will learn it thoroughly.

Though the different kinds of leather work occupied in 1901 only 2 per cent. of the total number of

Leather Work. working women in the district, these trades have in the past been more prominent, and it is possible that they may again increase. The chief divisions are :—

1. Military work, which is closely allied with the regular work in the next sub-division.
2. Harness and bridle manufacture.
3. Boots and shoes.
4. Fancy goods.

Military work is the lowest kind in the estimation of the workers, because it employs all the " vagrant

Military Work. labour " ; in other words, it has a small permanent upper class of workers, but as the work has periods of great pressure and great slackness there are numbers of workers who are discharged as soon as the rush is over, and such a class of men or women has a bad effect on any trade. Among women, however, there is a better class of intermittent workers, and these are the skilled married women who are glad of occasional extra work, but who cannot take permanent factory situations. Wages for women are low in any leather trade, and military work is the lowest in the social scale ; fancy leather goods, such as belts, purses, &c., occupy a very different set of girls.

Since the end of the South African War there has been much slackness in military work and harness-making, the latter being apparently also influenced by the rise of the motor industry.

In the leather trades, women's work consists chiefly of stitching, hand stitching in the heavy work and machining for light harness, boots and shoes, and fancy goods.

There was once a great deal of out-work in this trade, but this is rapidly decreasing, chiefly in consequence of the sub-contracting clause affecting Government orders. The suspension of this clause during the South African War resulted in a great temporary increase in the number of home-workers. It is not very long since the old "piece-master system" prevailed in these trades; that is, a foreman undertook a certain set of work and engaged and paid the hands in his department, making what profit he could out of the job.   **History.**

The harness makers, &c., are not a well-organised body of workers, and when this system led to the engagement of women because they would work at lower rates than men, the men had to come down to the lower rate of pay also. The pay used, under the old system, to be given out in a publichouse; now in the better firms every one is paid direct from the office, but the decreased rates still hold good. In saddle and harness work men and women's stitching is exactly the same, but where a man both prepares and finishes, a woman stitches only, and in common work a man thus earns 25s. to 30s. to a woman's 9s. or 10s. When, on the contrary, both man and

woman are on stitching only, and light goods are in
hand, a woman is quicker and has been known to
earn £2 to the man's 25s. Such wages are, however,
rare, and the present condition of harness and bridle
work offers, on a small scale, an instructive contrast
to the great cotton industries of the north. In both
women have, in many instances, replaced men. In
the disorganised leather trades this has been followed,
as already said, by a general decrease in wages. In the
cotton trades the inclusion of women in the already
strong organisation of the cotton operatives has kept
the wages of both sexes from sinking.

Leather stitching ranks as a regular trade, but, as
in other trades, the arrangements for training girls
vary considerably. Two years' learning
Training. or apprenticeship seems to be the most
general rule, though the term is sometimes as short
as six months or as long as three years. During this
time a girl earns from 2s. 6d. a week, rising to about
4s. 6d. before she finally passes on to piece-work. A
great many girls learn the trade from relatives or
neighbours before entering into factory life proper.
In heavy work the holes are punched with an awl,
and the stitching is done by hand. For light and
common goods the machine is used. Better-class
work is often the least profitable to the workers, as
the rates are not sufficiently increased to compensate
for the longer time required.

There are occasional instances of women harness
and bridle-makers earning as much as
Prospects. 20s. to 25s. per week when trade is good.
During the South African War high wages were very

general. At present women over eighteen are earning an average weekly wage of between 8s. and 10s.,
and many, both men and women, have either left the
trade or are earning less than the average for regular
hands, owing to short time. This is especially serious
in the winter when trade is always somewhat slack.

The same may be said of the boot trade, but here
we have an example of a trade dying out in one
district owing to its rapid increase in
neighbouring towns; owing, too, to the   **Boots and
                                               Shoes.**
flooding of the market with a cheap class
of machine-made goods, which have to a large extent
superseded the old, skilled hand-work. This work
has therefore decreased, as neither workers nor equip-
ment were suddenly adaptable to a change of fashion
against which they bitterly rebel. The home worker
has been the first to suffer, though there are still
many houses where the husband and wife work
together, and he makes while she machines the
uppers. In 1901 boot-and-shoe making employed
less than 350 women in Birmingham; of these more
than one-third were married women or widows, but
it is not possible to divide the latter into factory
and out-workers, though it is certain that many of
them belong to the second class.

When we come to fancy goods, *i.e.*, belts, purses,
cases, frames, &c., conditions in many respects are
very different. These goods are at present
fashionable, and consequently this branch   **Leather
                                                   Goods.**
of the leather trade is increasing. The
work is both light and skilled, from one to two years'
training being required in machining or purse and

pocket-book making. In both these departments
men do all the cutting-out and the girls machine in
a room by themselves. The work is also clean and
healthy, and all these conditions induce a superior
class of girls to learn it. Unfortunately, this is still
one of the trades where skill earns better conditions
merely and not increased wages. Learners begin
with 3s. or 4s. a week, 10s. is the maximum for
finishers, but adult workers in the other departments
earn on an average about 11s. a week. On the other
hand, head machinists and purse makers earn about
20s., so there are good openings for the exceptional
girls who have talent and application, and as the
trade is regular the workers have not the anxiety
of a periodic slack season. The light leather belts
which are at present popular are made chiefly by
power-driven machines under conditions similar to
pinafore making. Colonial pouches and belts are
much heavier, and are often embossed. Here men
do the actual embossing, stamping, and some of the
punching, while girls lay on the gold and silver leaf
and also do the stitching. This fancy trade is almost
entirely confined to the factories. It has grown up
under modern conditions, and employers prefer to
keep the work where they can personally superintend it.

When we come to the clothing trades we are on
more familiar ground than hitherto. So much has
already been said and written on this
Clothing Trades. subject, such careful investigations have
been made and published, and, in many
ways, the customer can deal so nearly with the

actual worker that we need not here go into detail as fully as in other classes of work, except in some particulars where the old order is changing and modern factory conditions are superseding the old principle of the skilled and all-round worker.

The student of textile industries will not come to Birmingham. Actual manufacture of material employs fewer than one thousand of the working women, and there are, roughly speaking, eleven thousand engaged in the making of garments. Of these, as is natural in a large centre of population, a great number (about 9,328) are engaged in tailoring, dressmaking, and millinery. Some branches of the "ready-made" trade complete the Birmingham list of clothing trades as far as women workers are concerned, except for very limited industries such as surplice and cassock making.

Taken as a whole the clothing trades are largely in a state of industrial transition, and they might almost be taken as a reduced picture of the whole manufacturing world.

As regards wages, sweating, competition of men and women, and, above all, the struggle between the old-fashioned worker who knew a trade throughout and the specialised factory hand, between the old form of workshop and the modern factory, we find here *in parvo* many of the problems and developments which are the theme of the economist, philanthropist, and socialist who are seeking to better industrial conditions.

Till comparatively recent times the factory system

was unknown in the clothing trades. They were learnt by apprenticeship, and the "one man, one garment" system prevailed.

Broad Divisions.

Now we have the two systems side by side, and the division adopted in tailoring may be roughly applied to the whole class of work, which thus falls into two broad branches: (1) the "ready-made," or stock work; and (2) the "bespoke" trade. Under the first heading the chief Birmingham industries are pinafores and baby-linen, corsets, and some tailoring and shirt and skirt making. The ready-made tailoring trade flourishes chiefly in Yorkshire and the Black Country, where it has attained to huge dimensions. Under the second heading we find the first-class tailors, of whom very few are women, and the majority of dressmakers and milliners.

The numerous costumes, &c., which are neither made for individual customers nor as examples of a dozen or a hundred dozen similar garments, form a borderland between the two classes of work. However, as far as working conditions are concerned, the majority of these may be classed with the "bespoke" goods.

In the matter of wages it is well known that the clothing trades give scope for sweating, though now this evil seems to be less prevalent in the Midlands than in London. On the other hand, the skilled and enterprising worker has prospects undreamed of in other trades, and, if really first class, a dressmaker or milliner may make as much as £3 a week, though this is subject to seasonal variations.

Wages.

The attention of the public has been largely directed to the existence of sweating in the clothing trades, and many people are genuinely anxious not to use anything made under **Sweating.** unfair conditions. In buying ready-made goods it is, however, very difficult to judge from the price whether the workers are fairly paid. For instance, at a recent meeting a lady much commiserated the work-girl who made a pinafore for fivepence. Such a girl is in reality one of the best-paid factory workers in the city, and is in all probability earning about 18s. a week, and this in spite of elaborate tucks and insertions. As factory conditions are rather good in the ready-made trades, such misdirected pity, especially when publicly expressed, does much to prejudice the employer against all attempts at befriending working girls.

It is only through knowing the conditions and character of individual firms that definite guidance in this matter can be found, and for this the co-operation of the shopkeeper is needed, not only for the goods made on his premises, but also in regard to the stock-goods, which pass through several hands on their way to the consumer.

Among employers and managers, of course, the general opinion seems to be that the girls are amply protected by the Factory Acts, that the skilled nature of the work renders it impossible to make conditions hard for workers who could always leave for better masters, and, as one gentleman expressed it, " The only sweating is among little Jewish tailors who sweat themselves."

But the fact seems to be that sweating is not confined to any class of work ; it is a question of individual character and conscience, and is found in high places as well as in low, and probably the intermediate classes in this industry are most free from its baneful influence.

All clothing trades are more or less skilled, consequently training has a definite and important place, *Training.* and, as one would expect, the workers as a whole are a higher class of girls.

Most of these trades are season-trades, *i.e.*, certain months of the year are always busy, while others *Seasons.* invariably bring slack time. The seasons vary in the different branches, but in most the slackest time is from October till Christmas.

The ready-made trade, properly speaking, includes all garments which are made in large quantities from *The Ready-made Trade.* a single pattern. As has been pointed out, it is an industry of modern growth, and is, indeed, still in its infancy. It is probable that as the supply of well- and tastefully-made garments increases, people will more and more take advantage of the opportunities thus afforded of saving time, trouble and expense, and a trade which began by providing the poorer classes with clothes will end by catering for all classes of the community. Some goods are already made in every grade of style and value.

Birmingham industries are chiefly confined to cotton and linen goods. Leaving out-work and ordinary shops for the moment out of the question, we find the work carried on chiefly in well-equipped factories, though they have generally been adapted and not built for the purpose.

The chief sub-divisions of work are (1) cutting, (2) machining, (3) ironing and folding. Some garments also require finishing, *i.e.*, buttons must be stitched on, and other details which are not done by machine must be added.

Where the seasonal variations of work are felt, as, for example, in the cotton skirt trade, there must be some overtime, but on the whole the hours of work are not long in these trades, and average about nine hours a day. It is a matter of general experience [1] that longer hours deteriorate the quality of the work, and where power machines are used, the power is too valuable to be provided for slack or tired workers.[2]

The general introduction of power has also an effect on the average wages, as girls who are not industrious or capable enough to earn a good wage (*i.e.*, 12s. to 14s.) when once they are thoroughly trained, are not worth keeping in the factory at all.

Although all the work is more or less skilled, machining is the most skilled and the best paid branch. Where the cutter is also designer or forewoman, her work naturally takes the first place, but apart from such cases the machinist has the best prospects.

---

[1] See also "Women and the Printing Trades," preface p. ix. and pp. 84–89.

[2] See also Note in Lecky's "Democracy and Liberty," vol. ii. p. 347, and Webb's "Industrial Democracy," vol. ii. p. 717.

Pinafore making is the largest wholesale branch of the ready-made trade in Birmingham, and it is therefore taken here as an example. Naturally every branch has peculiarities of its own, but there is a general similarity between all in the more important details.

Cutters generally teach the younger girls their work. They are paid a time wage, and **Cutters and Ironers.** are occasionally paid also for holidays and sickness. Ironers are also generally day workers.

In all these factories the bulk of the work is machining. This takes from six months to one **Machinists.** year to learn, and in many cases a regular agreement of apprenticeship must be signed. Other firms are less strict in this matter, but the system is practically the same. Generally the learner is taught by an older girl, but in one business the learners have a large room to themselves, and an experienced woman and a senior girl are employed only to teach and to superintend them. This employer considers that learners cost about 5s. a week at first, taking into account the value of spoilt materials, waste of power, light, rates, &c., and the time of the teachers. Many, also, either leave or marry soon after they are proficient. In a good place a girl learns all the machines, beginning with an ordinary treadle machine and passing on to the power machines, which end with the tucking machine, this being one to which many never attain. During this six months (the usual time) they have a pocket-money wage of 2s. to 3s. If especially quick, a girl may be promoted before her apprenticeship is over, but most are ready to "go piece-work" and earn what they can at the end of six months. Then an average industrious and capable girl will earn about 8s., with better prospects as soon as she shows herself fit to be trusted with more complicated patterns and the best materials. The latter are so valuable that a master must secure good workers; the demand at present exceeds the supply, and such a worker can make good wages, 18s. or £1 being not uncommon on full time and for senior hands.

No clothing trade suffers so little from short time, and this good condition will continue as long as the demand for pinafores continues to increase. Where the apprenticeship lasts one year a girl learns both machining and cutting, and can afterwards choose her special branch of work. Certain deductions are customary in these trades. Girls often have to supply their own machine needles and cotton, and they must frequently make some contributions towards the cost of the power. That such rules are liable to abuse every one knows. But sometimes all possibility of unfair dealing is removed by paying the girls an extra ½d. or 1d. on every dozen pinafores according to the amount of stitching, this being about the price that the cotton, if carefully used, has cost them.

Girls often prefer the smaller factories, as they think they have more liberty. There are fines of one penny or twopence for lateness, but the discipline is not very strict. They sing and talk while at work so long as they do not actually waste time. For instance, one master said he was obliged to interfere to save his power when he found the girls stopping to learn hymns by heart. There is generally a rule that spoilt work must be bought, but most masters only enforce this where real carelessness has been proved. Even so there is loss to the employer, as cutting out odd garments is a waste of material.

The pinafore makers are a superior class of girls; if they give their employers plenty of trouble through their high spirits and frequently unreasonable demands, they seem to be kindy treated in all good-class factories, and they certainly receive far more consideration and humane treatment than the majority of unskilled workers. In fact, we seem to be in a different world among them, and poor as many are they can have no cause to repent the months of short pay which have qualified them for their work.

As conditions stand at present, pinafore machining offers one of the best openings to bright girls who are about to enter industrial life.

Corsets are made both in factories and in workshops, which are either small, independent industries or attached to shops. Unlike London[1] the trade is not often carried on in the homes of the workers.

Corset Making.

Here again machining is the most important branch of work. There are subsidiary departments, *i.e.*, cutting and japanning busks, &c., but there would be no communication between the two sets of girls.

[1] See "Life and Labour of the People," vol. iv. p. 271.

The machinists generally serve for twelve months on a pocket-money wage of 2s. 6d. to 4s.

It is a little difficult to judge of their prospects when once they are on piece-work, as the period of depression through which most industries have recently passed has affected the corset trade, and the wages of adult women workers appear to be as low as for an unskilled trade. There is doubtless some compensation in the fact that their surroundings are comparatively refined. The work is very close and therefore rather trying, but the workers are a superior and quiet set of girls to whom it is of great moment to be amongst companions of their own class.

As corset making is not a staple industry in Birmingham, the most important factories are to be found elsewhere, and perhaps other towns would show better prospects in this trade.

Deductions have been introduced, but the introduction was accompanied by a rise in wages. In many firms girls provide their own needles and cotton, and they sometimes pay one halfpenny in the shilling for steam power, and an equal amount for gas.

In spite of the recent short time, prolonged beyond the ordinary few weeks which may be expected every year, the opinion of some of the senior girls is that " it is a good trade, but you must be quick and stick to it."

When we pass to tailoring we are on debatable ground between factories and home industries. There is not much " stock work " done in Bir-   Tailoring.[1]
mingham, and even the best " bespoke "

[1] Compiled from the investigation and report of Miss Hilda Joseph, Health Visitor, &c.

or "customer" orders are often executed in small workshops which are in many cases domestic, in that they employ the members of one family with perhaps a neighbour or one or two extra hands who are taken on in busy times. This prevalence of outwork is also noticeable in London. Workers employed in the workshops attached to the retail shops are paid at the same rate as those outside. The latter find their own cottons and silks (trimmings) machines, irons, firing, and working space. Notwithstanding, they make more money than indoor hands. They can obtain cheap female labour which is not admitted into the best shops. They take work from several shops instead of from one, and the men can work throughout the night if necessary.

The shopkeepers cannot be independent of their outworkers, because during the busy time by working late and by taking on extra hands they can execute very large orders which it would otherwise be necessary to refuse.

As Mr. Booth has pointed out,[1] and contrary to our experience in other trades, this system tends to increase. The cheapening of machines and the supply of female labour tend to make it advantageous to the ordinary tailor, and different authorities agree that the bad sanitary condition of many of the shops have driven the men to make their own working environment; the line of demarcation between the in and out work is, however, constantly varying.[2]

[1] " Life and Labour of the People," vol. iv. p. 147.
[2] See " Women's Work in Tailoring and Dressmaking "— Report for Glasgow Council for Women's Trades.

It is in the small secondary establishments that the majority of female tailors employed in Birmingham are to be found. The trade is very largely in the hands of the Jews. There are some newly-arrived immigrants among them, but Birmingham not being a seaport town there is not the same problem of over-crowding and a low standard of living as is found in parts of London where the foreign colony is constantly augmented by large numbers of aliens whose living requirements are almost as alien to British standards as their language.

The Jewish community is not too large to be well organised, and consequently, though there is some severe poverty, starvation conditions are not allowed to exist. Family life has the same cohesion as has been remarked in London [1] and it is therefore not surprising to find the Jewish work-girls alert, well developed, and too intelligent and well protected to accept work under the worst conditions. They are also very thrifty, and, unlike their English sisters, they do not expect to reserve out of their wages the 3d. to 1s. pocket-money, which is often spent on sweets, variety theatres, &c. Some of them have said when questioned on this point, "I'm no spender," or "What should I want pocket-money for?" As there are comparatively few of these girls they are also all within reach of the refining influence of their social workers, &c., an influence which is very perceptible when one visits their clubs and evening classes.

The majority of these girls are trained in one or more branches of tailoring, though the long hours

[1] Report of Commission on Alien Immigration.

and the sedentary nature of the occupation render it distasteful to many of them.

The "Jewish Ladies' Apprenticeship Committee" makes every effort to induce the parents of young girls to let them learn other trades. This is partly due to the objections just mentioned and partly to the conditions of the trade, which entail particularly close workshop association of men and women. The ordinary objections to tailoring from the point of view of health are more dependent on the usual conditions of the trade than on the nature of the work itself. Tubercular phthisis and diseases of the nervous system seem to be the chief enemies of the tailor,[1] and though the occupation necessitates the inhaling of a certain amount of dust, it is probable that improvement of exterior conditions would remove any stigma at present attaching to the trade.

Model factories now exist in this as in most other trades, but, generally speaking, tailoring has not up to the present benefited much by the reforming spirit.

Sufficient space, light, and ventilation are essential improvements, and probably in no trade would the effect of short intervals of change and relaxation be more apparent. The National Cash Register Co. (Dayton, Ohio) provide physical drill "where feasible, the young women of certain departments exercising under a trained instructress as they stand by their chairs."[2] Such a break of ten minutes' duration with all windows open, where outdoor

[1] Oliver's "Dangerous Trades," p. 152.
[2] "Model Factories and Villages," Budgett Meakin, p. 207.

recreation is impossible, has been found to result in increased vigour and efficiency, and therefore one ventures to mention it as a suggestion. Though it is naturally only applicable in this trade to factories or large workshops, some such arrangement should be contemplated in a trade whose workers are liable to nervous complaints.

Tailoresses are generally apprenticed for one or two years, except when they learn the trade in the workshops of their fathers or other rela- *Training.* tives. The half-time system is not un-known ; in such a case a girl between twelve and fourteen years of age works during the dinner interval and from 4.30 to 8 p.m. Others learn under the senior hands, who pay them a nominal wage until they go on piece-work, often at the end of six months. The regular apprentice may begin by running errands, &c. ; occasionally she pays a small premium and starts the definite work at once, but this is the less usual method. The initial wage varies between 3s. and 6s.

The trade is divided into the distinct branches of coat, trouser, and vest-making, and in these the women do only certain sub-divisions. *Sub-divisions.* Very few learn more than one branch, or sometimes than one sub-division of one branch.

Buttonholers and machinists often pay a home-worker 10s. to £1 to teach them the work before they enter a recognised workshop. Buttonholing is an especially good trade, and skilful workers can earn £1 or more per week, a wage that gives chance of saving for the inevitable slack season. It is, however, suitable only for girls whose eyesight is good, as the dark materials in general use are trying to the eyes.

As one would expect, the best "stock-work" seasons alternate with those for "bespoke" orders.

Seasons. The former class of work is the less highly paid, but as it is more sub-divided the output is greater and there is less seasonal fluctuation. Hence the average earnings are not on the whole lower than in the better-class businesses.

Waistcoat making is the poorest branch of the trade in Birmingham, where it is partly a home industry, and is often carried on by the elderly women, who can no longer easily find employment in workshops.

Vests.

In coat- and trouser-making, when the "one man one garment" system no longer holds, the work is generally sub-divided into:—

Coats and Trousers.

    a. Machining.
    b. Basting.
    c. Felling.
    d. Button holes.
    e. Pressing.

Occasionally a woman learns the trade throughout, and such a worker can make really high wages, *i.e.*, £2 or more per week during the busy season.

As a rule men do the heavy and most skilled machining and all the pressing, which is work that should never be left to women on account of the weight of the irons. Women may press the seams of a garment on which they are engaged, but they are never employed as pressers alone.

In all branches of tailoring, wherever the machine is introduced the woman-worker follows. The very best coats and trousers are made through- **Machining.** out by hand, and are consequently not touched by women. Much of the machining in coat-making is also done by men, as women are rarely skilful and strong enough to put a coat together. They can, however, do the plain machin- ing, which comprises the machining of sleeves, linings, and oddments. Trousers are often made throughout by women, but it must be remembered that "cutting" is never part of "making" in the clothing trades.

Basting, *i.e.*, tacking for the machine, is usually done by men in better-class work, but **Basting.** women are employed in many shops, and can earn good wages.

Felling and buttonhole-making employ the majority of tailoresses, and girls should always learn both these branches of work. Felling includes all the work which is put in by hand after **Felling and** machining, except buttonholing. Button- **Buttonhole** holes are made by machine in the cheapest **Making.** work. When done by hand 9d. a dozen is an average price, and, as has been said, this work ranks as a good trade.

Ladies' costumes form a small and highly skilled industry. They are often made in the same workshops as gentlemen's coats, **Ladies'** and the seasons for both kinds of work **Costumes.** are the same.

In conclusion, it may be noted that there is often

great poverty among tailoresses, that the trade is overcrowded with mediocre workers, and that both seasons and hours are apt to be irregular. On the other hand, really expert workers in any branch can earn high wages, and can therefore make provision for the slack months. Girls who wish to learn the trade need not be dissuaded if they have the application and ability to learn their branch or branches throughout, but their prospects are most discouraging if they do not aim at a high standard.[1]

There are nearly 7,000 milliners and dressmakers in Birmingham, and of these about 750, or 12 per
Dressmaking. cent., are employers. The majority of the latter have small private establishments, often carried on in private houses. As in London, a small middle-class business seems to offer the best training and most regular employment. Girls are generally apprenticed for one year, and during that time and the years immediately succeeding they learn the whole business, and not only bodice or skirt-making, as is often the case in the large workrooms attached to shops, &c.

Dressmaking is a season trade, but the fluctuations are most felt in the fashionable districts.

Individual effort can still make its way in this

[1] Report of Scottish Council for Women's Trades (Tailoring), p. 11 : " An intelligent woman-worker, who had a wide knowledge of the trade, has told me that if tailoring technical classes were started for women, and they could be induced to undertake the necessary term of training in them, she felt convinced there was nothing to prevent their taking as high, or almost as high, a place in the trade as men."

business, and a girl of taste and capacity who takes the trouble to train herself thoroughly can always hope for promotion ; but, as in tailoring, the trade is overcrowded with mediocre workers.

As far as women are concerned, probably more dressmakers are fined for breaches of the Factory Act than any other class of employer. The public who are so anxious to see girls working under ideal conditions would do well to bear this in mind. The dressmaker may be guilty of want of organisation, greed, or inhumanity, but the root of the difficulty lies with the customers who order their things at the last moment. We are too thoughtless in our purchasing, and this applies with especial force to dressmaking, where customer and producer are in such close contact.

Dressmaking would not be an unhealthy occupation were it properly regulated. The long hours of sedentary work form the chief objection to it, and, as might be expected, the girls often become anæmic from want of exercise. Girls who visit regularly at ladies' houses, making, re-making, and altering, have the healthiest life, and can make a good living when once they have worked up a small connection. For good workers or intelligent apprentices there is always an opening.

There have been various efforts made in London and elsewhere to start dressmaking establishments on a business footing, with good working conditions. Another promising movement has been the starting of public technical classes, arranged not to teach the trade, but to supplement the workroom training.

Some of the best London firms have sent their apprentices to these classes and paid their fees. It is to be hoped that both these movements will spread.[1] Meanwhile it is not necessary here to enter more exactly into the details of a trade about which so much has already been said and written.

The same may be said of millinery. It is a business which offers an excellent opening to the **Millinery.** skilled worker who is alert, artistic, and intelligent. For the mediocre workers who do not bring such qualities to bear on their work the prospects are as poor as in an unskilled trade. In any case a girl must be prepared to work three years before she can earn more than 5s. a week.

Socially, dressmakers and milliners would mix with the most refined warehouse girls. They must dress well, and as they are skilled workers, they are naturally "high-class" working girls. Season trades demand intelligence in another respect; only those capable of thrift and foresight can so arrange their irregular earnings as to provide for both short and busy times, and in this matter they need help and training as much as their poorer working sisters need more elementary help.

---

[1] The plan has been tried abroad with success, and there are districts in Germany, Switzerland, &c., where it is obligatory for apprentices in certain trades to attend the supplementary scientific classes at the local technical school, and the employers are obliged to allow sufficient free time to make such attendance possible.

Apart from actual process, the numerous small trades which are included in the miscellaneous division do not offer much variety in general conditions. The 2,324 food workers mentioned in the **Miscellaneous Trades.** Census are chiefly employed in chocolate, borax, and cooking-powder factories, and the majority of these girls are wrappers and packers. Some of the chocolate work is skilled and brings in nearly £1 per week, but otherwise wages are not above the general average. Many girls complain that they find powder packing unhealthy, but all these trades are carried on chiefly in modern factories and offer good conditions and surroundings to a superior set of girls, the principal disadvantage being the small chance of promotion. However, even this is true only in certain departments or in the few small factories which are not yet up to date.

The same may be said of whip-braiding, brush-making, glass work, wicker work, chemical appliances, cigar-making, and other trades too numerous to mention, much less to describe. A list of un-skilled work could also be added, to include such work as bottle-washing, rag-sorting, rope and twine making, &c.

With the exception of stone-polishing, a highly-skilled occupation, and some of the rubber processes, few of these trades are necessarily dangerous to health, and girls who choose a skilled branch may be as well off as in any better known kind of work, while careful inquiry will reveal excellent openings in some directions for the few who are really talented and persevering.

Specially Regulated Work.

On the borderland between the regulated and unregulated forms of work are two large groups of workers for whom there is special legislation. These are the shop assistants and the laundry workers, two groups which are almost at opposite ends of the social scale. These, with the unregulated workers, make up 47 per cent. of the total number of occupied women.

Work under Special Regulations.

Laundry work has recently been made the subject of detailed investigation both in London and Glasgow,[1] and needs therefore little description. The work is hard and exhausting, and, in spite of the cleanliness, and the absence of men from the workrooms, it is not considered a high-class trade. In large laundries there is a great deal of dangerous machinery, but the use of proper guards is being rapidly enforced by law. There were nearly 3,600 laundry workers in Birmingham in 1901. Of these a large proportion (63 per cent.) were married women ; in fact, in many laundries they include nearly all the ironers. Shirt ironers can earn about 16s. a week, but otherwise laundry workers do not earn more than the average unskilled factory hands, and in some departments the average is distinctly lower. There are no

Laundry Work.

[1] Report of Chief Inspector of Factories and Workshops for 1900, pp. 379–387. "Women's Work in Laundries" : Report of an Inquiry conducted for the Scottish Council for Women's Trades by Margaret H. Irwin (1905).

arrangements for training, and the work is "picked up," or rather, washing is one of the things which most women are supposed to do by nature. Where a higher level of skill is demanded it is difficult to find satisfactory workers, and there is very little short time in a well-conducted business.

In a provincial city the conditions of the shop assistants present less complex problems than is the case in the metropolis, where we find every class of business, from the mam- **Shop Assistants.** moth establishment of the universal provider down to the tiny general shop in a back street. In smaller towns there are a few large shops where the assistants live in, where the discipline is rigorous and is maintained by 150 or more rules with fines attached to each varying from 1d. to 5s. This class of shop has been fully described in the news-papers,[1] but the present investigation has dealt mainly with the medium and small shops, which are everywhere in the majority, though this majority is naturally more marked the smaller the town in question.

In the ordinary shops girls over eighteen earn on an average 10s. 6d. a week. In some cases dinner and tea are provided in addition, and most of the girls were well satisfied with the food supplied, if we except one little girl who was very hard worked in a restaurant and was tired of having stew every day. It does not seem to be general to give commission in this class of shop, but there are very few fines. There are also very few rules, six being the maximum

[1] Articles in the *Daily Chronicle*, 1899 (reprinted in 1900).

number, and even this is unusual. Some girls are
apprenticed for one or two years. They do not pay
a premium, and rarely "give time" for more than a
month. They receive no wages, but the familiar
"pocket-money" (2s. to 5s.) is almost always given
to learners.

The highest positions are in costume departments
in large shops. Here the assistants may receive
about 30s. per week, but such promotion is, of course,
rare. A few employers pay full wages in case of
illness, though this payment is often limited either
to a "short illness" or definitely to a fortnight.

The chief objection to this form of employment is
the long hours which are still worked in most shops.
Hours and Meals. Most girls have to be at work twelve
hours a day or ten and a half if we
exclude meal-times. As far as the
present investigation has reached, about 60 per
cent. have a short day, *i.e.*, once a week they leave
work either at 2 or 5 p.m. On the other hand, only the
fashionable shops are exempt from the long Saturday,
when the shops are kept open until 11 p.m. at the
earliest, and in some trades they do not close until
10 p.m. on Fridays also. Some girls have to work as
much as seventy hours per week exclusive of mealtimes, and anything between sixty and sixty-six hours
is very common.

The Birmingham assistants are fortunate in one
respect. Most of them have an hour for dinner and
half an hour for tea, but, as this provision is not as
yet enforced by law, cases are common where the
meals are unduly hurried, and as little as fifteen

minutes is occasionally allowed for dinner. A great many dine at home or in a restaurant, but the majority have their meals either in the shop dining-room or in the house attached to the shop. In small establishments they may be "called forward" to attend to customers or to find things.

The assistants who lived in were generally found to be satisfied with the food and accommodation provided, but sometimes living-in also meant longer hours of work. For example, a girl in a fish-shop earned 5s. and her board a week. Her hours were from seven in the morning till eleven at night, less three hours on one evening in the week. Another girl, who was employed by a tobacconist, earned 4s. a week, and was on duty from 8 a.m. till 11 p.m. She had no definite half-holiday or free evening, though she occasionally secured one by asking special permission.

The chief disadvantages from which shop assistants suffer are the long hours, the constant standing, and, very frequently, the inadequate arrangements for ventilation and sanitation. With the freedom at present accorded to employers in the distributive trade these disadvantages are sometimes removed, but they are frequently aggravated. It seems unfair that so much latitude should be allowed and that conditions which are not tolerated in factories should be permissible in shops or in offices.

The Shop Assistants Union is pressing for legal limitation of hours and inspection of sleeping and sanitary accommodation, and, if possible, for the total abolition of the system of living-in. At present matters are in a state of transition, and we cannot give any detailed account of the very varying conditions now existing, but the need for legislation is unmistakable. To-day hundreds of young people lose their health because hygienic principles are not enforced, while more sensible administration should make the occupation a healthy and desirable one for girls to enter.

Unregulated Work.

Unregulated work is almost as diverse as regulated, and far more diverse in the elements which go to compose this section. It includes such different occupations as the professions, domestic service, and charing. To enter upon a detailed discussion of the professions is not necessary here. Much has already been written on this subject, and what is more to the purpose, much is being done to co-ordinate and regulate the workers. Such action is as urgently needed as among other working women. Aimless competition and ignorance of economic principles have done much to lower the conditions of educated women workers, and this want of organisation is one of the causes which have depressed salaries to their present unsatisfactory basis, especially in the teaching and the clerical professions.

Nurses have also started an insurance society against sickness and old age. Some hospitals have **Nursing.** deliberately lowered their salaries in order to secure a higher class of applicants, *i.e.*, girls to whom the salary during training is not of primary importance. Sometimes no salary is paid during the first year. Taking the three years' training together, the usual salaries are from £10 to £30 according to the position of the nurse. Conditions vary a good deal; day duty lasts from eight and a half to twelve hours; night duty is eleven or twelve hours. About two and a half hours daily are usually allowed for exercise and recreation, and there is half or a whole day given once a month, occasionally half a day each week. The yearly holiday is three or four weeks' long, though some institutions give as little as two weeks. Nurses come from every class of society, and their prospects vary as much as their ability. We can only give an account of the years of training spent in hospital. Those who do not afterwards become staff nurses or sisters drift into many different kinds of nursing, much of which is in private houses or nursing homes, while many leave the profession altogether. Those attached to homes earn about £18 a year, while first-class private nurses, working directly under a doctor charge about £3 3s. per week.

There are nearly 25,000 domestic servants and charwomen and there is room for more in the former class. The pros and cons of domestic service are the subject of annual discus- **Domestic Service.** sions in many newspapers, and we will not add to matter so controversial and so little capable of generalisation. Among working girls there is a strong prejudice against service. Many owe this to a short experience as an overworked general servant, or else to the early experiences of their mothers or neighbours. Sometimes such girls are persuaded to take a carefully chosen situation and happy results follow, as may be seen from a short letter at the close of the present chapter. These instances are unfortunately rare compared with the number of girls who would be far healthier in service than they are in factories, but one cannot help sympathising with the girls' objection to loss of liberty. Domestic service will probably be re-adjusted in many ways in the near future, but even now prejudice and the mistakes of the past have much to answer for in the present state of affairs, and it is difficult to see how this prejudice is to be overcome.

If there are few good servants, there is always an army of charwomen available. Many women com-
Charwomen.   bine this work with taking in washing, and nearly every untrained woman who has fallen upon evil times turns to one or both of these occupations if she is unable to go to a factory and is within reach of people who can employ such help. Every working class is represented here. The City Council employ a certain number as bath attendants, &c., but these women keep regular hours amounting to fifty-two per week, for which they receive 14s. or 15s. Turkish bath attendants have 5s. per day, and there are also women who clean the Town Hall, Council House, &c. There are always a great many applicants for these posts, and among the ordinary charwomen the supply exceeds the demand. The usual payment is 1s. 6d. or 1s. 9d. per day with food, but there are a great many women who work for those who are scarcely less poor than themselves and in these cases the pay is very small and often takes the form of food or clothes.

Among the unregulated trades we could end with a long list of small and unusual occupations, each employing a very small number of women. Caterers, stall attendants, hawkers and even betting agents might be mentioned, while among the professional classes there are many openings for individuality and enterprise which are dealt with in books devoted specially to these ranks of workers.

We leave this section feeling that almost more has been left out than has been expressed. The main points are dealt with later, but if a general conclusion can be drawn from such a *Conclusion.* complex subject, it is that if working conditions leave much to be desired they possess at least the capacity for improvement. Such improvement can, however, only become general when it is demanded by an enlightened public opinion and assisted by the united efforts of the state, the employers, and the employed. We add a few letters from different workers, giving their views about their work, just as they were received :—

" I know that Factory work in its self is all right because I cannot see what there would be for them all to do, to get a living at, but there is also the danger for them to meet with those who will learn them things that are wrong and lead them to places that may be the ruin of them in years after. Those that work in Factorys have more time and more money in some trades and the work is nice and easy. but they have temptations that takes there money in Clubs that are healt in the Factory. and get things

they do not want, and when illness or short work
they have to go short and some cases the girls and
Women go into Biblick House and spent some of
there money before going home. But if a girl or
Woman as a strong will and don't mind be laught at
or being called skinney because they do not mix up
with them after work they are all wright.   Some places
have nice people in them that help you but not in
many places. I been in both. I could not tell you
when first that I went to work the dreadfull things
that was told me, and it would make parents more
carefull if they could see some that work in the rooms
befor there Children, when in them money is nothing
to what they will learn. Service in a good home is
better than Factory in some things, they have less
temptations for if there Mistress is good they have
good food and money for clothes, for girls in Factorys
spend there dinner money in thing that do them no
good, and servant have less holiday but better health.
I think they keep themselves cleaner and nicer
because the home they are in makes a differance. I
think they are better off anytime no short time and
are under some one else care while they are there and
I think it is much better."

" *The difference between factory life and domestic
work*.—When a girl first leaves school, she first wants
to know what work she is going to do for a living.
If she makes up her mind to go into a factory she
will find she has many things to contend with. In
some places there are no proper sanitary places.
Then in another case there are no places to wash

their hands. There is another disadvantage the factories are not well ventilated and it is very dangerous and unhealthy, and it often causes them to lose their lives. To give a girl a good advice I should tell her the best plan would be to go into office or warehouse because it is more healthier than in a close work room. Some factories you are aliable to be mixed up with bad company and get into their bad ways."

" *The Life of Domestic Work and why it is better than Factory Work.*—When a girl goes into service at a gentlemans house she is more aliable to get into better company than factory girls. To be a servant it is much more healthier and comfortable. Girls who are in service are generally much more quiter and more ladylike than those which work in a factory. In gentlemans houses there are proper lavertories and ventilators. There is another reason why servants are much more healthier, they have the more time for their meals than factory girls have."

"*Why I Pefare Working in a Factory Than going To Service.*—When I was about 14 years of age I went to service for about 18 months and I did not like it at all because you was on from morning till night and you never did know when you were done and you never did get your meals in peace for you are up and down all the time, you only get half a day a week their for you cannot go to Sewing Classes or Christian Indever or any other classes as we do and you never get very large wages in service. And you

never know when you are going to get a good place
That What I Think About Service."

" *Why I Perfare To Work In A Factory*.—Because
their is a fixed time for meals And you do know
when you are done. you are not all hours of the
day And you have only got one to serve and you
can go to has many classes has you like in a week
you have got Saturday and Sunday to yourself and
you can see a bit of life and we are not shut up all
day. We have only got one to serve and we have
only got one amount of work to do in a day and we
can help other girls to go the write way And you can
dress how you like in a factory And I Pefare to
Work In a Factory. I have got a Sister who is
about 15 and she works at the Gold Chain maker
And she likes Working in a Factory. There are
one or two things which can be approved of The
Master ought to have a Lavotary so that you can
come out respectable when you were done, there
hadent ought to be any bad words to be put out,
Most Factories their is, So I remain Yours Truly,
F—— J——."

" Shop life for a girl is like all other work it has
its good and bad uses a great deal depends on the
girl herself and a greater part with the Master for
one thing it is not such hard work for the body as
some other work is it is more head work it is very
clean work and a work which requires a great deal
of patience for when customers are very trying you
have to guard your temper and this is a very good

use of shop work training you to keep your temper no matter how trying it may be. You do not get such liberty in a shop as you do in a factory for the hours are much longer, but sometimes you get amongst girls who use language they ought not to in a factory, it is not very often you hear it in a shop for the girls have to talk properly and this is another very good use which makes up for the extra hours. There is one bad use in shop life and this is dress and following the fashions of the world such as regular theatre going and dancing and out somewhere every night of the week and if all the other girls in the shop follow these fashions you get a very trying life if you do not join them and it requires great firmness to keep from These pleasures which when taken too far are very wrong for we cannot do our duty to our Master the next day if every night we are seeking our own pleasures, but this can be turned into a good use for if you are a true Christian girl you have not only daily work for your Master to do but you have a great field of labour for your Heavenly Master by trying to come into close contact with the other girls and showing them the wrong of too much of there worldly pleasures and in this case you have good work cut out in your shop and by so doing making your shop life a very happy one."

"*An Essay on Why I prefer Domestic Service to Factory Work.*—Why I prefer Domestic work to Factory work in the first place, is, because I find it much healthier. All the morning you are moving about in the fresh air instead of standing or sitting closed up in a workroom.   I also have more time for sewing which is a great help to every one.   When you come home from work at seven oclock you dont feel much inclined for sewing.   Being in Domestic Service you avoid a great many evils to which you are subject to in a factory.   Of course, in a factory there are so many people of all kinds.   Some will want you to go with them to places where you would rather not be seen.   If you refuse, they laugh at you and then it is very hard to know what to do.   When you are in a Gentleman's house you associate with kinder people and learn to act and speak differently."

CHAPTER III

WAGES

IN the inquiry as to wages one of the outstanding facts elicited was, that whenever women had replaced men the former always received a much lower wage, and that this wage was not proportionate to the skill or intelligence required by the work but approximated to a certain fixed level—about 10s. to 12s. per week. The wage that the man previously received gave no criterion as to what the woman would get, though as a general statement, approximately correct, we may say that a woman would get from one-third to one-half the wages of a man.

But first, in order to clear the ground, we must point out that it is not proposed to discuss the relation of wage-earners as a class to the other factors of production, though, of course, our subject is part of the general wages question. Women are a part of the class of wage-earners and do not form a separate factor as land or capital does. Thus our discussion turns on the facts regarding women's wages and leads to an elucidation of the principles

by which women's wages are determined as compared with those of men.   A full discussion of these
points—which full discussion cannot exhaustively
be undertaken here—would answer the question,
which might be put thus :—When labour as a whole
receives a share of the national dividend why is there
the irregular distribution between the two sections
of labour, and what would be the effect upon each
of any attempt to alter the relative share of each ;
and further, what possibility is there of labour, men
and women included, increasing their absolute and
relative shares of the national dividend ?

The fact of the irregular distribution between the
two sections of men and women is admitted on all
sides as proved.[1] [2]   It has been found by this inquiry

---

[1] " This is the real opposition which men offer to women.
In Perth and Bungay, for instance, the women put in a bill
at the end of each week, worked out on the men's scale of
rates.   The cashier then divides the total by two and pays
the women accordingly.   In Edinburgh women's piece-rates
for composing average about two-thirds those of men.   At
Warrington women do machine ruling for prices ranging
from 15s. to 20s., whilst men are paid 32s. for same work.   A
more definite statement is made by a Manchester employer.
He estimated that a woman was two-thirds as valuable in a
printer's and stationer's warehouse as a man, and she was
paid 15s. to 20s. to his 33s.   A further example of this is given
in connection with a Scottish firm executing Government
work : ' As the Government insists upon the men's union
price being paid, the work is being done by men, although
in the ordinary way it would have been done by women.
But they (the employers) would never allow the women to
make such big money as that ' . . . "—(" Women in the
Printing Trades," Note, p. 47.)

[2] " Women's Work," p. 113.—Lady Dilke.

in Birmingham that for girls above 21 years of age wages move near 10s. per week, while an unskilled man's wage is 18s. to £1 at least. The following is the analysis of women's wages in the cycle trade:— For those over 21 the average wage is 10s. 6d. Nearly 50 per cent. of these are married women whose wages average 11s. Between 17–21 the average wage is 9s. 2d.; below 17, 7s. 1d. In the bedstead trade the cases investigated gave the following :—

Over 21	...	...	...	Average wage—11s. 6d.
Over 17 and less than 21 ...		„	„	8s. 11d.

The following table [1] shows the wages of women-workers in four of the trades investigated : —

[The names of the processes were given by the workers, and it is possible that in some cases more than one title is given for the same kind of work.

The maximum wages are in many cases exceptional, as they are sometimes given as a maximum by only one of the women working in the process.

The averages are obtained by taking the total amount earned by the employees in each class for a full week's work and dividing it by the number of such employees. The table takes no account of short time, holidays, or overtime. It is estimated that, in considering the *yearly* wages, on an average at least four weeks must be reckoned for short time due to various causes. In periods of depression of trade this is, of course, greater still. For example, one woman (aged 29) whose full week's wages was 12s. has for the last twelve months averaged 6s.]

---

[1] A full table of Trades and Wages investigated for the purpose of this book is given in the Appendix. In all cases where our evidence was insufficient to form a basis we have left wages blank.

Trade and Process.	Mini-mum.		Maxi-mum.		Average under 18 years.		Average 18 years and over.		Average Married Women.	
	s.	d.	s.	d.	s.	d.	s.	d.	s.	d.
BEDSTEAD TRADE¹—										
Cutter-off ...	—		—		—		10	0	—	
Lacquering ...	4	0	19	0	5	4	11	6	12	0
Painter	3	6	15	0	7	6	12	0	12	0
Ornamenting ...	4	0	15	0	6	6	9	0	12	0
Wrappers-up ...	3	0	16	0	—		11	6	—	
Wire Mattress Weaver ...	5	0	14	0	—		12	2	—	
Tube Charger ...	5	0	—		—		12	0	—	
Knob Solderer ...	5	1	12	0	—		10	8	11	0
Stover	—		15	0	—		10	0	—	
Warehouse ...	5	0	12	0	7	3	8	0	—	
Press Work ...	5	0	14	0	8	6	11	0	11	0
Polishers... ...	4	0	15	0	—		13	0	—	
Brass Casters ...	—		—		—		—		—	
Burnishers ...	—		—		—		12	0	12	0
Enamellers ...	3	0	20	0	—		—		—	
Wire Mattress Pounders ...	4	0	—		6	3	—		—	
Wire Mattress Grinding ...	5	0	—		8	6	—		—	
Knob Rounding	6	4	9	0	—		—		—	

¹ In women's work in the bedstead trade the system known as the "piece-master's system" is still in vogue in some firms. One woman contracts to do the work at a certain piece-rate, and then she engages girls or women to help her and pays them what she thinks fit. In one factory we found a woman "painter" who averaged 35s. per week after paying two under-hands at 9s. and 6s. per week respectively. There was also a married woman engaged as "wrapper up," and she averaged 35s. per week piece-work after paying four under-hands each 16s. per week day work. At "ornamenting" one married woman earns 30s. per week piece-work after paying one married woman 13s. per week and one girl of 15 7s. per week day work. The paymistress fulfils the function of fore-woman, but even recognising this fact the distribution of the total money earned seems unfair.

Trade and Process.	Minimum.		Maximum.		Average under 18 years.		Average 18 years and over.		Average Married Women.	
	s.	d.	s.	d.	s.	d.	s.	d.	s.	d.
BRASS TRADE [1]—										
Lacquerer	3	6	20	0	6	2	10	6	11	6
Polisher	5	0	18	0	6	11	13	6	14	9
Burnisher	5	0	12	0	—		11	2	12	0
Scratch Brusher	5	0	14	0	—		12	0	11	0
Press Worker	3	6	17	0	7	0	9	8	9	2½
Driller	4	0	13	0	6	4	10	9	—	
Nail Stamper	—		—		—		10	0	10	0
Nail Turner	4	0	11	0	—		9	0	9	0
Turner	4	0	13	0	—		11	9	—	
Riveter	4	0	14	0	7	0	9	0	—	
Stamper	3	6	11	0	5	10	10	8	—	
Solderer	4	6	12	0	5	9	11	0	—	
Tube Charger	4	0	17	6	9	4½	—		—	
Piercing Knobs	4	0	10	0	—		—		—	
Dipping Knobs	4	0	10	0	5	0	—		—	
Polishing Knobs	5	0	15	0	—		—		—	
Small Hinges	4	0	16	0	—		—		—	
Buttons	—		12	0	5	0	—		—	
Chains	4	6	10	0	8	0	—		—	
Small Taps	—		12	0	—		—		—	
Brass Rules	5	0	10	0	8	0	10	0	—	
Safety Pins	5	6	14	0	7	6	10	0	—	
Small Pins	6	0	14	0	—		12	0	—	
Warehouse	3	6	14	0	6	5	9	8	—	
Wrappers-up	3	6	12	0	6	6	9	4	—	
Packing	—		12	0	7	0	—		—	
Sorting	5	0	12	0	—		—		—	
Weighing	4	6	8	0	7	0	—		—	
Core Makers	6	0	30	0	—		17	5½	17	7
Dipping	3	6	—		—		—		—	

[1] The position of women in the Brass trade in Germany forms a striking contrast to the conditions prevailing here :— "Mr. Cohen (Secretary of the Brassworkers and Metal Mechanics of Berlin) said there were no women employed in polishing, or on the lathe, or at the vice, in the brass trades, except lacquerers, wrappers up, bronzers, and scratchers. Women have the same wages as men if they do men's work. There is a women's trades union of 3,500 members. The wages paid for woman's work are 14, 16, and 18 marks a week."—" The Brassworkers and Metal Mechanics of Berlin," by W. J. Davis.

Trade and Process.	Minimum.		Maximum.		Average under 18 years.		Average 18 years and over.		Average Married Women.	
	s.	d.	s.	d.	s.	d.	s.	d.	s.	d.
CYCLES AND ACCESSORIES—										
Press Worker ...	4	6	16	10	8	3	10	0	—	
Polishing ...	5	0	16	0	8	0	10	0	10	8
Enameller and Japanner ...	4	6	16	0	5	6	10	4	11	0
Lacquerer ...	7	0	14	0	—		12	0	12	0
Chains	6	0	—		6	0	10	0	—	
Valves	9	0	16	0	—		—		—	
Screws	4	6	15	0	8	6	12	0	—	
Testing	8	6	12	0	—		—		—	
Rims	5	3	9	6	—		—		—	
Hub Turners ...	—		—		—		—		—	
Wheel Webbing	9	0	12	0	—		—		—	
Machine Packing	—		—		—		—		—	
Cleaner and Packer	6	0	—		—		—		—	
Warehouse ...	5	0	14	0	—		—		—	
Office	5	0	—		—		—		—	
Wrapper-up ...	6	0	10	0	—		—		—	
Sorting Screws ...	4	0	14	0	6	4	—		—	
Spanners... ...	—		—		—		—		—	
Lathe Workers...	5	0	12	0	9	2	10	3	—	
Rubber Section...	—		15	0	—		—		—	
Drilling	9	0	19	9	—		—		—	
Plating Shop ...	9	0	11	3	—		—		—	
Lamp Solderer ...	7	0	18	0	6	9	—		—	
Fitting Burners...	6	0	10	0	—		—		—	
Fitting Backs ...	6	0	10	0	—		—		—	
Saddle Machinist	4	0	16	0	6	0	—		—	
Saddle Stitcher ...	5	0	12	0	—		—		—	
Saddle Frame Maker	—		10	0	—		—		—	
Bells	6	0	16	0	—		—		—	
Chains	9	0	16	0	—		—		—	
Nickel Plating ...	6	0	20	0	—		—		—	
JEWELLERS AND SILVERSMITHS—										
Gold Polisher ...	5	0	20	0	6	0	12	8	—	
Gold Cutter ...	3	0	16	0	—		12	0	—	

Trade and Process.	Mini-mum.		Maxi-mum.		Average under 18 years.		Average 18 years and over.		Average Married Women.	
JEWELLERS AND SILVERSMITHS (*continued*)—	s.	d.	s.	d.	s.	d.	s.	d.	s.	d.
Press Work (Jewellery)	4	0	15	0	8	6	10	5	10	9
Polishing (Jewellery)	3	6	20	0	6	9	12	2	—	
Soldering (Jewellery)	6	6	—		7	0	12	0	—	
Finishing (Jewellery)	4	0	20	0	—		9	10	—	
Brooch Gilder ...	4	0	18	0	7	0	11	6	—	
Charging and Soldering ...	3	6	—		6	0	—		—	
Studs	—		17	0	—		10	0	—	
Studs Burnishing	5	0	14	0	—		9	0	—	
Rings Polishing	3	0	18	0	—		12	0	—	
Gold Beads ...	4	0	12	0	—		10	0	—	
Masonic	—		14	0	—		10	0	—	
Medal Press Work	5	0	12	0	5	0	8	6	—	
Warehouse (Jewellers)	3	6	25	0	7	2	17	3	—	
Pearl Stringer ...	5	0	12	0	—		—		—	
Scratch Brusher (Jewellery) ...	—		12	0	8	0	—		—	
Burnishing (Jewellery)	2	6	17	0	3	6	—		—	
Gold Froster ...	5	0	12	0	—		—		—	
Gold Chains ...	2	0	20	0	6	9	14	6	16	0
Silver Chains ...	2	6	20	0	4	0	11	0	—	
Chains (various)...	2	6	20	0	9	9	12	0	13	0
Pencil Cases ...	—		—		4	0	—		—	
Photo Frames ...	—		—		—		10	0	—	
Press (Silversmiths)	6	0	14	0	—		9	0	10	0
Stampers... ...	3	0	16	0	—		10	0	12	0
Polishers (Silver)	3	9	16	0	5	4½	10	0	—	
Burnishers (Silver)	6	0	17	0	9	9	13	6	—	
Scratch Brushers (Silver) ...	5	6	—		—		9	0	—	
Finishers (Silver)	5	0	—		5	0	—		—	
Warehouse (Silver-smiths)... ...	5	0	20	0	—		12	0	—	

In considering the causes of this comparatively low wage of women, confusion will be prevented if we keep in mind the modern theory that under a competitive system such as ours, each worker, just as any factor of production, has to justify his or her position by work done. "The national income is distributed among these several agents in proportion to the need which people have for their several services, *i.e.*, not to the *total* need, but the *marginal* need. By this is meant the need at that point where people are indifferent whether they purchase a little more of the services (or the fruits of the services) of one agent, or devote their further resources to purchasing the services (or the fruits of the services) of other agents."[1]

This means that a man tends to get the more, the more he produces. His wage is determined by work done that consumers want, and not by any consideration of his wants or necessities. And this principle, so far as it goes, gives us a valuable lead, though from the point of view of the wage-earner it is subject to many important qualifications, since for it to be fully adequate, we must assume perfect competition and full equality of competitors.[2] However if we consider the nature and quality of the work done by women as compared with men, we shall probably get the solution of our problem. This becomes more evident when we remember some of the suggested solutions of the problem, such as, that women's wages are determined by demand and supply, or by the fact that a woman's standard of comfort is less, or that her wage is an

---

[1] Marshall, "Economics of Industry," p. 253.
[2] See discussion on this point in Chapter XII.

auxiliary one. In regard to the first of these, as
Professor Smart points out,[1] it is rather a statement
than a solution to say that if, on the average, wages
are not above 10s. per week it is because the demand
is met and the supply forthcoming at that rate. We
leave out of account "the factors, or influences, or
motives that induce, or tempt, or compel women to
take a wage below that of a man, and what are the
factors that guide employers to offer the low wage." [2]
We must remember that our question is as to the
share that falls to one class of labourers as against
another class.

Again, to say that a woman's standard of comfort is
less may, in the first place, be questioned as a matter of
fact. In many items, such, for example, as dress, a
woman's standard is higher than that of a man ; and,
secondly, the theory of basing a woman's wage on the
standard of comfort must be questioned, for it would
fail to explain the obvious fact that in some of the
"genteel" women's trades where the standard of life
of the class to which the workers belong is comparatively high, the wages are often lower than that of a
rougher and poorer class of worker.

On the whole, facts seem to show that it would be
more true to say that women's standard of comfort is
often low because of the low wages they get, rather
than the opposite. The fact is that women will, if necessary, exist at a much lower standard than a man, but
this is an effect of deeper causes, and is one of the
effects we must explain.

[1] "Studies in Economics," p. 109, &c.
[2] Ibid., p. 112.

Again, the third answer that a woman's wage is
low because her wage is an auxiliary one, because she
is subsidised by the other members of the family, is
not borne out by facts. In Birmingham, for instance,
in almost every trade the married woman gets the
highest wages. In the Cycle trade married women's
wages average 11s. while the general average for
women above twenty-one is 10s. 6d. The almost
invariable reply to the question whether married
women tend to bring down the wages was: " No, they
are more independent and better skilled and therefore
always get more on piece-work." A large employer in
the Bedstead trade when questioned on this point
said: " Married women are in responsible positions,
and are steadier and more skilled and so get better
wages." In the Pen trade a leading trade unionist
gave as his opinion that " married women's wages were
much the same as others, but better if anything."
And as pointed out above, in Birmingham the influence of married women has always been towards
the shortening of hours.[1] The only danger from
married women is when they come in as job-hands
in time of pressure, as they do in some branches of
the Bedstead and other trades. Sometimes they work
only for a few hours each day, and the fact that they
can be got in this irregular way must tend to keep
wages low. Still, on the whole, married women, as
against others, do not compete unfairly because they
are only part of a family, and others again are the sole
workers in the family. The assumption of this answer
is that the wage-earning unit is the " family," but this
does not correspond to facts, although we shall see in

[1] See Chapter on Legislation, p. 35.

the sequel that woman's position in the family is sometimes part of the complexity of causes which make her
willing to receive a low wage.   Here, again, it seems
that a woman is often subsidised because the low wage
which she receives would not suffice for the standard of
comfort of the family to which she belongs, and this
fact that women sometimes are subsidised must receive consideration in any final solution, but as usually
stated it is misleading.   As a matter of fact the worst
cutting of women's wages comes from those very
women who are not subsidised at all, such as widows
who are the sole wage-earners of the family.   It is only
in a few trades, such as typewriting, clerical trades,
and shop assistants, that we find the modern phenome-
non of a girl working for pocket-money, and thus
being content to take away the living of other girls
for the benefit of unscrupulous employers.   Evidently
the solution of women's low wages must be sought on
other lines, for at most this fact of women being subsidised is but part of the solution, and rests on some
deeper reason.[1]

The above attempted solutions fail to give the
answer because they have altogether missed the one
great fact pertinent to the question, viz., that generally
women do not do the same work as men, but follow
certain branches of the trade which both men and
women allow is peculiarly "women's work."   In Birmingham it is very difficult to get instances where
men and women do the same work.   In the large
majority of cases the answer to the question, "Do

[1] *Vide* C. Booth's "Life and Labour of the People," vol. iv.
p. 300.

men and women do the same work?" was, "No, women do certain branches in which the men never interfere." In the same way when asked what was the attitude of the men's union to the organisation of women, the reply was, "Indifference, because what the women do does not touch the men at all." In the Jewellery trade, the Printing trade, as well as in miscellaneous trades such as making swivels, studs, links and medals, women do the lighter and more mechanical jobs. The finer work in the Hook and Eye and Chain-making is left to men; and men do all the important and principal parts in Lamp-making and Japanning. In Harness-making, again, women work on certain well-defined articles, though this trade is in a state of transition, and women are in many cases supplanting men. This is also the case in the Cycle trade, in which women have supplanted men in almost all automatic and routine work.[1] In the Tailoring trade the men's and women's work seems fairly well defined, and it is generally in the case of a domestic workshop where a man employs his own family that the usual division is transgressed.

Thus we may note also, at this point, that the simple statement that a woman's wage is lower than that of

[1] In one section of a large cycle works the men employed in 1902 numbered 80; in 1905 men employed numbered 20, women having displaced the rest. The wages of the men were from 30s. to 40s. per week. The highest wages of women on identically the same machines and doing the same work is 18s. the average wage being lower. When the men were dismissed they were told to go home and send their wives back in their places.

a man, because her work is not so good, misses the more important facts of the case; for this would simply mean that better work got better pay, an advantage of more skilled work as against less skilled. In those trades where men and women seem to be doing the same work, there is usually some difference of quality or quantity due to the steadiness, strength, or skill of the man, *e.g.*, in machine-ruling the man can set his own machine, while the girl must have this done for her. Thus while in certain cases it is better pay for better work, generally the fact is that women are in certain branches of the trade in which men do not compete. This is borne out by various investigations. The recent inquiry in Printing trades shows that "except at occasional times of dispute their work is so well marked off from that of men, that the men's unions are coming more and more to the conclusion that it does not pay them to organise the women." [1] Again, Sydney Webb, as a result of extensive inquiries, says : " Usually, however, the women perform some branch of work which is wholly abandoned to them by the men ; and they refrain, whether willingly or not, from engaging in the branches monopolised by their male rivals. The line between the two classes is often subtle enough, and it varies from place to place. Moreover, wherever the dividing line may be in any particular locality at any given time, it shifts with almost every change in the industrial process ; moving, too, nearly always in the direction of leaving the women in possession of an ever larger industrial field. The economic boundary between men and

[1] "Women in the Printing Trades," p. 43.

women is constantly retreating on the men's side." [1]
It seems to be a fact, then, that women are in more
or less exclusive possession of certain branches of
trade, and if they monopolise a trade, in this trade
the commodities made are generally comparatively
"cheap," meaning by that, that the exchange value is
low. On the whole, men are in the better paid trades
or branches of trade, and women are in, and are constantly moving to, the low-wage trades; and, as
Professor Smart and Sidney Webb have pointed out,
this gives the question an altogether new aspect from
that ordinarily understood, for we have to consider
not merely a difference of wage between workers of
various degrees of efficiency, but a difference of wage
between two non-competing groups, and moreover of
groups whose level of wage is determined by a different law. "The question is not : Why are men and
women employed in equal work at unequal wages?
but, Why are men and women employed in different
groups of employment? and, comparing these two
groups, why is the wage level of skilled female labour
lower even than that of unskilled male labour?" [2]

Now, one of the most striking facts brought out
by our investigation about working women generally,
and also about employers, is the thoughtless way in
which they take women's work, its conditions and
wages, for granted. Almost invariably in answer to
the question, "Are you in favour of women's trade
unions?" the woman's answer was, "I have never
thought about it." And employers can usually give

[1] "Problems of Modern Industry," p. 75.
[2] "Studies in Economics," Professor Smart, p. 122.

no other reason for the actual wage than the fact that
such and such a figure is what women usually get in
Birmingham.   And in all cases piece-rates are fixed
by reference to this customary wage of the district,
and the rates reduced or increased till the wage earned
by piece-work approximates to what the girls expect
to get.[1]   And as we have already pointed out, in the
trades where women are replacing men they are
always content to do the work at a much lower wage
and usually get the wage that is customary in the
district.   We investigated one case in the Cycle trade
where a woman displaced her own husband at half his
wage.   Thus we get the fact that women are employed
on "cheap" goods, or less paid jobs, and men move
out of any line in which women compete with them,
because women's competition is bound to bring the
rate of wages down.[2]

So far, then, our conclusion is that women almost
invariably earn less than men, and nearly always this
low wage is co-existent with an inferior class of work.
And even where the work of men and women is more
nearly equal, such as in the case of shop assistants,

[1] *Vide* "Women in the Printing Trades," pp. 43, 52.
[2] The great exception, that of the Lancashire weavers, where
the men and women work under the same conditions at same
work for the same rate of wages, is explained by the other exception, that men and women are in the one union, and so both
sexes would consider their wages to be equally at stake in any
attempted reduction of the wages of either.   But if the union
broke down, then, as has already happened in Yorkshire and
other parts of the country, men would leave the trade entirely,
and women would soon be reduced to the customary wage of
the district.

teachers, clerks, &c., it is generally taken for granted both by men and women that a man *ought* to receive more than a woman. Thus, usually, men and women form non-competing groups in which the principle governing wages seems to differ, the woman's wage being fixed according to " use and wont." That is to say, the woman is usually employed in cheap lines, not that the low exchange value of what she produces accounts for her low wages, but the low wages are at least one factor in accounting for the cheapness. The woman earns less than the man, not merely because she necessarily produces less, but apparently because her wages are fixed at a comparatively lower level just because she is a woman. Thus we must ask why this disability attaches to one sex as against another. And the answer seems to be that generally it is because women accept the inferior position and take it for granted. But this general answer does not carry us very far, and we must seek out the reason why they are content to accept this inferior position.

And first we ask, Is there any reason at all for the level at which women's customary wage is fixed, or is it merely arbitrary ? Could the rate be lowered or increased and still be retained as the customary rate ? The answer to this, on one side, is evident. If an attempt was made to lift it, to say 20s. as against 10s. now, it is easy to see, that, *other things remaining the same,*[1] it could not be maintained, for the competition of unorganised women would break it down. Some

---

[1] *I.e.*, The want of independence and organisation on the part of women, and the cutting of price by unscrupulous employers.

women are almost independent of the work because
they are married, and at times of pressure come in as
job-hands in certain trades; others are independent
because they are subsidised by their parents, while on
the other hand some work because they are the only
breadwinners and would willingly take any wage
rather than not get the work ; and so the unscrupulous employer, hard driven by the stress of competition, would get women below the level and so would
tend to compel the other employers to do the same.
But why, then, does not the present value sink lower ?
The answer seems to be because it cannot.[1] In the
sweating trades, where, as recent investigations have
shown, the rate of wages is below the customary rate,
it always means either that the worker is slowly de-
teriorated as a worker, or else is subsidised by poor
law relief,[2] and private charity, or else finds money in
a way that is far more common than the average
respectable person thinks. This means, then, that
women's wages are already down as far as they
will go because they are often below subsistence
level, and cannot go any further without the rapid

---

[1] See Professor Smart's " Studies in Economics," p. 127.
[2] Miss Irwin, Glasgow, reports :—That the returns of the inspectors of the poor show that many outworkers, who are in
receipt of wages too small to support them, though working full
time, are aided from the rates. Moreover, although to an extent
impossible to ascertain, many of the outworkers on low wages
are assisted by the churches and by charities. Here evidently
part of the wages is paid by outsiders. . . . The cheapness of
goods made in such circumstances is balanced by the increase
in poor rates and in the demands on the benevolent (" Home
Work amongst Women," M. H. Irwin, Glasgow, 1897).

deterioration of the woman as a worker, and public opinion, unenlightened on these matters though it is, would resent any wholesale lowering of women's wages.

Whatever the reason why the rate is not higher, the fact seems to be that the limit is set against further reduction of women's wages by the sorry fact that the very existence of the women as workers demands at least the present level, for as a matter of fact even the present level is not sufficient for a girl or woman to realise the standard of comfort of the working classes, low though that is, unless the woman is subsidised to some extent, or gets a further income in some way or other. Any one acquainted with working-class life knows the low standard to which the widow, or the single girl left without friends, is obliged to adhere. Thus, as far as women are concerned, the workers have not shared in the progress of production of wealth, and are still at the stage where capital is all powerful, and while it does not take all the risks yet takes all the gains.

The reason of this inferiority of women, as compared to men workers, seems to be the same reason that accounts for their subjection and inferiority in other lines, such as politics, and education, and a full discussion of which would mean a historical account of the status of women from early times to the present day. But it is sufficient here to point out that women are governed by the customs, standards, and traditions of the past, not only in economics, but in many other ways as well. Working women usually accept the dependent inferior posi-

tion as right and just, because they have always
been accustomed to it, and from want of education
on broader lines. For instance, comparatively few
working women at any rate, appreciate the agitation
for political privileges. Again, the pathetic drudgery
of the ordinary working man's wife is accepted
as the proper thing, and one sometimes even hears
a woman boast of what really is her inferiority.
Where the man and wife both work during the day,
the woman accepts it as right that she should do all
the housework at night while the man amuses himself
in any way he thinks fit. And often where a working
man assists his wife in household duties he does not
like his mates to know. Thus the statement that
women's wages are determined by a customary standard, and that this standard is the lowest possible,
that of subsistence, is a general statement of a fact
really complex, and before we can consider any
possible remedies, it is necessary to detail as far as
possible the economic factors which make possible
this seeming economic anomaly.

First, then, considered as manual workers, women
suffer from physical and mental disadvantages which
are obvious, and because of the cumulative effects of
their narrow life in the past and the present a woman
usually lacks general ability and industrial experience.
Again, women are rarely able to look altogether after
themselves and their machinery or tools, and usually
a man must do this for them. This want of general
ability is a fact at present, although it may be
explained and remedied.

Secondly, if driven to it a woman will accept a

lower standard of living, not because generally their standard is lower, but—

(*a*) Because their past training, or want of training, has not contributed to develop independence, but has rather been the reverse;

(*b*) Because she is subsidised by family or husband, this subsidising being itself at once a cause and effect of low wages [1]; and

(*c*) Because women lack power of self-protection, due to their failure to combine, which failure itself is due to cause (*a*) mentioned above, and to the fact that few women expect to be life-workers, practically all looking forward to marriage as an escape from work.

Thus, on the whole, the conclusion is that the comparative want of economic progress and self-assertion on the part of women is due to their general subjection and lack of education, and their consequent narrow outlook.

Now, without entering at this point on particular remedies, we may note here a line of objection or warning that is given to would-be reformers by some writers. We are told that women are but part of the army of workers, and therefore any advance in their economic conditions may affect the men workers. Wages, just the same as interest and rent, come out of the national dividend, which is the product of the three factors, land, labour, and capital, and according

[1] In former times the husband himself would be at or near this subsistence level, but his greater mobility and independence has enabled him, in skilled trades at least, to get beyond it.

to modern orthodox theory the share of each factor,
by the principle of competition and substitution, tends
to equal the product of that factor towards the
national dividend. And thus it is suggested that
while it may be true that the women get a lower
wage than they are worth, yet labour as a whole gets
its fair share, and therefore any attempt to raise the
wages of women may necessarily result in lowering
those of men. This view is suggested by Professor
Smart,[1] as follows : " But here a doubt arises. Just
as we might assume that labour, as a whole, has
probably got its fair share as against capital, although
we should find the unskilled labourer at subsistence
level, so it may be that labour, as a whole, has got its
fair share although women's wages remain as they
were years ago. That is to say : as all the increase
may, in the one case, possibly have gone to the
higher ranks of labour, so, in the other, it may have
gone exclusively to men. If this should be the case,
there is reason for hesitation before suggesting a
remedy. For if labour, as a whole, is already getting
its full share of the annual product, any rise in
women's wages will involve a relative diminution of
those of men. To put it concretely : if the husband
is earning 20s. and the wife 10s., and if 30s. is all that
the national dividend can allow to the two, a remedy
which would raise the latter to 15s. would reduce the
former to 15s."[2]

[1] " Studies in Economics," p. 130.
[2] Professor Smart seems to throw this line of argument out
rather as a warning in regard to the complex nature of the
problem. He himself shows that even if this line of argument

This suggestion has the weight of authority, and undoubtedly, *taking the present competitive system for granted*, there is a limit to the rise of wages—although very difficult to define—for the amount of the national dividend limits what each or all the factors can take from it. It is from the national dividend that labour, land, and capital derive their value, because, as their product, it at once defines and limits the value of the productive factors which have produced it. But, while this is true, what must be shown is that competition is so perfect that it naturally determines that each factor gets its fair relative share, for if capital is stronger any way than labour, then it may be that labour as a whole does not get the share that ideal competition would give, and thus the difficulty of raising women's wages would vanish from this point of view at any rate. That is, it may easily be that labour, as a whole, is not getting its " fair " share of the increased dividend due to the progress in the production of wealth, and so a rise in women's wages would not necessarily mean a lowering of men's wages. And a consideration of the facts of the case seem to indicate that labour, as a whole, does not get its normal share. As Professor Marshall points out,[1] labour has several peculiarities which render it at a disadvantage in its fight with capital. In the first place, capital as compared with labour is much more aware of the conditions of the market, and can easily be diverted when

were valid, yet the attempt should be made to raise the wages of women (" Studies in Economics," p. 131).

[1] " Economics of Industry," p. 274.

necessary. But the mobility of labour and of the labourer are the same, and many causes, no less real because some are sentimental, hinder his mobility and thus place him at a disadvantage. Home associations, family connections, and the usual fact that members of the family are engaged in different trades, and a migration advantageous to one would be disadvantageous to another, considerably hinders the adjustment of supply and demand.

Again, labour is perishable, and the fact that the labourer, even when a skilled artisan, has little or no reserve fund, all militates against a fair bargaining. He is compelled to take not what his marginal efficiency makes him really worth to his employer, but what he can get in competition with his fellow unemployed worker, who is ever ready, hard-driven by poverty and want, to take the job. Thus, in Marshall's words, " It is, however, certain that manual labourers as a class are at a disadvantage in bargaining ; and that the disadvantage wherever it exists is likely to be cumulative in its effects. For though, so long as there is any competition among employers at all,[1] they are likely to bid for labour something not very much less than its real value to them, that is, something not very much less than the highest price

---

[1] This competition between masters is the exception rather than the rule. It is only in periods of exceptionally good trade that such competition would become effective for raising wages. The competition amongst the workers is much more regular and general, and becomes exceedingly keen in times of bad trade, and so is a more or less constant force tending to depress wages.

they would pay rather than go on without it ; yet anything that lowers wages tends to lower the efficiency of the labourer's work, and therefore to lower the price which the employer would rather pay than go without that work. The effects of the labourer's disadvantage in bargaining are therefore cumulative in two ways. It lowers his wages ; and, as we have seen, this lowers his efficiency as a worker, and thereby lowers the normal value of his labour. And in addition it diminishes his efficiency as a bargainer, and thus increases the chance that he will sell his labour for less than its normal value." [1]

Again, while it is easy to see that, in the case of various tradesmen together making one article, one trade (A) may be getting less than normal relative share, and thus allow one or all the other trades to get a greater share out of the total normal share due to labour as against capital, and that if (A) then gets its normal share, of necessity in the long run the overpaid branch must lower its wage or tend to diminish the demand for the article produced. Yet the same direct relation cannot be shown between low-paid women's labour and such a trade, say, as bricklaying. And, anyway, it is a big assumption to suggest that men are overpaid, for, even with all the combination of skilled artisans, the peculiar disadvantages mentioned above of limited mobility and industrial outlook must, on the whole, give the advantage to the capitalist. For example, it is well known that a rise in wages does not follow an increase in price of the goods produced

[1] "Economics of Industry," p. 276.

anything like as soon as a decline in wages in case
of a falling off in the demand ; and thus, while the
capitalist acts as the buffer which first receives the
shock of rising and falling markets, yet in the long
run he gets much more advantage than loss out of
this fact.[1]

Even in cases where the woman does a cheaper
branch of a trade in which the man does the more
skilled work, and where the total produce is sold
as a whole, it is by no means a necessary fact that an
increase in women's wages would bring down the
man's in proportion. For in many cheap articles
there must be a considerable consumer's surplus, and
thus the consumer would pay more rather than go
without. Excessive cheapness leads to waste, and
if the price of many things, *e.g.*, hairpins, pins,
matches, &c., were doubled, it would not decrease
the demand.

Further, there is the relation between wage and
efficiency, and in the case of low-paid labour this
is very important. A leading Birmingham manufacturer, who pays wages 50 per cent. above the
customary wage of the district, said that he feared
no competitor who paid low wages. Good wages
mean good business from the master's point of view.

Again, the warning may easily be taken as sound-
ing dangerously near an echo of the old wage fund
fallacy. And anyway, as Professor Smart himself
points out, a woman is not a mere appendage to a
man, and this economic inferiority has an ethical side

[1] See Chapter XII. with respect to the profits of Birmingham
Joint Stock Companies.

as well.   The relation of women's low wages to
early and improvident marriages, for example, and
to that dread trade which one hesitates to mention, would probably be interesting lines to follow
out.   And since there must always be girls who are
not members of any family, and widows and others
who are sole wage-earners for the family, it is imperative that, if possible, the economic status of
women must be raised ; for, while their economic
inferiority is due to their past subjection, yet in turn
the inferiority tends to perpetuate the subjection.[1]

[1] In the whole of this argument we take for granted the
competitive system with all the inequality of ownership and
distribution of wealth, together with the awful waste.   And
even then it is evident that to talk of the "fair" share of the
workers is closing one's eyes to the anomalies of the case.   If
the present share of the workers, which means that 10 per
cent. are in a state of primary poverty, and 20 per cent. more
are on the poverty line, is the full result that the competitive
system can offer, it is surely high time that the nation should
direct its attention to the possibilities of co-operative and
collective management of the industry of the country.   We
resent the opinion that it is "fair" that 1,250,000 rich persons
should take £585,000,000 ; 3,750,000 comfortable people should
take another £245,000,000 ; while the poor 38,000,000, who
bear the brunt of the industrial battle, should get only
£880,000,000.   On this point the reader should see Chiozza
Money's "Riches and Poverty."   Another estimate is made
by the Fabian Society as follows : Total National Income,
£1,800,000,000 : out of this Rent takes £290,000,000 ; Interest,
£360,000,000 ; Profits and Salaries, £460,000,000 ; i.e., the total
income of the legal proprietors of the three national mono-
polies of land, capital, and ability, £1,110,000,000, leaving for
the income of the manual labour class, the large majority of
the people, but £690,000,000 (see Fabian tract, "Facts for
Socialists," pp. 7, 8, 9).

CHAPTER IV

OUTWORK [1]

HOMEWORK (or, more technically, Outwork) has been described as the " Subterranean Department " of industry. The definition "home-worker " applies to any one who does work for an employer in other premises than those of factories or workshops which come within **General Notes.** the scope of the Factory Acts. We have taken the term in its broadest sense in order to include all the varieties of occupation by which women add to the family income without actually entering a place of business.

As regards home work proper, *i.e.*, home work that is done by *bonâ-fide* home-workers, and not as an extra by factory hands, present legislation demands only that accurate lists of those employed shall be kept, that no description of· textile goods shall be allowed to go into any house where infectious disease

[1] See article on " Home Industries in Birmingham," by Mrs. Muirhead, in *Women Workers' Quarterly*, Sept., 1899.

is known to exist, and that the particulars clause be observed as much as within the factory.

This group has been treated separately for three reasons ;—

(1) The isolation of the individual worker makes the enforcing of the present legislation difficult ;

(2) The dwelling-house is at once home and workshop ;

(3) The social effects of this class of work are more evident on some lines, and more hidden on others, than in the case of factory work.

In this group it is less satisfactory to consider the woman separately as a mere economic unit in the industrial world ; the conditions of work and wages are intimately related, both as cause and effect, to conditions of home life.

In a city like Birmingham, in which the small master and the small workshop still compete so largely with the great factory industries, the question of outwork is too large a one for any investigation to be absolutely complete. We hope, however, to give a general description of the conditions fair enough to form a reliable groundwork to any social student who may come into closer contact with the problems connected with this fringe of industry.

The home-workers belong to all classes of the industrial population. This is especially true of the unskilled workers, and is the reverse of the general rule we found obtaining inside the factories. The majority are married women or widows. A few are elderly spinsters, a few are young girls who work with their

Women who Work.

mothers or who live at home and do some work there in preference to entering a factory.

Nearly all the home-workers who answered the question as to why they worked gave one of three reasons. The most frequent was that the husband's wage was either too small or **Why they Work.** too irregular to keep the home. Fifty-two per cent. gave this answer in many varying forms, of which a frequent one was, " It's all very well at first, but what are you to do when you've three or four children like little steps around you ? " [1] Others had worked all their lives ; if the husband is a labourer earning at the best 18s. per week and liable to many weeks without work, no other course seems possible. When we consider the circumstances of those who did not answer this question, it is obvious that practically all the married women would belong to this group. Forty-six per cent. of those who answered, worked because they were widows or deserted wives. The widows, and they composed four-fifths of this number, had generally started work when their husbands became invalided, unless, indeed, the drunken or idle habits of the men had compelled such a course still earlier.

It is so frequently asserted that the married women work for pocket-money, or " to pass the time," that it was surprising to find that only o4 per cent did so. One of the latter indeed said, " What should I do without the hooks and eyes?" and one could but pity such lack of imagination. The few pence she would earn would not have a serious effect on the earnings of her

[1] See Rowntree's " Poverty," pp. 136–138.

neighbours.   Many skilled workers do not work for
the bare necessaries of life, but their standard of living
is relatively high, and they often work in order to
maintain this standard, especially with regard to their
children's clothes.

The houses in which work is carried on do not
vary much externally.   Some streets and courts have
a better reputation than others, but other-
Where They Work. wise all live in small houses either facing
the street or in a court.   The rent may be
anything between 2s. 6d. and 7s. 6d. and is most often
between 4s. and 5s. a week.   A higher figure usually
means that they keep a shop or take in lodgers.   Some
of the best-class workers are to be found in the back
courts, but they consider themselves above their surroundings and "do not neighbour."   The trade and
the interior conditions show the class of home at once,
and these are far surer guides than the kind of street
or court in which the workers are found.

Homework is decreasing in most trades.   Unless
the worker is an old factory hand who has left to get
married, the employer of to-day grows ever more disinclined to take the risk of giving work to be done
away from his supervision.   It is an extravagant system which has its advantages when adopted to meet
a sudden press of work to accommodate which the
factory premises are inadequate, but giving out the
work in small quantities, and fetching and carrying,
involve a great waste of time and effort, which does
not fall only on the employees, though it falls on
them most heavily.

In a city of varied industries like Birmingham, one

is not surprised to find an extraordinary variety of
home trades. For the sake of brevity the
following grouping has been adopted, but   **Groups of
                                               Work.**
there are many unfamiliar occupations
which can only be grouped together as miscellaneous
trades as they are too small for detailed description.
Such are gun-stock polishing, ginger-beer making, or,
for example, the lady who makes a "fair living" (*sic*)
by drilling holes in Spanish nuts and picking out the
kernels, engaging a neighbour for the latter job when
she is extra busy. Her husband earns over £1 per
week, and only one child out of the thirteen is still of
school age. Her work is regular, her home moderately
comfortable, but one would not have expected to find
such a good opening in this trade !

Homework falls into two broad divisions which we
may call : (1) trade work, and (2) extended domestic
occupations, *i.e.*, washing, lodgers, small shops, and
baby minding.

The most important "trade" occupations are :—
1. Unskilled work (chiefly carding and packeting);
2. Skilled work :—
>   i. Paper box-making.
>   ii. Leather work.
>   iii. Brush making.
>   iv. Polishing and burnishing.
>   v. Sewing and machining.

The chief of the unskilled industries is carding hooks
and eyes. Rumours arise from time to   **Unskilled
time that an American machine has been   Trades.
                                              Carding.**
invented to do this work, but up to the
present none has been found so quick and so

effective as the hand worker. " A few hooks and
eyes " are the great refuge of the labourer's wife,
and there are streets where as one passes along on
a summer's day one may see the carding done in
nearly every house.

The process requires only speed and neatness.
First the eyes are stitched on to a card, then the

Process. hooks are linked into them and finally the
hooks are stitched on. Thus each card
passes three times through the worker's hands. Many
say that it does not pay unless you have a child to do
the linking, and this work is left, whenever possible,
for the small deft fingers of children of five years old
and upwards. It is no uncommon thing to see an
out-of-work man doing his share, or to hear a woman
say of her neighbour, " Eh ! but he's a good husband
to her, you should see him nights; he's as quick as a
child at the linking."

The rate of pay varies from 9d. to 1s. 4d. per pack,
the higher pay being given for the small fine work

Rates of Pay. which is trying alike to eyes and fingers.
A pack consists generally of two dozen
gross hooks and eyes, i.e., a gross of cards with two
dozen hooks and eyes on each.[1] The worker must
provide her own needles and cotton ; the latter costs
about 1d. in the 1s., the needles about a farthing per
week. A great many get their work through middle
women, who fetch and carry the goods in a peram-
bulator or small hand-cart, weigh it out, and take the
risk of loss, and charge 1d. or 2d. per pack. The
women consider this well worth paying to save trouble.

[1] 3456 about, i.e., 384 hooks and eyes for 1d.

The middle-women are generally respected and have a good position among their neighbours, and we heard of only one exception to this rule. One, who was very much respected, earned from 7s. to 10s. per week as middle-woman, but she might fairly be described as the aristocrat of her business. The work is fairly regular, slackness, if any, coming in the summer time. At the best, "It's scandalous work, and there's no living in it," as one woman said who carded with her aunt, the two earning about 6s. per week with hard work. Another delicate woman, prematurely old at 44, earned 5s. when alone with her children, 15s. when the two elder girls were at home and helped her; the boy of seven sat down to the linking as soon as he came in from school. The husband earned about £1 per week, and two girls brought in 11s. 6d. per week between them. This family of nine and a baby were living in a house with a private yard, and "didn't neighbour;" they paid 8s. 6d. for rent, and gave up one room for the man's workshop. All was neat and orderly, and by dint of incessant and united work they kept up a standard of respectability to which the mother had always been accustomed.

If such a family is to be found at one end of the social scale among the carders, there are plenty where the worst conditions of the casual labourer prevail. In considering the social conditions in connection with home workers, various questions suggest themselves. What kind of women are working, and what did they do in their early days? What is the family history, and what are husband and children doing? What are the homes like as regards cleanliness, furniture, and crowding? Need they be so poor, and how do they spend their money?

Almost every trade will bring different answers. As regards the carding business, we will ask the reader to accompany our investigators on a first visit to a characteristic street, and to draw his own conclusions from a straightforward account of some of the visits made. A distant mission has advised the visit, a gentleman has even collected some names to start us, and, as we find later, " there's been a lot of jealousy because he's took some and left others."

It is a dull August day, the street is perfectly colourless, the wind seems to blow into it all the newspapers of the neighbourhood. There is a tiny dilapidated mission hall, and one or two houses have been fitted with shop windows, otherwise the dingy rows are only broken by the three-feet-wide passages which lead us to the courts behind. Some of the houses are closed, some condemned. Others have been recently renovated, and are at least decently papered and painted. In others, again, the renovations have not been effectual, and the new paper is already peeling off. In some, whole patches of the wall are bare, the brick floors are uneven, the woodwork is bursting from the walls, and occasionally there is a heap of fallen bricks in the corner.

The houses nearly all consist of a kitchen and pantry, one bedroom, and a garret, and cost from 3s. 3d. to 4s. 6d. per week. In most of the kitchens we find a wooden bench or settle, with or without all the boards of the seat, a table, and some wooden chairs. Most have pictures, and some sort of muslin curtain over

the windows, which is, on the average, cleaner than
one might expect.

The street swarms with children, mostly ragged and
dirty.   Naturally there are many pale faces, but it is
a comfort to see also many rosy cheeks and bright
eyes.   Clothes are often held together with safety
pins.

We have been advised to start with Mrs. A., and
her four pale dirty little girls follow us in with two
or three friends, and stand in a row and stare.   Mrs.
A. is a cheerful bright woman, and quite ready to be
questioned.   She married at 20 and is now 41.   Before marriage she was a screw-worker, and earned 10s.
to 13s. per week.   Has she always worked during
married life?   Yes; she went to the factory till she had
three children, then she took to washing and hooks
and eyes because she could not leave home.   She
would rather work out " than be bothered with children all day, but they lost by neglecting them."   She
has had nine and seven are living.   The eldest son is
away in the militia, the second, aged 18, is a filer and
pays her 7s. out of his 10s.   The husband is an iron-
caster, but work is slack and he can only give her £1
per week.   She adds 1s. 6d. to 2s. 6d., according to
the help the children give.   They lived for fourteen
years in a two-roomed house, and moved here two
and half years ago.   The house has been condemned
by the sanitary authorities; it is less dirty than
some, and could hardly be clean in its present condemned state.   Rent is 4s. per week, and burial clubs
for the family and her mother amount to 1s. 7d.,
leaving about 23s. 5d. to feed and partly clothe the
family of nine people.

Mrs. B. is sitting at work on her doorstep. She is a robust-looking woman of 51, in a spotless apron. She was a screw-worker before marriage, since then she has worked for twenty years on and off at hooks because her husband was often short, but he would never allow her to enter a factory again. He is a gas labourer and gives her £1 per week out of which she must feed and clothe him and "find his baccer." The only living child, a delicate girl of 15, works at rivets and brings home 6s. per week. The house costs 4s.; it has an extra room downstairs and is "one of the three best in the street." She herself "does hooks and eyes more to pass the time than anything else—it all helps," and she does not sit to them every day. She "learnt from mother, but in those days you got 1s. for what now earns 9d."

Mrs. C. has lived for four months at the top of her court and had no luck there. She was seventeen years in her last house. She has also worked for twenty years at hooks and eyes and can now earn up to 5s. per week, but her eyes will not let her make more. She was a general servant and earned up to £16 a year, and would go back if she could. Her present husband is a labourer, but is "mostly out of work and has to be kept: he has never been *seen* drunk in the street." Of her first husband she says, "Didn't he just treat me well." He helped with the children, no woman could beat him at carding, and together they earned up to 14s. per week. "He was very miserable in his beer," and she thinks it hastened his death. She has had "more comfort since she lost him." The house is very bare, but

cleaner than some, and the same may be said of the
five school children. Two girls are at work. The
eldest, aged twenty, earns good money at a button
factory (up to £1), and keeps herself very respectable. Nellie, aged eighteen, gives her mother 5s. 6d.
when she is well enough to work. She has lately
been very ill, and her work was blamed as the cause.
The mother does not really know, as she never
inquires into her daughter's affairs, and the girl has
always been delicate. The boy of 15 sells papers,
gives his mother 10d. per day and wastes the rest.
The joint family income averages about £1 per week
(excluding what the girls keep for themselves). The
mother is never ill ; she has always been a teetotaler
and brought her girls up the same. She says everything has to be neglected for hooks and eyes, and
she would rather wash and clean. They pay 3s. 6d.
rent and 5d. for the children's burial clubs, and the
girls pay 2d. for her. She is a lady of much activity,
aged 48 as near as she can tell ; she washes on
Tuesday and chops wood sometimes in addition to
her carding.

Mrs. D. is now bowing at her door and begs us to
walk in, as she also cards. She also washes, but
does not make more than 2s. 6d. per week. Her
husband is a cycle brazier, but, as work is short [1]
and he is very delicate, he never gets more than 7s.
He helps with the carding and the children and has
never been seen the worse for beer. He takes a bit
of bread and butter and goes out all day to look for
work, returning at tea-time when the hooks and eyes

[1] Work very short during year of visit, August, 1904.

come in. Four children died of consumption ; the
other five have been very delicate, but two are now
quite healthy. The boy of fourteen brought home
his first earnings, 4s., last week, for keeping watch
outside a pawnbroker's shop. He also gets all his
meals except breakfast, and his Jewish master is
very kind. One little girl of eight is hopelessly
paralysed. She tries to link the hooks with her
useful hand, and is very clever and a beautiful singer.
The house is almost bare, but everything they can
possibly spare is at her sister's, for fear of the bailiffs.
They have always been chapel members, but have
no clothes for chapel now, so go to any open-air
meetings. The house costs 3s. 6d. and is on the
better side of the street. They never need to buy
bread, as they live mostly on the broken bits a
doctor gives them. "We live on bread and butter
with sometimes a bit of dinner on Sundays." The
family has been twice in the workhouse at times
of special misfortune : she wishes they were there
now, "It's more comfortable than clemming."

We find out Mrs. E. only by accident. She is the
widow of a sawdust dealer, and her failing health
has made her give up washing for carding. They
chiefly card in the bedroom, "as it looks so poverty"
if any one looks in.

The reader must be getting tired, so we will pass
by many more cottages and pay only one further
visit. Whenever we ask any question of broader
issue than their own immediate concerns, every one
says, "Ask Mrs. G——," and to Mrs. G—— we go.
She is now 58, has been married thirty-three years,

and her husband has been paralysed for the last
nine years. Two sons live at home, and though
trade is bad and they can hardly pay their share
of the household expenses, things seem fairly comfortable. Mrs. G—— has always worked, but never
in a factory. Now the shop brings in about 30s. a
week, and the house, which is a double one, costs 6s.
a week. We rest with relief in the spotless kitchen
while our cheerful hostess, who has lived here for
many years, tells us about her neighbours and about
the open-air concerts, which come at very rare
intervals to one of these courts and which are one
of the joys of the street. These and occasional
open-air services are the only means of recreation other than the public-house, but attempts are
being made to use the little mission hall to more
purpose. The workmen who told us where to
get off the omnibus said that what they wanted
most was a girls' club or evening home where
their daughters could learn sewing and nice
ways.

We could give many more instances of carders
and their histories, but we have literally fulfilled our
promise of not going beyond one street. It has
been often visited since that first day and the first
impressions have been confirmed. It is the home
of many loafers, many who seem to be only half-
developed human beings, of much drinking and
wickedness, and of much kindness and patient
struggle that amounts to heroism in deeds that
remain unknown.

To turn once more to general statements, we have

found the hook-and-eye carders earning, on an
average, 3s. 3½d. per week. The husbands
Summary.   brought home about 19s. 6d. and the
average rent was 4s. In 23 per cent. of the families
provision was made for burial expenses, but this
does not include several whose payments had run
out owing to exceptional ill-luck. The women
themselves had been in every grade of work before
marriage, from a bolt maker at 5s. per week to
a schoolmistress at £80 a year.

The other kinds of carding do not show much
variation. The best paid are the smaller groups,
such as toy carding or carding brass
**Other Carding
Industries.**   cabinet fittings. One of these women
made on an average 11s. 3d. per week.

Buttons and safety pins are the other "cardings"
which occupy a considerable number of women.
With constant work the button carders we investigated seem to earn an average of 5s. 3d. a
week. The husband, where there is one, brings in
about 16s. to 22s., and 4s. 3d. goes to pay for the
three- or four-roomed house. Children who are
at work help a little, but they rarely do much
beyond paying their own share of the household
expenses.

Pearl buttons are the best work, though the tinfoil
generally used as a background makes the work
rather trying for the eyes. These buttons are paid
for at rates varying from 2s. 9d. to 6s. 8d. per
hundred gross, *i.e.*, 1d. to 2½d. for 432. There is
also some special work which fetches 1½d. per gross.
This is thread-work, and consists of carding the

large buttons, which have a horizontal hole from side to side and which have to be threaded before being stitched. It takes one hour to do two gross of these as against five hours to do twenty gross where the rate per gross is lower, so the profit is probably the same in either case.

The payment for linen buttons is from 2s. 9d. to 4s. 2d. per 100 gross, and a quick worker can card four gross in an hour, earning approximately 1½d. an hour. Trouser buttons fetch 3s. per 100 gross.

There was less variation in social status observable among the button carders. Many of them are desperately poor, but the homes, if bare, were nearly always clean.

Safety pins are also carded by the very poor. There are nine to twenty-four pins on a card, generally arranged according to size, and payment varies from 2½d. to 6d. per gross of cards, *i.e.*, on an average 580 pins must be put in for 1d. In connection with safety pins there is a curious side industry. This is opening the pins ready for japanning ; they are sometimes fetched to houses for no other purpose, and 1s. is paid for opening 100 gross.

One finds similar unexpected work, such as putting curtain hooks on pins at 2s. 6d. per cwt., at which one can earn 5s. per week by sitting all day ; [1] binding iron split rings with fine wire to keep

---

[1] "Sitting all day" generally means working from 8 a.m. to 11 p.m., when not absolutely prevented by household interruptions. It is impossible to gauge the length of these interruptions.

them from springing apart after hardening, and unbinding them again when cool—dirty work which brings in 1d. per gross, *i.e.*, about 1d. per hour ; and other "oddments," all undertaken to supplement sadly inadequate family incomes, sometimes only when the man is out of work.

Boxing and packeting are not far removed from carding. Hooks and eyes, hairpins, stationery, and other small articles are often boxed or packeted by outworkers. These things also are generally done in very poor but respectable homes where some addition must at all costs be made to the low wages of the husband or older children.

Boxing and Packeting.

In the case of hooks and eyes, the worker makes the little paper cases, pastes and labels them. She then counts in either 23 hooks or 17 hooks and 17 eyes, ties up each packet with cotton, and threads on a sample outside. For hooks alone she gets 3½d. per gross, for hooks and eyes 4½d. Cotton and glue cost 4d. in 3s. Where children help it is possible to make 6s. or 7s. a week at this work, but this necessitates very long hours and the work itself often runs short.

Hooks and Eyes.

Hairpins can bring in a similar amount. They have to be assorted sizes and are put into boxes containing 50, 100, or 150. These boxes are filled and counted for 3d. the gross. Others are wrapped in packets containing 27, at 1d. or 1½d. the gross.

Hairpins.

Stationery packets are filled by a favoured few

who have generally worked for many years for some particular firm. It takes about one hour to earn 2d. when the worker has acquired **Stationery.** the necessary knack.

So far as we can find, women usually resort to these unskilled home-trades in order to supplement other income. Many women have to exist on 3s. or 3s. 6d. a week in old age, and it would, of course, be possible to exist even by carding hooks and eyes. As a matter of fact no one does this. The woman who has both the time and the ability to earn so much, can more profitably work the shorter factory hours, earning in this way double the wage and not necessarily neglecting her home more. If she is too old for a factory she can rarely sew fast enough to earn more than 2s. a week at the most, and children or parish help her unless she is able to keep a tiny shop or to take lodgers. Many of the home workers are mothers of young children; they have often apologised for their untidy rooms, but cleaning and washing must be indefinitely postponed, for, as they say, "It's either wash the children or feed them, and it's better to earn the few pence for a bit of bread."

Skilled Work.

The simpler kinds of paper box-making are generally taken as homework by women who have learnt the trade as girls. The cardboard comes to them cut and prepared (*i.e.*, **Paper Boxes.** scored) for bending, the coloured paper with which it is to be bound and fixed, or else covered entirely, is also cut out, and the woman practically shapes and fixes the box, providing her own glue, which costs from 9d. to 1s. 6d. per week according to the amount of work. A pennyworth of glue suffices for 1½ to 2 gross of boxes. Cheap small work earns 3½d. per gross and best work 1s., *i.e.*, 12 to 40 boxes for 1d.

It is not uncommon to find a mother and daughter working at home together. A few women do it for pocket-money, or to save against a rainy day, others from force of necessity, and naturally the amount of work varies ; but however urgent the necessity, we commonly find only decent and cleanly houses belonging to this class of workers. The earnings average 9s. a week, rents 5s. 6d., and the number of rooms four ; facts which all point to conditions above the poorest. It must, however, be remembered that this improvement is generally due to the better mental status of the workers, which enables them to keep up the determined struggle, and prevents them from sinking to the level of unskilled workers. Among the latter we often found the same fight successfully and untiringly waged, but while there it was the exception, and marked the woman who had been ground downwards by misfortune, here it is the rule.

There is another kind of trade in the paper line which is met with occasionally, *i.e.*, making and hawking paper flowers, windmills, &c. An outlay of 1s. 2d. on paper, sticks, and colouring matter, makes three shillings-worth of flowers, which seem to sell readily in the winter. In the summer this occupation is probably varied by some other casual trade.

In the leather trades we again find all extremes.

There was a great rush of work during the South African War and workers of all classes were attracted into the trade. Since then there has been a period of depression, and now the outworkers are few in number, and mostly "old hands" at their work. Different firms give out different parts of their work. We know women who do harness, saddlery, belt and purse stitching, military chain lining, and there are also a comparatively large number in the boot-and-shoe trade, though this seems to be dying out in Birmingham.

Leather Work.

Taken as a whole, the miscellaneous leather workers are poorly paid, and they have to provide their own thread and awls.

One woman lines chin-straps for soldiers, police, and firemen's helmets. For the firemen she stitches brass rings on to the leather, lines with a leather strip, and sews on the buckle and tab for ¾d. The other straps are larger, and numerous steel rings are sewn on with double white hempen thread. For these she receives 11d. per dozen, with 1d. in four dozen for thread ; this allowance does not cover the cost, for which she reckons 2½d. deduction in 5s. 6d. She works from five in the morning till eleven at night, and does not succeed in earning 10s. a week. This may be an extreme case ; the widow is a woman of 60, and is helped by her son and the parish, but the average earnings of the cases investigated amount to only 6s. 9d. per week. These women had all been in good work before marriage, generally at an indoor branch of the same trade, and they had earned from 15s. to 25s. a week. The fact that very few of them were insured against burial expenses points to much poverty, either chronic or the result of recent trade depression.

Boot machinists and repairers seem to do rather better, especially where man and wife work together. However, the introduction of electric power-driven machines into the factories has affected the amount of work given out, and the Birmingham manufacture seems to have decreased before the growth of the trade in other towns. There are many such survivals of dying trades in Birmingham, and the new and growing ones will not add to the homework industries.

One woman who worked with her husband, when questioned as to the family income, answered, "We just make a do of it," and that answer would probably serve in most cases. With those who were in the trade in its more prosperous days the "do" represents rather hard times. Other workers who live in the carding districts would, on the same earnings, consider themselves much above their neighbours.

There are other lingering trades. Brush-making and drawing is one which is carried on in poor but, in many cases, well-kept houses. Some of the women have been at other trades before marriage, but the best workers have taken home a trade which required from one to two years factory training to learn thoroughly.

Brushes.

One lame woman often starts work at 4 a.m., because later the house and children will claim her. When there is work to be had, by working all the hours she can spare up till 11 p.m., she can make up to 10s. She started to work at home, as so many do, a few years after marriage. The three children are still at school, and her husband's regular employer failed in business—a common source of extreme poverty among working people.

One old lady of 86 has worked for a well-known firm for nearly 60 years. She can now make only 1s. 6d. a week, for she is old and feeble, though she still "draws" without glasses. In her younger days she earned 10s., but prices were better then, and she could do a brush in an hour. The parish allows her 3s. 6d., a kind old lodger pays 2s. and also helps with the housework. She has worked all her life whenever it was humanly possible, bringing up the survivors of her sixteen children to do the same, for the husband was always slow and delicate. She complains that there was no good schooling when the children were young, and so they have grown up ignorant. Her other grief seems to be that she was "reg'lar throwed away" when she married at seventeen, and that she is now "growed out of date."

The old brush-makers could detain us a long time with their stories. We will stop only for one other, an old lady who had worked so long that when she was sent for a fortnight by the sea she was homesick for her brushes. Her friends got her afterwards into an almshouse, but she kept her bench at the house of a married daughter, and went there from time to time to have the treat of a little work.

Pearl work is still carried on in a few homes and small workshops, but pearl grinding is very unhealthy, so the decadence of this **Pearl Work.** trade is a gain to the community.

Different kinds of polishing are done in the homes, but not to any very great extent. There are some **Polishing.** French polishers who can earn as much as the indoor hands when there is sufficient work. Chains, brush handles, and gun stocks employ scattered women, but the chief trade of this class is burnishing.

This is a trade which a woman can always take up again in her own home, as it is a rule in the factories **Burnishing.** that the burnishers provide their own tools, and the only other materials needed for ordinary work are suds and beer for polishing and sawdust for drying. In the jewellery quarter of Birmingham, where there are hundreds of small factories, outwork is easy to get, and many of the women work for two or three employers.

A small table is generally set apart for the work, which is clean, and in no way detracts from the comfort of the living room. The homes are almost always well kept, and these workers belong to a superior artisan class. They do not generally work for the bare necessaries of life, but to save against illness, &c., to clothe the children, or to supplement an income which is otherwise not large enough to keep up the standard which they desire. The husband's wage, or, in some cases, contribution to the home, averages 24s. 6d.; the woman's earnings, 8s. They are generally of the class which " have no neighbours," preserving an aloofness that seems hard and sad when contrasted with the rough-and-ready give-and-take which almost amounts to communism among the very poor. Yet, if they are to see the children tidy, to bring them up in good ways, and to start them well in life, they have no time for the gossiping which plays such a large part in many women's lives, nor can they afford to mix freely amongst those who have no share or sympathy in such efforts to maintain a relatively high standard. One woman said that she always saved in good times, but she kept the money herself as she did not believe in banks. She had never been in debt and never used a pawn or huckster shop, " They make many a woman poor." She was a fair specimen of her class, the backbone of her home, and one respected the very stiffness which her determined stand against illness, the uncertainty of her husband's work, and the depression of her own trade had engendered.

Chair-caning is another of the high-class trades which is decreasing : fashion has changed, and most people buy rush-bottomed chairs now. **Chair-caning.** When there is work to be had, the caners receive 12s. or more a week, but they have to supply their own materials, and it must be remembered that cane is very expensive, and often costs 50 per cent. of this sum.

When we come to sewing and machining, we find on the one hand the most cheering, on the other the most depressing, conditions of homework. The young machinist who has married a **Sewing and Machining.** skilled workman, and who occupies her spare time by taking a few dozen pinafores from the factory where she used to work, is at one end of the scale ; at the other is the elderly woman, often left alone in the world, who is just keeping herself alive,

with the dread of the workhouse ever before her.
Speaking generally, the women who sew or machine
at home are relatively very superior. All the skilled
work is undertaken either by those who have been
properly trained, or by girls who have been in service.
It is only among the plain sewers that we find the
class mixture which was so noticeable among the
carders.

The occupations given are numerous: as one would
expect, there are a great many small dressmakers
working on their own account; in addition we find
tailoring, "ready-made" machining, and shirt-making,
and finishing, and a number of small trades, such as
gun-bag making, girth-stitching, umbrella mending,
&c., &c., trades which have often been discovered or
learnt through the ingenuity of the woman herself.

Smocking is a large home industry, but, like the
ready-made suit trade, it exists mostly outside the
Birmingham district. Young girls learn the trade
and then leave their employers to work at home,
where they earn 10s. or 11s. a week.

Many of the pinafore and shirt machinists work
very intermittently, applying for work when the
husband's trade is slack, or when for any reason
they want a little extra money. Others work in
order to save, or to occupy their spare time profitably.

The wages earned vary with the trade and the
home conditions, and any averages are apt to be mis-
Earnings. leading because the amount of time given
to work varies so much in different
families. The Pinafore machinists whom we investigated earn about 9s. 6d., to add to the husband's 35s.

Tailoresses can earn 11s. 6d., but the varying seasons
affect them considerably and few women are capable of stating an average to cover the whole year.
All the odd trades investigated seemed to pay fairly
well, but it was so largely a matter of individual character that this is not surprising. For instance, we find
a widow who was left with six children and started
cleaning clothes. Her children have always been
distinguished for their neat appearance at school and
the regularity of their attendance, and, most remarkable of all, the three youngest (girls) have each been
sent to a higher grade school after passing a standard
qualifying them to leave an ordinary school.

The way in which women of this stamp keep a
home together and bring up their children often
seems little short of miraculous. We may mention
here another, who was left penniless with eight children and no trade to which to turn. She only says
she "did not sit down under it;" by dint of incessant work, washing, cleaning, and nursing, those
children have not only been kept alive without parish
relief, but they have been brought up in respectable
refined ways and belong to the rare few who are glad
to spend their evenings at home.

However, this is a digression. As far as the
clothing trades are concerned, more can be learnt
from a study of the conditions in London, Glasgow,
&c.[1] Compared with these towns Birmingham possesses a very small group of workers.

[1] See Reports of Women's Industrial Council, Scottish
Council for Women's Trades, "Life and Labour of the
People," &c.

Among the hand-sewers and waistcoat makers extreme poverty is often found, combined with respectable surroundings, the survival of more prosperous days.

The homes among these workers almost always attain a relatively high standard. The records of dirty or ill-kept houses are rare, though **Homes.** in the case of women who are dependent on their work there is naturally something to be desired in this respect. The average rent is some guide as to the class of home, and as this is 5s. we see at once that, though privation may be great, we are no longer amongst the poorest of the poor. Leaving out of account the dressmakers, who are very often single women, we find a large proportion of widows in this group of trades, especially among those who do plain sewing, chiefly for their neighbours who are nearly as poor as themselves.

Many firms disapprove of outwork on principle, and only give it to their old indoor hands, or to women who started working for them when it was more general than it is now. Such masters will not turn away their old workers, but the system of outwork will die with them. For example, there is an old lady of 87 who cuts out the best surplices and makes them with the help of one woman : she has worked for one employer for more than forty years, but when she retires the work will not be given out again.

This decrease of outwork in the clothing trades is satisfactory for manufacturer and purchaser : the former sees the materials properly and carefully used, and the latter has not the fear that clothes have been made in dirty or insanitary homes, a condition frequent enough in the past, however satisfactory present conditions may be in this particular city.

Extended Domestic Occupations.

The chief "domestic" trade is washing, and when we come to consider this business we cannot but be reminded of the traveller's account of certain islands whose inhabitants "earned **Washing and Cleaning.** a precarious living by taking in each other's washing." This exactly describes what seems to be taking place in many Birmingham courts. First one takes in washing, then another; a woman washes at home or gives it out according to the state of household finances, or a regular worker is temporarily relieved of her business obligations during illness, and so a neighbour is benefited and she does not lose her trade.

As in other home industries, many women do a little work but make no effort to maintain themselves. Many, on the other hand, are thrown suddenly on their own resources,[1] and to try to obtain washing and cleaning is the first thing that suggests itself to them.

The rate of payment may be as low as 6d., but is usually 8d. or 9d. for a dozen articles, irrespective of size or quality, though, as one woman **Earnings.** sadly remarked, "You needn't look to find many pocket-handkerchiefs or such things in

[1] Frequently happens on death of husband.

the dozen." The expenses, *i.e.*, soap, starch, blue, and coals deduct about 4d. from every shilling earned. Washing is pre-eminently a trade for married women. All the " home-workers " are either married or widowed, and among laundry workers 63 per cent. are married, a larger percentage than is found in any other trade.

It is not conducive to home comfort; the actual washing is generally done in the " brewhouse," which

Homes. may be shared with as many as ten neighbours, but ironing and much of the drying take place in the small family living room, causing a hot, steamy atmosphere, which is very trying for the family, while it is naturally impossible to maintain any standard of order and sometimes of cleanliness.

These washerwomen are among the first to suffer in any period of trade depression, for as the first economy in bad times is to do your own washing, the tiny laundry with a very local connection is soon emptied.

We find as many types or groups among the " washing and charing " women as we did among

Women. the carders. There are many who have fallen upon evil days and keep up the appearance of cleanliness and order in spite of adversity. There are others who seem to work in the intervals of drinking and quarrelling, and whose homes are wretched in the extreme. Between the two ends of the scale we find literally every grade of respectability, but, after prolonged investigation, it is gratifying to note that only 19

per cent. of the homes are classed as dirty and
neglected. A great many of the women are members of mothers' meetings or kindred institutions.
Many have parish help.

Before marriage these charwomen had followed
every variety of trade, but about 35 per cent. of
those investigated had been domestic servants. Many
of these women bitterly regret this fact in after-life,
because they say that had they learnt a trade they
would have been better equipped for taking their
share in the struggle to keep the home: their rela
tives are apt to think they feel their difficulties and
privations more keenly because of the immunity they
enjoyed from such anxieties while in service : on the
other hand, many of them have learnt thrifty household ways and are excellent managers.

The average earnings per week among this class
of washerwomen are about 4s. 2d. Those who earn
more are generally women who have to keep the
family, and they combine various home industries :
they take in sewing, go out cleaning, mind babies,
cook and clean where a neighbour is ill, and are
often paid as much in kind as in cash, earning a loaf
by scrubbing floors, an old frock for a child by
cleaning, &c. For instance, one woman, the mother
of eight children ranging in age from 19 to 5
years, was such a mainstay of her home. The
husband had ruined his health and his reason by
early indulgence, and, though recovered, could do
no regular work, and brought home as little as
10s. for an exceptionally good week. The two
eldest girls (aged 19 and 18) earned 6s. a week

each, and the mother was content because they were learning respectable, clean trades. The son of 17 was a brass caster and earned 8s. 6d. or 9s. 6d. All three retained 1s. or a little more for their own clothes. The next boy, aged 15, was temporarily out of work; the son of 13 was in the blue-coat school; the little girl of 11 was allowed to save all the pennies she got for carrying home washing, and had so been able to go into the country for two weeks. The elder children had gained prizes for exceptional attendance when at school, and went regularly to evening continuation schools. They paid 4s. rent for a front house with four rooms, but they had been regular tenants for seven years and the landlord showed them consideration in consequence. The home was very poor, but the mother managed to pay 1s. a week for family burial insurance.

Some women mind children in addition to other work; a common charge is 6d. a day, out of which the child's dinner must be found. The care of older children who can go to school brings in less, *i.e.*, 1s. or 1s. 6d. a week, but in these cases no food need be provided.

When minding babies is the only occupation, a woman may take in two or three, and sometimes she does a little carding in addition.

Babies. Many of these women are exceedingly kind to their charges, and even help with food when the mothers cannot provide anything. Very often older women mind their own grandchildren in this way, and thus preserve their independence when

they are past more arduous work. They generally
do washing for their married daughters as well, for
which they charge 1s. or 1s. 6d. a week.

In spite of the care and kindness with which the
little ones are so often treated, it is a very general
opinion among the working women that children
put out to mind do not thrive, and after a little
experience of this a great many women leave the
factory and start as homeworkers in order to watch
over their own children. Others resign themselves
to taking the risk, because, as they say, "What is
the good of staying at home if you can't give them
anything to eat."

Adult lodgers are a very frequent aid to paying
the rent in houses which have four or more rooms.
The lowest charge for a man is 2s. a
week for room and washing. One "real   **Lodgers.**
Christian gentleman" let an aged widow have half
an attic for 9d., and superior rooms bring in as much
as 5s. Girl lodgers can be housed and boarded for
between 5s. and 7s., the price they would pay if
living at home; they are then treated as members
of the family, and often do their share of cleaning
up on Friday nights.

The average earnings of these working-class
lodging-house keepers are 9s. 3d. per week, but it
must be remembered that we are dealing only with
the poorer branches of the business. As soon as we
rise to furnished apartments of a higher class 10s. to
14s. is charged for two rooms, and a working man
pays 1s. a night for his room, though even in this case
board and lodging may be given for 12s. 6d. a week.

One old woman had brought up first her own family, and then a family of orphan grandchildren, in spite of a drinking husband who was a hopeless invalid for the last seven years of his life. She said she had "got along by providence," but she had done her share by caning chairs and letting rooms, mostly to professionals (*i.e.*, theatrical visitors). She let two or three rooms and charged 8s. or 9s. a week for room, attendance, and cooking ; and paid 7s. 6d. rent for her five-roomed house, which was beautifully clean.

Small shops of every variety occupy a great many women. The most common are small general shops where every oddment seems to be sold.

Shop-keepers. They are often carried on in an adapted kitchen, which may be the family living room as well. There is usually a bowed window fitted with shelves, and a table or counter is fitted up inside, behind which the lady of the house does her cooking in the intervals of business. She sells sweets, butter, soap, soda, pickles, cotton, ginger-beer, &c., her stock varying according to the capital she can expend in filling the window. Home-made ginger-beer, pickles, and cakes, are generally prominent features among her wares, and she may add to her trade by cooking workmen's dinners or early breakfasts. Trade is chiefly among the immediate neighbours and is often in farthingsworths or ha'p'orths. One frequently finds a woman with an empty shop, and with the business in abeyance because she cannot buy anything to put in the window. Even in the poorest shop the legal regulations as to scales and weights must be strictly observed. These are expensive articles to buy (or to fetch out of pawn when a fresh start is made), but it is much more profitable to sell by weight than in packets. In very low streets the contents of the shop (*i.e.*, window) and the scales are taken up into the bedroom every night for fear of theft.

Where there is a counter and a bell, &c., the cheapest fittings are valued at about 30s., and the average profits come to about 11s. a week. Of course there is every class of shop in this one branch, from the little window in the poorest street to the regular business in a little corner shop, though even this may only bring in 10s. per week in bad times. We asked the owner of such a shop how she managed : she answered, " We trust a bit above, you know, and we don't tell people everything ; what we can't get, we do without." She was seventy-seven, delicate and cheerful, one of those who had learned good ways in her country home and in service long ago. The husband was nearly twenty years younger, but he had been blind for seventeen years ; he chopped wood for the shop, scrubbed the floors, and did much of the cleaning. He rejoiced in a pension of £10 a year, imperturbable good spirits, and the respect of his neighbours and friends.

Shops selling only one class of goods seem to pay the best, and we have found special prosperity in fried fish, and in second-hand clothes.

The average rent for houses with shops of this

class is 6s. 8d. per week, and taking all trades
together the women earn about 17s. 6d. Their
homes have generally four or five rooms, but, as
position is of great importance, they are naturally
dearer than houses of the same size situated in
courts.

Though the average earnings appear high in the
thirty trades of which some knowledge has been
gained, it must be remembered that the sum mentioned gives the best view of the situation. The
number of small shops is very variable; many
appear for a short time and then fail, either from
lack of custom or business capacity, but more frequently in consequence of an accumulation of bad
debts. On the other hand, a great many of the little
shops with a small trade exist for many years, and
the women who keep them become almost local
potentates among their neighbours.

We have a few records of dirty and neglected
homes (one of them unfortunately attached to a
tripe shop), also of drinking shopkeepers, but the majority seem to main-
tain a fair standard of cleanliness and order, though
many are too poor to attain to much comfort. Shop-
keeping is a trade that is soon ruined by drinking
habits and the attendant irregularity, consequently
a high level of respectability is the only one that can
survive, and it is not surprising to find small shopkeepers as a class on a fairly high grade in the social
scale. Many of the women have been in service or
shops before marriage, though it is not uncommon
to find former factory workers among them. The

Homes.

husbands are very often in an allied trade or working in connection with their wives. These men earn considerably more than the labourers; but among the shopkeepers, as in every other class of women workers, many are obliged to work because the husband either will not, or cannot, provide for his family.

Taking over eighty of the cases investigated, we find that an average family of three workers (*i.e.*, over fourteen years of age) and two children (under fourteen) has an income of 39s. per week when the father is not on short time.[1] They are poor, but rich compared with some of the home-workers described earlier.

The last home trade we will mention is wood-chopping and selling, a business only partially carried on in the home, as the selling **Wood.** is practically hawking. Hawking salt is the only thing more wretched than hawking firewood, and, when we come to consider this business, we find ourselves plunged again among those who may almost be called "submerged." It is not so difficult to sell the wood as to get it to chop, as there is only a limited supply of waste wood in the market, and in bad times there are so many customers that each one is limited in the amount they may buy.

The women earn about 6s. a week when they make a regular trade of it, and their husbands are men who can earn about £1 if they are willing to work

[1] 86 families. Total over 14 = 240, average per family 2·79; under 14 = 196, average per family 2·28; total income 3,360s., average weekly income 39s.

and can get jobs as labourers.   Many people turn to
this trade for a few months to tide over a bad time.
We find again representatives of the lowest social
classes mixed with many who, through the illness
or death of the breadwinner, have been driven to
it as a last resource.

WOMEN WORKERS

CHAPTER V

WAGES AND EXPENDITURE

IN describing the general conditions of work we confined ourselves to the work itself, and left untouched the many social and economic questions that arise out of the present state of affairs with regard to working women of all classes; in other words, we described the work, leaving to future chapters what we may call "the human side" of the question.

Such a distinction was no longer possible in describing the different kinds of home-work. Here the work and the home life are inextricably intertwined, and no consideration of the work alone would allow us to get quite away from viewing the worker in relation to her family. Home-work thus formed a connecting link between the two views of our subject—women viewed in relation to their work, and the work, or rather working conditions, viewed in relation to the women.

At the same time home-work touched many points which are not so apparent when a woman's working and home life are definitely separated in place, hours, and companionship.   On the other hand, in some respects home-workers can be considered with the great army of women workers.   One of the most striking of these points is the question of wages.

Women's wages were discussed in Chapter III., but there is one point on which a few more remarks may be made, viz., the effect of low wages on the women themselves.

In discussing the wages of women as contrasted with those of men it is always assumed that a woman has only to keep herself.   Leaving therefore out of consideration the large number of women who must keep, at any rate partially, more than themselves, we are faced with the question as to whether the average working woman can keep herself in a state of efficiency, and in this we include in a way not derogatory to her own self-respect.

When calculations are made as to what a woman, or for that matter a lady worker, can live on, an important social factor is generally neglected or ignored.   Payment is commonly calculated for a grade below the standard of the worker in question instead of a grade slightly *above it*.   What does this entail ?

At the present time more sympathy is felt and expressed than ever before for the difficulties of the nation's workers.   In spite of this the common tradition of payment tends, as far as women are concerned, not only to counteract in them the race tendency to struggle upward, which is essential to national progress, not even to make women content with the place in which they were born, but actually to force them into contentment with a *lower* grade.

This applies to all women workers whose payment is regulated by the fact that they are women, *i.e.*, with certain exceptions; the only professions generally exempt are art, letters, the stage, and medicine.

In considering the woman's station in life let it be distinctly understood that we have no wish to condone the pernicious love of luxury and display which ruins so many men and women, in leading them to emulate those whom they are pleased to consider as their social superiors. The instinct to which we have referred is far sounder and, let us hope, more deeply rooted than the pitiable weakness which so often serves to obscure it. The emulation of our superiors in matters of thought, education, and refinement is a tendency we all feel, and one we encourage in efforts to improve the condition of factory girls, &c. How, then, can we tacitly acquiesce in a system that demands a course of the severest self-denial and necessitates the suppression of this very instinct of emulation?

When the salary of almost any worker is discussed one hears almost invariably the easy reply, " Oh, she *can* live on it." She generally can live on it, but that is not the question. The vital point is, Can she improve on it? Can she live as her education and class of work demand? Can she keep pace with the times and the rising standards required in her particular work? Can she have the necessary minimum of recreation (a point rarely noticed as a necessity)? and Can she, whoever she be, save against sickness, loss of work or old age?

We must at least give women the chance to save, to use leisure profitably, in some cases to keep themselves neat and respectable, before we assert that any given class is incapable of improvement.

In dealing with women common custom permits us to calculate not the worth of their work, not even what they can live on, but, if we consider the question at all, what they will consent to live on.

Take, for example, the case of a teacher in an ordinary school or family. She must be educated in a way to stimulate every intellectual and refined instinct, also in a way that makes the greatest demands on her parents, and then we trust to her the most important and exacting work (next to that of a mother) in the world. We ask her to arrange to be housed, fed, and carried to and from work for about 30s. a week, to dress well on about £15 per year, and if we leave her about £7 per annum for keeping herself up to date, books, longer journeys, doctor's fees, and savings, we consider that she is very well paid.

How many of the ladies and gentlemen who make these calculations would like to carry them out? Of course it can be done; if there is no professional work to take up the time it can be done easily, but we rarely realise that economy is a matter that takes much time. Take the question of dress. A girl can considerably reduce her expenditure if she gives her time and attention to making, repairing and altering her clothes, but we expect the worker to dress equally

well on equally little and yet to give all her strength
and mind to her work.   We expect her to spend her
spare time in care and thought for economies of dress
and food ; to " put up " with accommodation that is
often unsightly, cramped, and rough ; to resolutely
shut her eyes to all anxiety as to the future ; to be
always well dressed, well in health, and cheerful in
spirits ; and we complain at the premature narrowness and hardness that overtakes so many teachers
and others.   We shelve them in early middle age,
and unless they have been fortunate in making a
firm position in some good school, we force them
into the lower grades of the profession, and fill their
places with bright, eager girls, fresh from college,
and full of the vitality and enthusiasm of their early
womanhood.

The case of the experienced clerk, secretary,
typist, &c., is worse.   True, less is required of her
in the way of appearance, training, and intellectual
effort, but her hours of work are longer and her pay
less.   30s. a week is often the maximum pay of this
class of worker, and though the average differs slightly
in different towns it is rarely more than 25s.   We
need hardly enter into an analysis here.   The fact is
obvious that a lady cannot live on 30s. a week unless
she be content to spend *all* her spare time, and often
more, in doing so, or unless she lower her living
standard to that of the board-school girls who are
trying to capture this kind of work.

Among "charity workers " (*i.e.*, district nurses,
missionaries, Biblewomen, &c.) the standard is still
lower, though educated women are often wanted for

the work. "Charity on the sweating system" has an ugly sound, but it is a truer expression than is generally known, and both men and women are frequent sufferers. Such work is always exacting, and is often both mentally and physically exhausting. The usual remuneration is a nominal salary which, for women, varies between £20 and £60 a year.

What answers are generally given to these well-known objections? It is said that girls live at home, that they spend their holidays with their friends, that they go home when they are ill, &c. This is all true in the majority of cases, but we are not therefore justified in taking women's lives and getting our work done partly at the expense of their relations because we pay them less than enough to live in the standard to which they have been brought up. Few men would like to think that they were educating their daughters at the expense, rather on the charity, of other men; that their office expenses were kept down by the kindness of men whom they would hardly know in society; and yet this is only too often the case.

We are not considering the girls who may be considered as still in training, *i.e.*, under twenty years of age; and now, turning to working-class girls, we shall not assume that girls under eighteen are of an age or capability to warrant the demand of a full living wage.

Shop assistants form a class by themselves for many reasons. Among the mass of working girls we have shown that there are a few trades where they can earn a sum enabling them to live rather above than below the standard of their own class. We refer to such trades as the highest class of lacquering, machining, dressmaking, just as among professional women we might refer to first-rate positions in schools and in Government and private employ; but these cases are exceptional as compared with the rank and file of workers.

The mass of unskilled workers have one alleviation, they rarely take any thought for the morrow. They go on from day to day, spending about 7s. per week on their keep and the rest of what they earn on clothes and amusements. Opinions vary as to how much these girls should spend, but probably about 14s. is not an extravagant estimate for a girl to keep herself respectable and healthy. The average wage in Birmingham for unskilled women over seventeen is barely 10s. The reader should also remember that four to six weeks each year must be deducted for sickness and slackness of trade, when the girl would get no wage at all, unless in the former case she had qualified by weekly payments for benefits from a sick club.

Where she falls below this, charity or subsidy in some form must play its part. If it does not or cannot—and how very often this is the case—there is nothing but a life of semi-starvation which must be attacked by the cruellest and worst forms of temptation.

How is this anomaly of taking a woman's life and giving her less than the living wage of her standard affecting the women of England? We have men-

tioned the results in the premature narrowing or
ageing of many of our educated workers; we could
mention more if we could get statistics of nervous
collapse and illness, or search the lists of homes and
institutions.   Fortunately some women who have
not the ability or good fortune to reach the top of
their profession escape the results of under-payment
through their private circumstances.   Many of all
classes accept the downward pressure as inevitable,
and quietly shrink out of sight and descend step by
step.   Take the lower classes, and we come to the
great crowd of those who just live, are content with
their lives, and remain where they are in an easy
acquiescence, marry, and work on in one way or
another until death cuts them off, or old age and
infirmity make them turn to indoor or outdoor relief.
And the great crowd of those lower still, who just do
not make enough on which to live, who are always
underfed and underclothed; what of them?   To all
who have gone in and out among them it must be a
matter of continual marvel that so many of them
are so good.   There is a heroism rarely seen or
recognised in the lives of these thousands who "keep
respectable."   For the rest, "There is one ghastly
investigation still waiting on the economist.   It is
the aid to wages which is got from 'the oldest trade
in the world.'   That this is an economic element in
the wage question is beyond all doubt.   All of us
know it.   None of us has yet had the courage to
measure it.   Not till we do so will the world know
the true cost of 'cheap labour.'"[1]

[1] "Studies in Economics," William Smart, p. 129.

When the British and Foreign Bible Society reduced wages in 1833, the workmen addressed a
petition to the society, in which they wrote, " Your
memorialists respectfully submit that the making it
more difficult, and in some cases impossible, for
females to earn an honest subsistence by their labour,
is in the same proportion to give potency to the
seducers of female virtue." [1]

How, then, does the present system of payment
affect women ?   There is first a waste of nerve and
spirit, a continual temptation to overwork in order to
maintain a standard that ought to be maintained,
and hence much ill-health and early deterioration of
physique ; lower in the scale we find an acquiescence
in conditions which are, to say the least, not conducive
to progress ; and lower still there is no possibility of
escape from actual physical deterioration.   It is not
a hopeful prospect for the mothers of the coming
generation.

A woman should be paid at a rate based on the
quality or quantity of her work.   It is not fair that
the rate should be based on the fact of her sex and
not on her living requirements as a human being ;
that she should give the chief and best part of her
life to hard toil, whether intellectual or manual, and
yet be partially dependent.   At present, if society
does not openly advocate this, it at least tacitly
acquiesces and refuses to face the question at all.

[1] "Women in the Printing Trades," pp. 32–33. We are
well aware that there are other factors in this monstrous evil,
but until this one is removed it is almost impossible to deal
with the question on the moral side alone.

CHAPTER VI

LIFE IN THE FACTORY

THE life of the workers in any particular factory depends so largely on the character of the manager or the proprietor, that any general remarks on this subject must be taken with the reserve rendered necessary by numerous exceptions. At the same time the prevalence of inferior conditions, as of inferior wages, in a few factories is very apt to depress a whole industry, especially when the work is unskilled and in the hands of small firms.

Where many masters spend little or no thought on the comfort of their employees, it becomes doubly difficult for the few who wish to introduce improvements to face the actual initial outlay necessary. This does not apply in the case of skilled work ; here the master wishes to secure the best workers, and, consequently, either in wages or in general conditions, his factory must be made attractive.

For example, the pinafore workers would never be asked to work in a room which is considered quite good enough for a polisher, and shorter hours, provision of time for tea, &c., and other arrangements are noticeable as we ascend in the social scale of work.

Many kinds of work are fashionable or popular among girls for the only reason that they cannot be carried on amidst dirt and disorder. The apathy of working girls with regard to these matters is very often given by masters as an excuse for not attempting improvements. As a matter of fact, many of them are apathetic because the desire for wholesome surroundings has never been awakened, except in the school ; but school influence ceases at a most impressionable age, home and factory influences remain, and the growing girl quickly adapts herself to her surroundings, which are as depressing physically as they are mentally. Small wonder then that the little learner, who hardly counts as a unit in the great organism of her " works," does not show any marked desire for cleanliness or refinement by the time she is sixteen.

Cleanliness, &c.

In describing the general conditions of metal workers we showed how necessarily rough and dirty most of the work must be. It is rarely recognised that the very roughness of the work necessitates a strong counter-influence to compensate for its effect on the workers. Hence girls are allowed to come and go as untidy as they will, to spend their dinner-hour in the dreary workroom, or else in a dining-room whose only advantage is a change of air ; in short, so long as the work does not suffer, they may become as dirty as the machines they tend. Fines and penalties are frequently imposed for carelessness or unpunctuality ; occasionally they are imposed for bad language or untidy appearance.

Press-girls working in a factory where no one may

wear hair-curlers, where boots must be clean, &c., are refreshingly proud of these rules. They consider themselves quite above the ordinary press girls, and many whose desire of refinement has been awakened in social clubs will continue to do the roughest and dirtiest work in factories where such rules are enforced.

The same class of girls earnestly protest against another condition of most metal shops. This is the indiscriminate mixing of men and women.

Men and Women. Here again we are most anxious not to appear to condemn the workmen or the foremen as a class. Some mixing is indispensable in many industries, but most social workers are agreed that there is grave moral danger in the present arrangement. The factory life is a hidden stage even to many who are in most intimate contact with the girls outside, but from time to time the curtain is lifted, and the picture revealed may well dishearten those who are trying to elevate and " level up " our workers.

It is a matter in which statistical evidence cannot be obtained. During the course of this inquiry some hundreds of girls have been questioned, on applying for fresh work, as to their reason for desiring a change. As one would expect, either short work or low wages caused many to make an effort to " better themselves," but there remained a considerable number who had no such complaint to make. With these, the reason for leaving was generally that some one in authority was " forward," or " spoke as they didn't ought." This is only a hint as to how matters stand and how the girls feel on the subject. Where they must work or starve, and where work is distributed according to the will of the foreman, girls are appallingly helpless if personal favouritism or feeling of any kind are allowed to have influence in the " shop."

Allied to this difficulty is the mixing of married and single women. It is a matter of common complaint that the men and married women talk in a way unfit for the ears of young **Married and Single Women.** girls. Many social workers deplore the presence of married women, and object strongly to their employment. Apart from the vexed question whether they should be allowed to enter the factories at all on account of their home duties, it seems rather drastic to suggest that they should not be admitted on account of the bad moral influence they may exert.

In many factories there are strict rules against swearing, &c., and these rules are thoroughly appreciated by the girls employed. It is a pity that such regulations are not the rule rather than the exception, as is at present the case.

Another difficulty with which girls must reckon is the temptation to drinking or gambling. The temptation to drink takes different forms, and **Drink.** here the girls themselves are largely to blame. Customs vary very much in different parts of the city, and after twenty or thirty years of factory life women will mention one of these customs as a grave abuse, and another may be absolutely unknown to them. Sometimes the custom prevails

of treating the forewoman on pay-day in the hope
of propitiating her, and influencing her distribution
of work in the coming week ; for this purpose the
party adjourns to a public-house. Christmas and
birthday parties, &c., are another much abused
custom. A group of girls forms a party club, *i.e.*,
each subscribes 1d. or 2d. for several successive
weeks, and on the appointed day perhaps the foreman or forewoman stops work half an hour earlier,
and allows them to stay rather late, and they enjoy
cakes and tea, with which they mix rum or gin.
The foreman is, of course, treated, if he does not
actually start the collection. For birthday or wed-
ding parties the contribution of 6d. or 7d. is paid in
one sum, and sometimes a present of spirits is made
by some one in authority with a thoughtless kindness.
The girls may or may not get partially intoxicated,
but at least they are engendering a vicious habit, and
in many cases young girls dare not refuse to join,
and they thus start the taste for a dangerous indulgence. More open drinking is too apt to follow ; a
present of a bottle of rum is sometimes made by an
enterprising publican, and younger girls may be
absolutely forced by their fellows to swallow the
stimulant.

It is of the utmost importance that temperance
workers and others should know the actual material
temptations their girls will have to face, for a few
words of kindly and encouraging sympathy in face of
a fact are far more stimulating than the most im-
passioned exhortation to courage, where the audience
know that the teacher is ignorant of their special

temptations. As a matter of fact, even in a most strictly-managed factory, the teetotalers, both men and women, must often face unlimited ridicule, a weapon to which the usual factory employee is keenly sensitive.

We have mentioned the party clubs, but they are part of a vast system. The average factory girl buys almost all her clothing through clubs. These are managed by senior girls, who **Clubs.** generally act in conjunction with some shop which allows the club-holder a discount [1] on the amount of custom she secures. A clever club-holder frequently ends by giving up all other work and devoting herself to the business, out of which she will make a good livelihood. The management is very simple ; for example, fifteen girls wanting boots will agree to pay 6d. each for fifteen weeks. Each pay-day they draw lots, and the fortunate one takes the 7s. 6d. and gets her boots. Cases of dishonest dealing are comparatively rare, and the system has something in its favour, as few girls can save at home for themselves, and by these means they get jackets, boots, drapery, &c., &c. The chief disadvantages are :—

1. An element of gambling is introduced which is almost as risky in one way as the cup of tea with its spoonful of rum is in another; as the girls say, "You may get your things before you've paid for them."

2. Girls are very apt to waste their money by entering for things they do not need, because they have not the courage to refuse.

[1] Generally 6d. to 1s. in £1.

3. They do not get the best value for their money; the purchases must generally be made in a specified shop, and, as one woman said, " The man know's you're a club member, and you have to buy from what he chooses to show you, and he puts away his best things; if you save your own money you can look round everywhere and get the clothes you like best."

It seems a pity that some effort is not made to capture and adapt this system of co-operative purchase. It is absolutely suited to the needs of the women, and careful and disinterested administration would rob it of the disadvantageous elements.

It is well known that many girls share the craze for betting, which is becoming more and more common among working women. It is probable **Betting and** that it is carried on by individual and not **Gambling.** by concerted action. It is a point on which it has been found very difficult to obtain exact information. A widespread evil exists, and many girls bet on coming out of the factory, but the practice seems to be more common among married women who are at home.

In our chapter on the general conditions of work, we alluded to the depressing moral and physical effects of dirt, noise, monotony, and bad atmosphere. Leaving suggestions for a later chapter, we may point out here that the very existence of these conditions, and the fact that they are often inevitable, shows that counteracting influences should be brought to bear.

We are not referring now to the non-working hours. The employer is responsible for the hours passed inside his place of business, and if the conditions are such that the average worker is checked in development, or is actually deteriorating, the employer is running into debt to the country. If he uses up human capital instead of the interest in energy, &c., which can be repaired daily by an average constitution, his business is aided either by the worker's relatives or eventually by the rates, which must provide for those who are prematurely disabled. Women especially fall off in capacity in consequence of early overstrain, and this has a disastrous effect on their offspring ; while many in middle life drag on a miserable existence on the diminished wages they are able to earn. In so far as this is due to work and not to the home life, our labour conditions need reform, and employers and the consuming public must be held jointly responsible.

CHAPTER VII

RULES AND DISCIPLINE

I F the average unskilled work-girl seems to have much in her work and home life against her chances of self-improvement, it must not be forgotten that the present conditions have some important advantages, and that a few employers recognise that efficient, contented, and superior workers produce the best work ; in a word, that it pays to have good conditions.

We have already mentioned the pride of the girls in places where cleanliness and order of person and language are demanded. This brings us **Rules.** to an important question, *i.e.*, the question of rules and discipline. In a young life just freed from school, free too often from all parental control, surrounded by examples of lives unregulated by any form of restraint, factory discipline is the only controlling influence, and the necessity for promptness, regularity, and obedience may benefit the worker as much as the master.

The commonest method of maintaining order is by means of fines and deductions. Before legislation interfered, many trades might have been aptly included in the description of one prominent instance, that it was "a gigantic legalised fraud." The extension of the Particulars Clause, and the Truck Act and Factory Act of 1900 have done much to stop the old abuse by which an employer profited by the delinquencies of his employees, and, in the majority of cases, and apart from the deductions which we mentioned as customary in the clothing trades, the only fines and penalties are for unpunctuality or spoilt work.

The general method of dealing with unpunctuality is by "locking out." At the stated time for starting work the doors are locked, and late comers must wait half an hour, one hour, or lose the half-day, according to the rules of the particular factory. Sometimes the doors are opened twice—half an hour and one hour after starting time, the pay for the time lost is stopped, and sometimes a small fine is inflicted. Occasionally where piecework is the rule, very little notice is taken of the time when girls begin work, but in all cases an employer dismisses a girl who by her persistent "bad-time" does not utilise to the full extent her machine, or place in the workshop.

The other rules refer chiefly to meals, *i.e.*, morning lunch and tea. In industries where no food may legally be taken in the workshop, most stringent rules are essential, but in the generality of industries either these extra meals are forbidden altogether or time is given for them. Fifteen to thirty minutes are often allowed for tea when work is carried on after 6 p.m., but where tea is a forbidden luxury the rule is rarely strictly enforced, and most women secure both lunch and tea with such regularity that one wonders why the few minutes necessary are not granted as a matter of course.   With work starting at eight, and the prevalent habit of getting a hurried and insufficient breakfast, girls naturally want something to eat before one o'clock, and even when the work ceases as early as six o'clock, girls cannot get home until 6.30 or later, and they find the afternoon too long without food of any sort.   As a matter of fact these prohibitive rules are generally quietly ignored, and it seems a pity that a minimum break of ten minutes in every spell of four or more hours of work is not generally given for refreshment and change of position.   Just as reduced hours have resulted in increased output during the actual hours worked, so the loss of output involved in granting time for lunch or tea might conceivably be rendered negligible, by the reduced loss of physical energy in the workers.   In any case it is to be hoped that the maximum spell of uninterrupted work will be reduced from five to four hours in the near future.

More serious in moral effect are the regulations against washing that are still found in many factories where excellence of work does not depend on cleanliness of handling.   Painters and japanners are generally provided with turpentine, &c., but the rank and file are fortunate if they can get a bucket at the sink, and there do exist places where there is a fine of 6d. for washing!   Of course, there is the employer's complaint that where basins are provided the girls do not use them, let them get stopped up with rubbish, waste time in gossip, &c., but the employer has power to regulate such matters.

There are many complaints about the roughness and uncivilised habits of the machine girls, but few pause to remember that a girl who is free, even if not obliged, to go through the streets in a dirty condition has small chance of preserving self-respect, and the fact that this is the necessary condition attached to many kinds of work, induces an acquiescence in dirt and disorder that easily spreads to the other sides of life. As a matter of fact, more girls than one would expect rebel and deplore the roughened condition of their hands. We must all hope that some day masters will recognise that it is not to the credit of their establishments that any employee should enter or leave with unwashed hands or face.

A few masters forbid "curlers" or unblacked boots, and wherever "sumptuary" rules of any kind come into force the best workers available for the particular work are at once attracted. They are grateful for the chance of respectability thus given, for a girl must have sunk very low indeed before she loses all interest in her personal appearance. With women, at any rate, the supply of labour available is so large that even if a few objected to the restriction that forced them to be clean, their places could easily be supplied, and, as the timekeeper is already an essential member of all factories except the very small ones, the machinery for carrying out such a rule is not wanting. That many would welcome it is shown by the fact that there exists a company in Birmingham which supplies clean towels in workshops, charging each subscriber 1d. per week for the convenience.

We may mention that the want of cleanliness in their own apartments in a factory is a great grievance to many girls, and here again the fact that the majority are acquiescent, or even disorderly, is no excuse for dragging to the lower level the minority who have either gained or preserved the elements of refinement.

Many employers have encouraged their workers to make provision against sickness, and though the Shop

Thrift. Clubs Act of 1902 has checked many sick clubs, a great number still exist which pay subscribers a certain sum per week during illness, while the balance is equally divided into " bonuses " at Christmas time. Sometimes the master gives direct encouragement to such clubs, adding a percentage to the amount subscribed. Other sick clubs are entirely in the hands of the workpeople. The fines for unpunctuality or spoilt work often find their way into this fund, or are used for the purchase of hospital or dispensary notes which are given to employees who need medical advice. Very often these notes are granted by a firm without reference to sick club or other payments.

Where lead is used it is compulsory to provide medical advice and attendance, and the best firms in other trades both in England and abroad are beginning to voluntarily follow this precedent. Such improvements have an effect in the rejection of weakly applicants for work,[1] but at the same time, the gain of proper medical supervision is great both to employer and employed, for the ignorant application

[1] See final chapter, pp. 293–294.

of remedies results in permanent injury to the health of hundreds of working women, while anything that ensures health, regularity, and hence efficiency, is a gain to the employer of labour.

The maintenance of ordinary order is often a very difficult matter, and all classes of girls are apt to give trouble in this respect. Very often the best circumstanced are the most difficult, and in such cases strict rules against insubordination are often necessary.

On both sides far greater acknowledgment and, in some cases, knowledge of the mutual dependence of employer and worker are needed. The spirit of antagonism and the belief in opposing interests, where many interests are mutual, cause endless friction and waste of all kinds. While strict justice and impartiality are essential on the part of the master, some check is needed for the ignorant opposition and grumbling which disturb the most model factories. Here the social workers could do great service by teaching the girls their legal rights and powers, and at the same time showing them where these end, and submission is a fair demand that is advantageous to all concerned.

Many girls prefer to work in small factories because they think there is more liberty, even if the wages are less than in larger establishments. This is undoubtedly true. In a small factory the character of master is often merged in that of co-worker, and even where the place is large enough for the employer to have a distinct position as such, he still knows each of his workers, and can deal personally with all questions that arise. A large factory employing hundreds of hands is like a vast complex machine, in which most perfect organisation and rule are necessary, and the individual touch is of necessity much diminished and usually entirely lost. Between the two extremes there is naturally every grade of difference, and, wherever the number of hands is small enough to be manageable, a master who thinks of the matter at all generally considers every case that comes before him on its own merits. This frequently happens in the skilled trades, where an employer often considers it best to allow the maximum of liberty, and to dismiss any girl who is too idle or inefficient to earn enough to be worth her place in the factory. Liberty is thus kept within reasonable bounds on both sides, and the girls are free to enliven their work with singing or talk.

On the other hand, large firms which have a reputation for fairness and superior conditions attract a good class of workers who are anxious to stay with them, and they have therefore great power of enforcing any reasonable code of rules.

A director in such a firm has kindly given the following sketch of a method which has been found very successful where many hundreds of women are employed :—

"Each girl's name is recorded on a card (see illustration) giving full particulars as to age, &c. Each forewoman keeps a record of any breach of discipline of the girls under her care. This record, giving date and nature of the offence, is then sent up to the office and transferred to the girl's card. The girl is always told when, and why, her name is being

SPECIMEN OF RECORD CARD.

Alice Smith

No.			BORN 4·20·86	CAME 9·8·01	LEFT 6·11·03
5360	3·26·02 Loitering in Dressing room	6·30·02	Bad time keeper		Cautioned 7·10·02
40397	10·17·02 Untidy place	10·29·02	Leaving room before time.		Suspended 1 week 11·5·02
	5·31·03 Bad time keeper			Discharged	
			For general bad conduct		

On the other side of the card are entered particulars of health, state of teeth, educational acquirements, &c., of the girl employee.

To face page 206.]

sent forward. At the end of each month the cards with bad records are collected together, the forewoman, and the girl concerned, appear before a director and the head forewoman; the forewoman states her case, the girl has an opportunity of giving her version of the matter, and the penalty is then settled. The whole matter is decided as coolly and judicially as possible, the various factors of previous record, character of the girl, and nature of the offence are taken into account. The penalties are a reprimand, a week's suspension, or dismissal, and the added penalty of a list of offenders, offences, and penalties being posted in every department. This publicity has a most deterrent effect both on the girl and on the department concerned. The whole idea of the system is to be reformatory and not vindictive. Seeing the girl in this way gives the director and head-forewoman the opportunity of giving a little advice, especially to first offenders. The elements of unfairness, and spite, are as far as possible eliminated, the forewoman having to justify her action in reporting the girl. The really unsatisfactory girls, and inefficient and careless workers, are gradually weeded out, which fines and deductions would not do. A forewoman who has to report many girls is considered unsatisfactory, as discipline should be maintained without resort to punishment. The directors are also brought into touch with their employees, and get to understand their difficulties, their character, and their point of view. In order that a girl may be able to redeem her character, after an interval of two years' good behaviour her bad

record card is destroyed, and a clean record given
her. With regard to late time, and absence from
work, this is entered on the cards in the same way,
although a girl once or twice late in the month is not
dealt with. Late time often proceeds from thought-
lessness, carelessness, late hours at night; but in
many cases if there is illness in the home, the
daughter often has to do a great deal of nursing,
and a great deal of housework, before coming to
work. But in a large factory, excellent as these
reasons for unpunctuality often are, it is impossible
to allow irregularity in coming to work, and it has
generally been found to be the case that those who
are most devoted to their home duties are the most
punctual. Other factors are distance and bad
weather; the former is overcome by only taking on
girls from a two-mile radius, and in the latter, in the
case of snow, or exceptionally heavy rain, or thick fog,
special latitude is allowed. To sum up, on the one
hand fines have no good moral effect, and tend
towards the debasing rather than the elevating of
character, often being arbitrary in their action, while
not eliminating the worst offenders. On the other
hand, some such system as outlined above, if carefully
and sympathetically worked, strengthens the character
of the girls, raises the moral standard of the factory,
and, above all, is just. The time taken is very small ;
in a factory of many hundred girls, it takes a director
less than an hour a month, and he considers no time
spent yields such a return, both in promoting the
moral welfare of the employees and the economic
efficiency of the factory, and it certainly pays. The

raising of the moral standard of the girls, and the abolition of fines and deductions, have attracted to the factory a better, more intelligent, and more efficient class of girls."

This extract is given as a suggestive example, and probably every individual employer could suggest some modifications, if he applied it to his particular trade.

In conclusion, factory discipline may be looked at from two points of view: (1) The efficiency and economy of the factory, and (2) its relation to the happiness and welfare of the worker, though these two views are complementary.

This second point is too often overlooked, but if the two could be recognised as inseparable, factory discipline might become a potent educational instrument, and no mean factor in the raising and building up of a more efficient industrial class. Such an instrument will, however, always be inoperative among people whose earnings will not allow of their living in elementary decency.

CHAPTER VIII

MARRIED WOMEN AND THE HOME

I F we consider the total of wage-earning women in Birmingham and the district we find that the married women and widows together number 27,194,

Proportions of Married and Single Women. or about 23 per cent. of the whole. A large number of these women belong to the trades which we have called the unregulated trades. Among charwomen 83 per cent. are married women, and nearly one-half of the female shopkeepers and hawkers also belong to this division of the population. Taking the factory workers alone, we find that about 21 per cent. are married women, who belong chiefly to the metal, leather, and clothing trades, accounting for about one-fourth of the whole number of women in these sections. A great number of the married women in the clothing trades are homeworkers, and when the census was last taken the same would be true in the leather trades, though here circumstances have since undergone some modification. It is in the metal shops that we find the most frequent mixing both of married and single women and of men and women, and many employers hardly inquire of a woman whether she is married or single. In some factories, on the other hand, no married women are admitted at all, though an exception is occasionally made in favour of former employees who have lost their husbands. The prohibition is sometimes made on moral grounds,[1] in some cases because the employers think that married women should stay at home, and sometimes because they have been found unreliable as to regularity and punctuality at work. Where married and single women are employed indiscriminately no distinction is made, and naturally latitude cannot be allowed for the performance of home duties. Many reformers are in favour of legislation to prohibit the employment of married women in any factory. It is obvious that no woman can do all the home work required by a growing family and at the same time spend the day in the factory. A great many try to lead this double existence, washing and cleaning on Saturdays, and paying parents or neighbours for a little care and supervision of the children during the week.

A great many women go back to the factory as a matter of course immediately after marriage. Sometimes this is caused by an independence of spirit that does not wish to be beholden to another for everything. As one

Cause of Work.

[1] "In a large London firm of clothiers, on the contrary, two or three married women are generally put to work in each workroom, and the manager employs these as an unofficial medium through which to check or reprove undesirable conduct on the part of their juniors."—*Women's Industrial News*, December, 1905. See also chapter on "Life in the Factory."

old woman, after sixty years of factory life, said, " A shilling you earn yourself is worth two given you by a man." Others know that the husband's wage will never be sufficient for comfort, and the skilled women who marry labourers are often in reality the chief supporters of their homes, for the labourer's work is subject to frequent seasonal variations, and is the first to be affected by trade depression or depressed by improved industrial appliances, &c. Two elderly women, when questioned on this point, wrote as follows :—

(1) " I wish to say that I should prefer domestic service for respectability, but I think it is every married woman's place to work and help if the husband is short of work or does not earn sufficient to support the home. I should like the factory on account of the hours then, and if she should be a widow factory work would be a lot better for her because she would be able to see to her home and little ones in the morning and when she returns in the evening ; but there are lots of factory work that is too degrading for women who do it and have no need to do so, and it would find more work for men if they did not. I have worked in a factory and I have been in domestic service and I find you can keep yourself respectable in either, so I like them both."

(2) " I think that if a woman has enough coming in to keep them all she ought to stay at home because the children would get better food and be seen to better, but some would rather go to work than mind them. The women ought to help only in cases of illness or

shortness of work. What can a married woman do if not in factory? There is not enough work in going to houses to work as charewomen or washing, and if she goes in factorys she can get good money to help at home ; but I do think it ought to be because they are oblidge to go to work. Little children get neglected and allouged to run the streets and do things that stay with them all their lives, and their husbands get careless and go to the public house to get more comfort, then drink and spend what would keep the wife at home, so what better off is she in the end."

The whole subject of married women in factories is a vexed question. There are different views as to why they work, the effect of their work on homes and husbands, and not less as to the measures which should be taken to check the practice. It may, perhaps, be interesting to compare the two large groups of women who have come before us in the course of this inquiry, viz., nearly 700 married women and widows who work either in factories, in laundries, or as charwomen, and a still larger number who do not leave home to go to work. Our knowledge of them is not derived from one casual visit, but from investigators who have known them for years, and who could therefore be trusted to form a reliable opinion as to their circumstances, the character of the family, &c.

The following table shows comparisons of the earnings of the husbands of the two groups of women :—

TABLE I.

	Women Occupied in Factories, Laundries, or as Charwomen.	Women Unoccupied except with Home Duties.
	Per cent.	Per cent.
Husbands earning 25s. and over ...	26·26	50·00
„ „ under 25s. ...	32·20	35·79
„ wage not stated ...	15·43	10·17
Widows	25·52	3·77
Unmarried women keeping house for fathers	0·59	0·27
	100·00	100·00

First, then, we see that of the group of occupied married women and widows nearly 26 per cent. are widows, a fact which makes it compulsory for them to work. Among the married women and widows who have no outside employment we find that very few are widows (not quite 4 per cent.). The following tables show the habits of the husbands of the occupied married women :—

TABLE II.

Habits of Husbands Earning 25s. and Over. (Wives Occupied.)	Per Cent.
Steady, sober, industrious, &c. (2 delicate) ...	36·72
Fairly steady (1 delicate)	15·82
"Indifferent"	22·60
Unsteady, idle, brutal, drunken, &c.	20·34
Habits not stated	4·52
	100·00

TABLE III.

Habits of Husbands Earning Under 25s. per Week. (Wives Occupied.)	Per Cent.
Steady, sober, industrious, &c. (12 in ill-health) ...	39·63
Fairly steady	9·22
"Indifferent"	16·59
Unsteady, idle, drunken, &c.	27·65
Habits not stated	6·91
	100·00

The two following tables show the husbands' habits where the women are unoccupied except with home duties :—

TABLE IV.

Habits of Husbands Earning 25s. and Over. (Wives Unoccupied.)	Per Cent.
Steady, sober, industrious (5 in ill-health)	59·89
Fairly steady	10·03
"Indifferent"	3·62
Unsteady, drunken, violent, &c.	14·76
Habits not stated	11·70
	100·00

TABLE V.

Habits of Husbands Earning Under 25s. per Week. (Wives Unoccupied.)	Per Cent.
Steady sober, industrious	62·26
Fairly steady	6·62
"Indifferent"	3·11
Unsteady, drunken, idle, &c.	11·28
Habits not stated	16·73
	100·00

The foregoing tables eloquently set forth the difference between the lot of the occupied married women and their more fortunate sisters who have no occupation except the duties of home.

It will be seen (Table I.) that 50 per cent. of the husbands of the unoccupied women earn 25s. or more per week, and 60 per cent. of these men are steady, sober, and industrious (Table IV.), while only 26 per cent. (Table I.) of the husbands of the working women receive a similar amount, and barely 37 per cent. of them (Table II.) can be thus described. This undoubtedly shows that a large proportion of the married working women are compelled to work because the wages of the husbands are insufficient for the needs of the family.

Throughout the tables it is shown that where the women work the habits of the husbands are worse than where the wife stays at home. In the class of earnings under 25s. per week, 62 per cent. of the husbands of the unoccupied women are sober and industrious (Table V.) as against 39 per cent. of those whose wives are occupied (Table III.), and the larger percentage of the working-women's husbands who are unsteady, drunken, and idle, or only fairly steady or "indifferent" should also be noted. These figures lead to two possible conclusions: either the women are compelled to work because the husbands are unsteady, drunken, or idle, or the husbands develop bad habits because their wives remove the burden of responsibility from them. The former seems the more probable theory, but the influences are apparently interacting and cumulative, the two evils perpetuating each other in a vicious circle.

Mr. Rowntree has pointed out[1] that for a man and wife and three children the minimum necessary expenditure per week in York, on the lowest possible basis, would be 21s. 8d. This, he says, would suffice only for the bare necessaries of merely physical efficiency *in times of health*, and would allow *nothing whatever for travelling, recreation, or luxuries of any kind, or for sick or funeral clubs.* In Birmingham, taking the actual life of a working-class family, which includes a certain amount of sick and funeral payments, and higher rents, and also remembering that often a family consists of more than five persons, 25s. per week can hardly suffice for providing efficient conditions, even taking for granted the low standard of comfort of working-class life. This proves, then, the necessity, as economic conditions now are, for the woman to become a bread-winner even where the husband is described as "fairly steady," and our investigation shows, in addition, that 14 per cent. of the sober, steady, industrious husbands (of the working-women) earning under 25s. per week are in bad health.

The figures of the whole of the foregoing analysis are appended in one table (with the percentages calculated to the nearest unit) in order to show the comparisons more clearly :—

---

[1] " Poverty," chap. iv. p. 10.

TABLE VI.

	Occupied Married Women. Widows 26 per cent.		Unoccupied Married Women. Widows 4 per cent.	
Husbands' Wage ...	25s. and over. 26 per cent. of total.	Under 25s. 32 per cent. of total.	25s. and over. 50 per cent. of total.	Under 25s. 36 per cent. of total.
Husbands' Habits :—				
Steady, Sober, Industrious	37 per cent. of group	39 per cent.[1] of group	60 per cent. of group	62 per cent. of group
Fairly Steady or Indifferent	38 per cent. of group	26 per cent. of group	13 per cent. of group	10 per cent. of group
Unsteady, Drunken, &c.	20 per cent. of group	28 per cent. of group	15 per cent. of group	11 per cent. of group
Habits not stated	5 per cent. of group	7 per cent. of group	12 per cent. of group	17 per cent. of group

The remaining cases, which could not be classified according to wage, as wages were not stated, work out as follows :—

TABLE VII.

	Occupied Married Women (15 per cent. of Total).	Unoccupied Married Women (10 per cent. of Total).
	Per cent.	Per cent.
Husbands steady, sober, industrious	16	48
Fairly steady or "indifferent" ...	9	3
Unsteady, idle, drunken, &c. ...	29	4
Invalided	10	4
Living apart or deserted	23	1
Habits not stated	13	40
	100	100

The following table, showing the occupations of the married women and widows investigated who are

[1] 14 per cent. of this number are in bad health.

employed in factories, laundries, or as charwomen, &c., is of some interest :—

TABLE VIII.

		Per Cent.
DOMESTIC OCCUPATIONS.	Charwomen	28·04
	Laundry...	2·08
	Minding Babies, Nurses, Cooks, Caretakers and Waitresses	4·90
	Miscellaneous Domestic Occupations	1·19
FACTORY OCCUPATIONS.	Press Work	11·13
	Polishers	7·86
	Solderers	3·26
	Lacquerers	1·04
	Burnishers, Japanners, Painters, Stencillers, Transferrers, and Scratch Brushers	2·98
	Bag and Box making	2·51
	Leather Stitchers and Machinists ...	3·41
	Sewing (Tailoring, Needlework, Slippers, &c.)	5·34
	Warehouse	1·19
	French Polishing	2·67
	Other Factory Occupations	12·31
MISCELLANEOUS OCCUPATIONS.	Hawkers	5·34
	Rag Collectors, Packers, Sorters ...	1·19
	Public-house Keepers, Barmaids ...	1·19
	Shop Assistants, Teachers, Collectors, Carding, Brickmakers' Carrier off, and Boatwoman ...	2·37
		100·00

All recent statistics show that infant mortality is high in districts where the majority of mothers go out to work, though this does not necessarily reflect on the care or devotion of the "minders," who are often near relatives.

Effect on Homes and Families.

We have shown that, at any rate in Birmingham, poverty is the predominating cause which sends married women to the factory. A great many work intermittently, dropping factory work whenever a good time sets in for the husband. If a man is lazy or a drinker, the fact that his wife takes the responsibility off his shoulders will only emphasise his defects, and in very few cases will her work act as a stimulus to him.

Where poverty is the cause of the woman going out to work it becomes a question of choosing the lesser of two evils, *i.e.*, whether the children are to be almost starved or more or less neglected.

Inquiries were made as to the care, health, and attendance at school of the children of each family of the two large groups of women from which our former tables have been taken. It was found that 86·59 per cent. of the unoccupied married women had on an average three children under 14 years of age, and 84·93 per cent. of the occupied married women, 2·52 children [1] under the age of 14 years.

The following table shows a comparison of the care of the children of the occupied and unoccupied married women :—

TABLE IX.

Care of Children.	Occupied Married Women.	Unoccupied Married Women.
	Per cent.	Per cent.
Children well cared for	41·12	61·61
„ fairly well cared for ...	20·39	11·61
„ uncared for, neglected ...	35·33	17·10
Care not stated	3·16	9·68
	100·00	100·00

[1] The average number of children of the widows (26 per cent of the occupied married women) is 1·80.

The following table shows a comparison of the health of the families of the two groups of women :—

TABLE X.

Health of Children.	Occupied Married Women.	Unoccupied Married Women.
	Per cent.	Per cent.
Healthy children	63·10	74·52
Fairly healthy children	7·73	3·39
Weakly and delicate children ...	23·02	12·74
Health not stated	6·15	9·35
	100·00	100·00

The following table gives a comparison of the school attendance of the families in each group :—

TABLE XI.

School Attendance of Children.	Occupied Married Women.	Unoccupied Married Women.
	Per cent.	Per cent.
Regular attendance at school ...	27·77	50·48
Attendance fairly regular	18·45	14·68
Irregular and bad attendance ...	35·15	21·77
All the family too young for school	8·44	5·81
Attendance not stated	10·19	7·26
	100·00	100·00

The above tables, therefore, clearly show that where a married woman has to augment the family income it is greatly to the physical and moral disadvantage of the children.

There are cases where a woman works through

restlessness, dislike of housework, &c., but, as our figures show, these form a small minority.

When, however, we compare the homes of the women who work with the homes of those who stay at home, there is less discrepancy than one would have expected. This points to the conclusion that the fact that a woman goes out to work is very often a sign of strength of character in the woman. It also shows how many women keep up the intense and pathetic drudgery entailed by doing the two kinds of work. For workers or non-workers alike the houses resemble those described in our chapter on " Outwork," *i.e.*, a great many are in courts, and they consist of a kitchen and pantry with two or three bedrooms. Better-class houses have two living-rooms and may have four or five bedrooms. Rents vary from 2s. to 13s. per week, 4s. 8d. being a fair average.

For the purpose of comparing the condition of the homes we have divided the two groups of women as before, according to the income of their husbands, and the three following tables give the result of the analysis :—

TABLE XII.

Husbands earning 25s. or more per Week.	Occupied Married Women.	Unoccupied Married Women.
	Per cent.	Per cent.
Homes clean, tidy, comfortable ...	55·36	63·51
Homes poor, neglected, untidy ...	40·68	28·13
Comfort of home not stated ...	3·96	8·36
	100·00	100·00

TABLE XIII.

Husbands earning under 25s. per Week.	Occupied Married Women.	Unoccupied Married Women.
	Per cent.	Per cent.
Homes clean, tidy, comfortable ...	44·70	49·42
Homes poor, neglected, untidy ...	52·53	35·02
Comfort of home not stated ...	2.77	15·56
	100·00	100·00

TABLE XIV.

Husbands' Wage not stated.	Occupied Married Women.	Unoccupied Married Women.
	Per cent.	Per cent.
Homes clean, tidy, comfortable ...	46·15	32·88
Homes poor, neglected, untidy ...	45·20·	19·18
Comfort of home not stated ...	8·65	47·94
	100·00	100·00

Comparing these tables we find that the non-workers have a balance in their favour, but the difference is not so great as one would have expected when the fact that the workers are absent eleven hours of the day is taken into account.

The widows form a separate class, and where the comfort of home was stated, the following table shows that both those occupied and those unoccupied stand very high with regard to the cleanliness of their homes :—

TABLE XV.

Widows.	Occupied (26 per cent. of Occupied Married Women).	Unoccupied (4 per cent. of Unoccupied Married Women).
	Per cent.	Per cent.
Homes clean, tidy, comfortable ...	62·66	75·00
Homes untidy, neglected, poor ...	37·34	25·00
	100·00	100·00

With regard to the neglected, comfortless homes it was thought worth while to make a separate analysis in order to ascertain the habits of the husbands, and the following tables give the result :—

TABLE XVI.

Dirty, comfortless Homes. (Husbands earning 25s. and over.)	Occupied Married Women.	Unoccupied Married Women.
	Per cent.	Per cent.
Husbands drunken, unsteady, &c.	75·00	51·49
Husbands fairly steady	11·11	17·82
Husbands sober and steady ...	9·72	28·71
Habits of husband not stated ...	4·17	1·98
	100·00	100·00

TABLE XVII.

Dirty, comfortless Homes. (Husbands earning under 25s.)	Occupied Married Women.	Unoccupied Married Women.
	Per cent.	Per cent.
Husbands drunken, unsteady, &c.	67·55	31·11
Husbands fairly steady	7·90	11·11
Husbands sober and steady ...	21·05	48·89
Habits of husbands not stated ...	3·50	8·89
	100·00	100·00

TABLE XVIII.

Dirty, comfortless Homes. (Husbands' wage not stated.)	Occupied Married Women.	Unoccupied Married Women.
	Per cent.	Per cent.
Husbands drunken, unsteady, &c.	51·06	21·43
Husbands fairly steady	6·38	—
Husbands sober and steady ...	4·26	42·86
Habits of husbands not stated ...	10·64	14·28
Living apart, deserted, &c. ...	21·28	—
Husbands invalided	6·38	21·43
	100·00	100·00

Taking the two groups of untidy, comfortless homes, regardless of difference in income, we found that 75 per cent. of the workers' husbands were drunken or only fairly steady, and of this number 25 per cent. of the wives also drank; and 54 per cent. of the non-workers' husbands were drunken or only fairly steady, and 48 per cent. of their wives were of similar habits. Whether the state of the home affected the habits of the husbands, or whether those habits caused apathy and indifference on the part of the women must remain an open question, though extenuating circumstances might be pleaded for the occupied women, who, in addition to their factory labours and their home duties, have the burden of drunken husbands in three-fourths of the cases of these untidy homes.

Pursuing this investigation still further and from another point of view, we give the following tables relating to those women of both groups who give way to the drink habit.

15

The table given below shows the habits of the husbands in cases where the wives drink :—

TABLE XIX.

Husband's habits where Wife drinks.	Workers.	Non-Workers.
	Per cent.	Per cent.
Wife and husband both drink ...	59·38	66·66
Women drink—husbands steady, industrious	9·38	15·00
Women drink—husbands live apart from wives	6·25	—
Women drink — husbands fairly steady	3·12	16·67
Widows who drink	21·87	1·67
	100·00	100·00

The following table shows how this habit in the women affects the comfort of the homes :—

TABLE XX.

Comfort of Home where Woman drinks.	Workers.	Non-Workers.
	Per cent.	Per cent.
Women drink—homes dirty, neglected, &c....	92·18	98·33
Women drink—homes fairly clean	4·69	1·67
Women drink—homes clean, tidy, &c.	3·13	—
	100·00	100·00

We next turned our attention to the way in which the leisure of the women was spent, and we found there was very little variation between the two sets. The answers are given below in tabular form :—

TABLE XXI.

Leisure.	Workers.	Non-Workers.
	Per cent.	Per cent.
Housework, children, reading, sewing, &c.	33˙53	31˙76
Mothers' meetings, chapels, missions, &c.	9˙94	13˙93
Gossip (no intelligent recreation)...	19˙88	10˙86
Drinking	10˙24	9˙05
Little or no leisure	8˙16	—
Enjoyment, visiting friends, &c. ...	2˙52	10˙17
Employment of leisure not stated	15˙73	24˙23
	100˙00	100˙00

Among the women who said that they had little or no leisure were several who worked outside as well as inside the factory. For instance, one made lace, another stitched umbrellas, two did carding, and another sold papers at night.

The conclusion is inevitable and generally accepted that it would be advantageous if married women were not compelled to go out to work, and the figures given above show that the occupied married women taken as a class have a hard and striving life. Among the married factory women we find every grade of work, from bottle-washing or rag-sorting to gold laying-on and lacquering. The earnings of these women vary considerably, but 9s. 1d. is the average when all are taken together. Cases of widows or deserted wives who bring up three or four children on 12s. to 14s. a week are not uncommon. The parish help of a shilling and a loaf per child per week is not sought by all, and even when it is granted there is still far too great a strain on the mother. The question of adequate provision for widows ought to receive speedy attention. Women who are left unprovided for ought not to be compelled to attempt to fulfil, more or less inefficiently, the duties and responsibilities of both parents, and for the fatherless children the least that should be ensured is healthy and sufficient food and home care during their school years.

Where a man's habits drive a wife to work the immediate cause is simple, difficult though it is to apply a remedy ; but when the husband earns only a labourer's wage (up to £1 per week in Birmingham) we are on more complex ground. All we can do here is to state the case, for it is not a problem connected with women's work alone. In Birmingham at present a labouring man works 10 hours a day, or 56 hours per week, and earns 17s. 6d. to £1, *i.e.*, not enough to rent a house in a court and to efficiently feed and clothe himself. If his wife works at home for the same hours she can barely earn enough to feed herself. If the wife works at a factory at unskilled work she may earn as much as 10s. a week, but if she cannot work a man's hours at a factory and in addition do a woman's work at home, she must lose most of the advantage by paying some one to do the home work for her. Where the father and mother are earning barely enough to decently house, clothe, and feed themselves, how are the children to be fed and clothed ? [1]

[1] " The necessaries for the efficiency of an ordinary agricultural or of an unskilled town labourer and his family in

This is a question of national importance, for the children belong not merely to the parents but to the community as a whole.

We need not look far for one cause of physical deterioration when we realise that all over the country thousands of children are growing up who are chronically underfed and insufficiently clothed, notwithstanding all the efforts of the parents. The situation is one that repeats itself. Those parents cannot afford to apprentice their children, who grow up into another generation of unskilled labourers. If we could get some scheme of free apprenticeships, maintenance grants during learning, &c., in connection with our schools and technical institutes, we should at least be doing something to ease State burdens in the coming generation. We need permanent measures which would make it possible for every individual to lead a healthy and rational life. In addition, temporary measures are urgently necessary to rescue many of the rising generation from

England in this generation, may be said to consist of a well-drained dwelling with several rooms, warm clothing, with some changes of underclothing, pure water, a plentiful supply of cereal food, with a moderate allowance of meat and milk, and a little tea, &c., some education and some recreation, and, lastly, sufficient freedom for his wife from other work to enable her to perform properly her maternal and her household duties. If in any district unskilled labour is deprived of any of these things, its efficiency will suffer in the same way as that of a horse that is not properly tended, or a steam-engine that has an inadequate supply of coals. All consumption up to this limit is strictly productive consumption; any stinting of this consumption is not economical but wasteful" (Marshall's "Economics of Industry," p. 44).

the apathy and indifference which, at present, is their inevitable heritage from the past, and to give them the chance of becoming citizens with the capacity to benefit by a fairer and more enlightened social administration.

The fact that some men and women contrive to better themselves must not blind us to the multitudes who can make no effort to raise themselves or their children, or to the many who lose heart and give up the struggle.

It is practically impossible for a man and wife to bring up under efficient conditions even one or two children on a labourer's wage, and to make any attempt at this would necessitate a rigid economy and abstinence from recreation and luxuries which are not common in any class of society, and would demand on the part of the wife a skill in management which is the natural gift of a few, but which in all classes would need specialised training before it could be instilled into the many, especially the many whose only home life has been spent in surroundings of dirt, disorder, and hunger.

CHAPTER IX

SOCIAL LIFE OF UNMARRIED WOMEN

IN previous chapters we have touched on several points affecting the lives of working girls, viz., the effect on their health of monotony, dirt, and bad ventilation, the general effect of factory discipline, companionship, &c.

Many social workers hold the view that girls and women are now so well protected by legislation that no further efforts need be made to better their working conditions, but that all charitable efforts should be centred on their lives apart from their work. Those who hold such views can hardly have been in contact with all the social and working grades to which we alluded in describing general conditions.

In our accounts both of married women-workers and outworkers we tried to give some idea of the kind of homes from which the poorer girls come. In such small and overcrowded houses there can be little home comfort, even if the conduct of the inmates be unimpeachable. It is not wonderful, therefore, that most young people spend their evenings away from home, though it is a matter for regret that this habit is so prevalent among the better-class work girls.

Most girls pay their mothers a fixed weekly sum for board and lodging, and find their own clothes, &c. This payment varies between 5s. **Expenditure:** **I. Food.** and 7s. in different parts of the city, and workers occasionally pay as much as 10s. or 11s. per week, though sometimes the payment is as low as 3s. 6d. and 4s. 6d.

The fact that the girls in lodgings do not pay more than the girls at home in the same district shows that this sum is supposed to cover expenses. Lodgers are sometimes taken for profit, but very often a girl who is uncomfortable at home takes up her quarters with a friend's family, is treated in all ways as one of them, and is not expected to pay more than the daughters of the house.

What the girl gets for her 5s. to 7s. depends on the status of the family and not on the girl herself. Where the family is in a good position and all its members are in work, the girl undoubtedly gets more than she pays for, while in very poor families it is quite possible that the girl's payment has to keep two members, if not more.

In a certain girls' club well known to the writers eleven girls kept an exact account of expenditure and meals for one month. The district is very poor, and the books were kept in the early part of 1904 when wages were not good. All these girls paid 5s. a week to their mothers, though their wages varied between 5s. 6d. and 9s. a week, 30s. 2½d. being the average for the month in question. They were all unskilled workers, nearly all being on different kinds of presses. Most of them had to go without some meals, but if food ran short at home during the day they generally bought some dinner for 1d. or 2d. Supper is the meal most frequently omitted, and two went without it thirteen times, one missing also one dinner and one tea.

In most cases "meat" is entered once or twice a day. Further inquiry elicited the fact that "meat" most frequently meant stew, liver (with or without thickened gravy), "faggots," chitterling, or pig's fry, three dishes which the girls explained to be various kinds of "inside of pig"; occasionally they had a chop or steak, while beef and vegetables were very frequently provided for Sunday. The "pig" dishes or one pennyworth of fried fish and potatoes also form a frequent accompaniment to supper, especially at the beginning of the week. Breakfast nearly always consists of bread and butter and tea, three pieces of bread and butter and two cups of tea being a frequent entry. The same fare is provided for tea, unless this meal is combined with supper, in which case one of the dishes mentioned above, cheese, or an egg, are often added. Lard or dripping are often used instead of butter. The absence of fruit and vegetables is very noticeable. The diet as a whole is not calculated to give the most nourishment possible at the price, and it must be remembered that the supply is often insufficient for the family. In consequence of the shortness in quantity some of the girls suffered distinctly from partial starvation, and most of them were thin and undersized. When there was an accident, a cut hand, &c., the wound nearly always gathered, a sure sign of absence of fruit and vegetable food and of poverty of blood. The signs of chronic underfeeding were very apparent when these girls were compared with a set from a better district, where most of the girls came from good homes and themselves earned 15s. or more each week. The "press girls" visited a better-class club. There was very little difference in dress, as both classes of girls were in drill costume, but at the beginning of the evening, while the two groups were as yet apart and too shy to mix, the difference between them would have struck the most casual observer. On the one side there were some traces of delicacy, but the girls were well formed and there was the buoyancy and ease of movement which are incompatible with exhausted physique. On the other side, there were equal good spirits and possibly a greater power of enjoyment, but the faces struck one as strangely pale and the figures of the girls were small and thin. In short, the two groups might almost have been the children of different races.

The better-class girls take more fresh meat, vegetable, and milk dishes, &c., and in one district, where a determined attempt has been made to teach the value of fruit as an article of diet, tomatoes and other fruit are often added for breakfast and tea.

Probably the striking difference in the appearance of the girls is partly due to the different food during

childhood. The artisan's wife is very thankful when
the boys and girls begin to earn, but she does not
wait for this in order to feed them properly. The
children have the same kind of food as they will
provide for themselves when old enough to do so,
and, unless there are times of special misfortune,
they start their working life with a constitution
unimpaired by privation. The labourer's children,
on the other hand, fare worse during infancy than
at any other time, unless indeed they grow up to
marry labourers and try to bring up families on
an irregular 18s. or 20s. a week. These children
often live for weeks or even months at a time
chiefly on bread and tea, and it is no uncommon
occurrence for the supply of these to run short.
Even where the mother is a good manager many
children are enfeebled for life by recurrent periods
of underfeeding. The average child often seems to
thrive in spite of these disadvantages, but entrance
into working life is generally accompanied by a
rapid falling-off. Attention has recently been drawn
to this deterioration [1] in young girls, and it is suggested that this is chiefly due to their work. This
may be the cause in some cases, but we must
probably look farther to find the root of the evil,
and it is not fair to lay the whole blame on work,
when the girls have not had their constitutions
built up by proper food and care during infancy.
The mothers are well aware of this and know that
the appearance of health in the young children is

[1] Report of the Inter-Departmental Committee on Physical
Deterioration, vol i. Summary of Dr. Eichholz, pp. 13–14.

often deceptive. They do not expect a girl who was "clemmed when she was a little one" to develop into a strong woman.

It is so well known that the "food tradition" is in itself partly to blame for a great deal of ill-health that little more can be said on this point. Much has been done in the last twenty years to train girls in hygiene and home-management, but the school days are too short to make sufficient impression and few girls are sufficiently interested to voluntarily attend such classes when they are older. If the girls' clubs would form parties, and if the teachers would attend the classes and learn with the girls, perhaps something might be done to arouse interest and to overcome the disinclination of the girls for serious occupation after their long day's work.

A plan which is common in Switzerland and other countries is also very helpful. The cookery class begins with a lesson on food-management, home hygiene, &c., and then the girls cook a well-planned meal and eat it together. This not only trains them in orderly and cleanly ways, but it is incidentally an education in healthy and rational taste.

This question of taste is another great obstacle in the way of food reform. Where means are sufficient children are often much spoiled, allowed to refuse simple food and to indulge their fancies. When they grow older and begin to feel the stress of life this want of self-control stands them in bad stead. Many growing girls are disinclined to eat a hearty breakfast, and the majority spend their dinner-money unprofitably, choosing tarts, buns, and ginger-beer in preference to more nourishing food. Even where special restaurants are provided and hot meat and vegetables can be obtained for 3d. or 4d., a large number of girls prefer to spend an equal sum in cakes or tarts. In some places fruit, custard, or milk puddings have been introduced with success, but in others the practical certainty of loss hinders any attempt to provide them. Among the poorer girls hard work and impaired physique combine to produce a jaded appetite which craves for highly flavoured and "tasty" food, and is a great temptation to take intoxicants. Better training and teaching would doubtless help them to cultivate more healthy tastes, but any remedy demands a more adequate income, and a higher standard of living on the part of the working classes. Among the higher-class working girls the chief obstacle is a personal lack of self-control and discrimination.

We have wandered from the question of expenditure and Account Books.

After subtracting the weekly 5s. for board, nearly all the wages left were needed for clothes. One or two saved their money at home and one girl entered 5s. 1d. for a Sunday **II. Dress.** dress. She was asked whether she could get a dress for that money, and after much hesitation she said that her mother had pawned her best dress and she had just managed to redeem it. Whereupon a group of her companions cheered her by exclaiming, "Don't you mind saying. 'T'aint no shame to you if you didn't pawn it yourself, was it!"

Most of the clothes were got through clubs, as already described, and, for part of the month at least, out of the eleven girls—

7 girls paid into boot clubs from 5d. to 1s. 6d. per week ;
6 girls paid into drapery and dress clubs from 2d. to 1s. 6d.
    per week ;
5 girls paid into money clubs from 1s. to 2s. 6d. per week.

It was not the season for party clubs, against which some of these girls are struggling hard in their efforts to keep their temperance pledges. A few minor articles of dress, such as belts, collars, &c., are entered, but these naturally figure more prominently in other account books which were kept by better-paid girls.

But few pence were left for pocket-money, and these went largely in sweets and fruit, the latter hardly a luxury when the general diet III. Amusements. is considered. There are a few tram-fares, an occasional twopenny visit to the music hall, and one or two spent as much as 6d. in an Easter outing. Every one paid 1d. per week to the girls' club, where they enjoyed drill and sewing lessons, or at least brightness and warmth if they were too tired to take a more active part.

Taken altogether, during the month these eleven girls spent between them 16s. 7d. as pocket-money, and this 16s. 7d. may be divided as follows :—

	s.	d.
Sweets and Fruit	9	6
Music Hall (at 2d., 3d., and 4d. a visit) ...	1	1
Tram Fares		6
Music and Song Books		10
Gipsy Party (one girl)[1]	1	0
Evening Home Subscriptions (1d. per week)	3	8
	16	7

There may be some inaccuracies in the books, which rarely balance exactly. On the other hand we have evidences that they are true in the main. They were examined weekly at a kind of criticism class, and the girls' own injunction to new-comers was, "Mind, there's to be no lying about this."

These girls are typical of their class, the unskilled factory girl, except for the fact that the club has refined them in many ways. They were often very badly off for clothes, but had reached the stage of trying to be clean and tidy, and, as we all know, these first efforts are generally combined with a love for cheap finery. When it is due to the awakening of self-respect there is much in its favour. Those who remained under the club influences for some years outgrew it to a large extent and showed a marked improvement in taste. They were wonderfully contented with their working conditions, but had their own views on the subject of insufficient

[1] A "Gipsy Party" is an excursion arranged by the workpeople of a factory. Any one who wishes to join in the party pays so much a week for about six months beforehand. Each pays what he or she can afford, and if at the end any one has paid more than the amount needed, the money over is given back.

pay.   One evening a strange lady failed to understand something they had said, and one of them
apologised, saying, " We're rather rough, Miss, and
don't rightly know how to speak to a lady."   " Never
mind," was her answer, "we can all get on together
so long as we keep ourselves respectable."   " Well,
Miss," answered the girl, "we all mean to, but when
work's short the master puts us piece-work instead
of day-work, and we don't know and come short
the end of the week.   These things make a girl lose
heart and then she doesn't care what becomes of
her.   You should see some of the girls cry pay-day."

Girls of this class nearly always have dirty, monotonous work.   Their working surroundings are often
degrading, and though the last ten years have shown
an increase in the number of good factories, the girls
leave their work needing change, recreation, and enjoyment, as much as exercise and fresh air.   What
wonder, then, if they " walk out," and if this walking
is accompanied by noise and rough behaviour.
Repressed by monotony, the craving for excitement,
inherent in most people, breaks loose, and sheer
recklessness leads many into difficulties more or less
serious.   When a girl has not the young man com-
panion described as " her friend " or " her feller,"
she goes regularly with one or more chosen companions until they fall out, are no longer "speaking," and a redistribution of friends takes place.

They need, above all, wise and sympathetic friends
to guide their misdirected energies and to give them
wholesome amusement.   There may be many failures,
many deceptions, many disappointments of every

kind, but such girls, in spite of all drawbacks, are
very lovable. They are very like big children, and
will take advantage of any teacher who is not firm
and just, but they are warm-hearted and faithful,
and when once a worker has " made friends " with a
group of such girls, she soon finds that she is receiving infinitely more than she gives. "The glamour of
the slum " is upon her, human nature in its sad, dis-
torted, yet withal kindly and affectionate aspects sur-
rounds her, and few indeed who have once found the
road to such intercourse would care to be without it.

Among the skilled workers and warehouse girls
we are on different ground. These girls have also
to face much monotony, and very often work in
ill-ventilated rooms. They have more resources in
themselves, but on this account they feel more need
for change and pleasure. Their dress is in good
taste, though often money goes in smartness which
were better saved. They feel privation more keenly,
and their readiness to sacrifice necessaries in their
efforts to keep up appearances is responsible for
much suffering among middle-aged women who are
obliged to be quite independent.[1] As they come
from better-class homes they could comfortably
spend some at least of their free time with their
parents. Unfortunately many of them have no
capacity for usefully occupying their leisure time,
and if they do not care for novelettes and similar
literature, they are too restless to stay indoors. It is
often less easy to deal with them than with the

[1] See Charles Booth, "Life and Labour of the People,'
vol. iv. p. 321.

rougher girls, but their need of friends, though different, is as great, and to train them to fill their leisure when at home is to confer on them a priceless gift.

We have not sufficient data to show the difference in food, but the summary on the following page shows how the clothing and recreative expenses were met by 13 girls who were skilled workers, earning from 8s. to 16s. per week, or an average of 44s. 8d. per month.

Some of these better-class girls pay occasional visits to theatres and music halls, and a few join dancing classes. For others the churches and chapels find the recreation, and choir practices, Bible-classes, and missions fill all available time. An objection to this form of spending leisure time is that the girls are seldom or never at home, except on Friday evening. That is "candlestick night," or the universal night for house-cleaning, leaving the Saturday half-holiday free for marketing and outings with friends.

As most of their parents have little idea of saving for anything except possible funeral expenses, so the girls rarely save except for some immediate object, either through their

Thrift.

clothing clubs, or for a bicycle, piano, sewing-machine, or country holiday. Out of nearly 3,000 of the women investigated by us, only 13 per cent. saved apart from such objects. Among these were four unskilled metal workers who saved a little, two who supported their homes on about 10s. per week, and one who kept herself and her child on 11s. These evidences of thrift were found under very diverse circumstances.

Occupation	Cycle Bell Maker.	Gold Polisher.	Gold Polisher.	Watch Keys.	Watch Keys.	Under-linen Machinist.	French Polisher.	Ware-house.	Ware-house.	Draper's Assistant.	Shop Assistant.	Clerk.	Lathe Burnisher.
	£ s. d.	£ s. d.	£ s. d.	£ s. d.	£ s. d.	£ s. d.	£ s. d.	£ s. d.	£ s. d.	£ s. d.	£ s. d.	£ s. d.	£ s. d.
Earnings per Month ...	2 14 0	2 12 0	2 12 0	1 16 0	2 2 0	1 14 0	2 16 9	1 16 0	1 12 0	2 9 0	2 4 0	2 8 0	2 5 1½
Home Payments ...	1 4 0	1 4 0	1 4 0	1 0 0	1 6 0	1 0 0	1 6 0	1 12 0	1 2 0	0 6 0	1 6 0	1 12 0	1 0 0
Extra Meals	0 0 6	0 3 6	0 1 0½	—	—	0 0 8	0 0 11	—	—	1 5 4	0 0 6	0 0 5½	—
Clothes and Boots ...	0 1 0	0 12 9	1 2 2	0 1 6	0 2 0	0 7 5	0 5 6	0 1 1	0 4 5½	0 7 10½	0 1 6	0 3 5	0 5 11
Clubs, &c.—													
Sick Club	0 1 2	—	—	—	—	—	—	—	—	—	0 0 8	—	0 1 0
Clubs	0 2 11½	0 1 2	0 3 9	0 3 9	0 5 2½	0 0 9	0 1 2	—	0 0 6	0 2 4½	—	—	—
Sewing Class... ...	—	—	—	—	—	—	—	0 2 0	—	—	—	—	—
Doctor Club	—	—	—	—	—	—	—	—	—	—	0 0 9	—	—
Life Insurance ...	—	—	—	—	—	—	—	0 0 5	—	—	—	—	—
Early Closing Association ...	—	—	—	—	—	—	—	—	—	0 0 4	—	—	—
Savings Fund	0 9 6	0 0 11	0 0 3	—	0 1 9	0 2 0	—	0 2 1	—	—	0 9 9	0 2 0	0 16 3½
Charities...	—	—	—	—	—	—	0 4 2	—	—	0 0 6½	0 0 5	0 2 4	—
Train and Tram Fares...	0 0 4	0 0 11	0 0 7	0 3 8	0 0 10½	0 1 7	0 1 4	0 0 7	0 0 2	0 3 1½	0 3 1	0 2 2	—
Sweets and Fruit ...	0 1 2	0 1 0	0 0 8	0 0 4½	0 4 0	0 1 4	0 0 9	0 1 3	0 0 9½	0 1 6½	0 1 3	0 1 1	0 1 3
Papers	0 0 6	—	0 0 4	0 0 3	0 0 7½	—	—	0 0 2	—	—	0 0 2	—	0 0 8
Sundry Expenses—													
Ticket for School Party	—	—	—	—	—	—	—	—	—	—	—	0 3 0	—
Sewing Machine payments	—	—	—	—	—	—	0 8 0	—	—	—	—	—	—
Medicine	—	—	—	—	—	—	0 1 0	—	—	—	—	—	—
Holidays&Excursions	—	—	—	—	—	—	0 3 0	—	—	0 2 5	—	—	—
Father's Tobacco ...	—	—	—	—	—	—	0 2 10½	—	—	—	—	—	—
Library Fee	—	—	—	—	—	—	—	—	—	0 0 8	—	—	—
Watch Mended ...	0 2 0	—	—	—	—	—	—	—	—	—	—	—	—
Sundries	0 0 6	—	—	0 0 6½	—	—	0 0 8½	0 0 2	—	0 0 5	—	0 1 5½	—
	2 3 7½	2 4 3	2 12 9½	1 10 1	2 0 5½	1 13 9	2 15 5	1 19 9	1 7 11	2 10 7½	2 4 1	2 7 11	2 5 1½

One would expect to find a good percentage of girls in the clothing trades alive to the duty of providing for bad times, and about 21 per cent. of the dressmakers, who were earning from 10s. to 15s. per week, saved sums between £1 and £5 yearly. The better-class jewellery workers, who earned an average weekly wage of 12s. 1d., were equally careful, and 22½ per cent. of the cases investigated paid on an average 5s. 7½d. to their mothers, and saved from "a little" and a "few shillings" up to £10 a year.[1] Sixteen per cent. of the paper-bag makers saved from 2d. per week to £5 per annum from an average weekly wage of 11s. 10d., with 6s. going towards home expenses. Among the French polishers 15 per cent. were saving, some "a very little," several as much as £5, and one as much as £10. These women were all in the higher branches of their trade, and earned on an average 14s. 4d., paying 7s. 10d. per week for board and lodging. We will not complete this list, painfully short though it is, but will conclude by mentioning three out of twenty-two bottle-washers, who saved £1 to £2 per year from a wage of 10s. per week, out of which they paid 8s. at home. However, in these cases the home payment must have included clothes as well as board and lodging.

These savings are often drawn out at the end of the year, and only in very few cases are they accumulated in readiness for a marriage outfit or to meet the possible demands of illness, loss of work, &c.

Only 379 out of nearly 3,000 of the women ques-

[1] One of these girls earned 18s., kept herself and her mother, and saved 4d. every week.

tioned on this point saved at all, and the following table shows the amounts which these 379 were able to save :—

158 = 42 per cent., saved "a little," "not much," or "some-
                times saved." [1]
  79 = 21   ,,   ,, from 20s. to 30s. per year.
  44 = 12   ,,   ,, from £2 to £3 per year.
  36 = 9   ,,   ,, £5 a year.
  36 = 9   ,,   ,, "a few pounds."
  18 = 5   ,,   ,, over £5 and up to £10.
   8 = 2   ,,   ,, over £10 and up to £20.

The following table gives the percentages of savings in each trade, as shown by the above 379 women :—

Trades.	No. questioned as to Savings.	No. who Saved.	Percentage of each Trade.
Clothing and Sewing Trade	284	70	25
Jewellery, &c., Trades ...	231	52	22½
Food Trades	59	10	17
Leather Trades	128	20	16
Wood Trades	122	20	16
Paper, Cardboard Trades...	212	27	13
Metal Trades	1,299	125	10
Miscellaneous (regulated) ...	342	37	11
,, (unregulated)	235	18	8

Both inside and outside the factory the lives of working girls are too often barren of all that gives wholesome relaxation and brightness. It is this want of change and recreation that makes them wild and restless and inclined to seek undesirable

[1] This in most cases means only a few shillings in the year.

amusements. The restlessness often finds a vent in frequent change of work, particularly during the first three years of working life. In the first flush of freedom the girls are very independent, and as soon as they feel out of sorts, or quarrel with neighbours or master, or as soon as work runs short, they try a new place. They soon get tired of low wages, and many who start at a real trade give it up and drift into the ranks of unskilled workers. Sometimes they candidly acknowledge that they like a change. With many this restlessness soon gives way to an acceptance of things as they are, a girl learns to dread being out of work, and settles down for several years at her job. If she is suspended because work is short she will seek another place during the interval, but her foreman sends for her when there is a change for the better.

The common practice of taking on extra hands when there is a press of work, only to discharge them unconditionally when work slackens, encourages thriftless and improvident habits among men and women alike, and only the best workers are exempt from its influence. Hundreds of people are literally incapable of looking beyond the present day or week, and the master who makes an effort to equalise things for his employees and so to keep them on during slack times is frequently placed at a disadvantage by less scrupulous neighbours who draw off his workers by the offer of high wages, which can, however, last only a few weeks. There is a tendency to create a vagrant class in industry, which has a very bad effect on the workers them-

selves.   These " casuals " are always the lowest class
in any trade, and their presence is a constant menace
to the better workers, while they themselves alternate
between plenty and starvation, and too often become
vagrants in character if not in mode of life.

Restlessness, improvidence, and craving for excitement are well-recognised social evils, but it should
be remembered that they are rarely prominent
among those for whom a real home life is possible.
There are many social remedies, all valuable in their
way, but the chief hope of the future seems to lie in
fostering the home spirit in the individual, and in
making the possession of a home in which men and
women can take pride a possibility to all.

IMPROVEMENTS, PRESENT
AND POSSIBLE

CHAPTER X

WOMEN'S TRADE UNIONS IN BIRMINGHAM

WHEN one comes to consider possible means of raising the wages of women-workers, one's first thought is, since trade unions are recognised as being a considerable factor in getting men a greater absolute, as well as relative, share of the national dividend, to recommend organisation to women. But the same want of independence, the narrow outlook and want of foresight which is the main explanation of the low wages, at once makes this an almost impossible remedy—in the near future, at any rate—except in the case of the more skilled workers. Then the fact that girls always look forward to marriage, and few expect to be life-workers, means that the will to organise demands a clearer idea of the common good than even a man need have. The good that a man expects to get is at once more permanent and more evident. Again, considerations of sex and family life make it almost impossible that a girl or woman could have the mobility required to make organisation effective. Then, again, since the work of the common run of women-workers is practically unskilled work, needing little or no training, there would always be the effective competition of large numbers of unemployed who could easily take the place of the worker in case of any dispute.   There is a great deal of truth in what Sidney Webb says:[1] "Where, as is usually the case, female labour is employed for practically unskilled work, needing only the briefest experience ; or where the work, though skilled, is of a kind into which every woman is initiated as part of her general education, no combination will ever be able to enforce, by its own power, any Standard Rate, any Normal Day, or any definite conditions of Sanitation and Safety. . . . Mutual Insurance and Collective Bargaining, as methods of enforcing the Common Rule, become impotent when the work is of so unskilled or so unspecialised a character that an employer can, without economic disadvantage, replace his existing hands in a body by an entirely new set of untrained persons of any antecedents whatsoever."

This view is also given by the Commission on Labour,[2] in the following : "Various causes are alleged which make it very difficult for women to combine successfully.   One cause, no doubt, is that which also affects a large class of men, viz., that many of the occupations in which they are employed are not protected from competition by the necessity for much skill or strength, and are overcrowded.   But even in the case of those occupations which require a

[1] "Industrial Democracy," p. 758.
[2] Royal Commission on Labour, Fifth and Final Report, Part I., p. 96.

degree of skill and training, corresponding to that which would probably enable men to organise successfully, women appear to have the same difficulty in combining by themselves. This has been attributed to the fact that unmarried women frequently consider their employment as one which will be terminated by marriage, and not as a life affair ; to social divisions and distinctions existing amongst them ; to hereditary incapacity for transacting business in common ; to difficulties in way of meeting ; and by special dislike felt by employers to their organisation."

Our inquiry into the subject of Women's Unions in Birmingham bears out the above pessimistic outlook, for although efforts have been made more or less spasmodically in different trades to organise the girls, the result in the main is extremely discouraging. Attempts have been made to organise the women in the Bedstead, Bookbinding, Pinafore, Tailoring, and Leather trades, but failed in some cases partly because of want of experience on the part of the organisers, but in all cases more because of the apathy and indifference of the workers on the one hand and the open opposition of the masters on the other.

An attempt to organise the women in the Chain-making trade at Cradley Heath was more successful. The union was formed in 1886, but the women are becoming apathetic, and only about 200 out of at least 1,000 women are now in the union. This trade is carried on almost entirely in domestic workshops, husband, wife, and daughter often working

together. Very few girls work in factories, and the
pay is even smaller in the factories than outside.
Strange to say, the men workers are more or less
indifferent to the progress or failure of unionism
amongst the girls. The union has not prevented a
decrease of wages.

A union under the name of " The Birmingham and
District Lady Clerks' Society" has been formed for
lady clerks, typists, bookkeepers, invoice clerks, and
girls engaged in office work generally. The origin
of this society was due to the success which had
attended the working and management of the Birmingham and District Clerks' Provident Association
in this city. A few ladies who were originally
members of the Birmingham Shorthand Writers'
Association decided to start a society from which
they could derive the same benefits as were conferred
upon male clerks by the society referred to above,
and they were fortunate in obtaining as secretary a
professional gentleman who for some years had been
a director of the male clerks' society, and who also
for many years was connected officially with the
Birmingham Shorthand Writers' Association. The
lady clerks' society was started and registered under
the Friendly Societies' Act of 1896. The first meeting was attended by about fifteen lady clerks, and it
was decided to proceed in a businesslike way. A
set of rules were drafted, and were registered by the
Registrar of Friendly Societies, and applications for
membership were thereupon invited with a very
gratifying result. The number of members has
steadily grown to 190. During the 3½ years the

society has been established it has paid to members
or paid on their behalf the following sums :—

	£	s.	d.
Out of employment pay to members ...	140	6	8
Medical attendance and medicine ...	88	16	4
Death payment	7	10	0

The society is well organised, and offers to its
members the following advantages : Situation
bureau, out-of-work pay, medical attendance, special
grants in cases of distress, annuities to aged
and disabled members, and funeral expenses of de-
ceased members.   The pecuniary benefits received
are in proportion to a graduated scale of subscriptions.   The secretary complained that a few members
had left the union on getting employment at a well-
known firm in the suburbs, where some of the above-
mentioned advantages are provided free by the
employers.   This throws an interesting sidelight on
the effect on trade unions of the advantages offered
to employees by this firm.   It is to be regretted that
there is not a more enlightened opinion and a greater
feeling for the common good amongst these more
fortunate of the lady clerks.

A large number of applications for trained girls
are constantly being received from employers, and
although a large number of situations have been
secured for their own members by the union, many
of the situations could not be filled owing to the lack
of suitable candidates.

The society is managed by a committee of lady
clerks engaged in some of the largest establishments

in the city and district, and it has been of great
assistance to those members who, through no fault
of their own, have been thrown out of employment.
There is a great demand for lady clerks of good
general ability, and also for lady shorthand clerks
and typists and bookkeepers with experience.

Although its membership is somewhat small
compared with the male clerks' society, which now
numbers upwards of a thousand members, the committee feel that greater benefits could be conferred
if a larger number in the city and district were to
take advantage of the benefits offered. The social
entertainment of the members is not overlooked, as
social evenings and summer excursions are arranged.

The women Penworkers in Birmingham have had
a union since 1895, though it had to be restarted in
1898. It came into being through an agitation
started by Miss Tuckwell and Lady Dilke, together
with some well-known Birmingham trade unionists
and other people. The two ladies mentioned were
at the Trade Union Congress, and took the opportunity to hold a public meeting of women-workers,
and from this meeting originated the Penworkers'
Union. During the following week other meetings
were held which led to the formation of at least two
other women's unions, both of which, however, failed
to attain any permanent success. Even the Penworkers' progress was slow for some time, but
different methods brought improvement. The small-
ness of the contribution—2d. per week—and the
undisciplined character of the members necessitated
careful action. On one occasion 250 women pre-

sented an ultimatum to the officials, saying that unless they allowed them to come out on strike they would leave the union. As the officials wisely refused their permission, 150 tore up their cards. But in spite of their poverty the union met with a fair measure of success. The chief result was the application of the Particulars Clause to this trade. This soon became almost a dead letter, because there was no one to enforce it. Still the advantage has been gained, and can be insisted upon at any time when supervision becomes more adequate and there are more inspectors.

The indirect advantages were greater than the direct, and were largely the effect of moral pressure brought to bear by the union. Fines and deductions, which in the past were scandalous in this trade, were reduced, and better sanitary conditions were provided. In this way the union has done a great deal of good, and has helped the women and girls to a sense of their rights as to hours, work, and wages.

The membership at first was about thirty, and the union was kept steadily going till, in 1899, it reached its highest membership, about 600 girls having joined. At present there are five nominal members. The chief reasons for the decline seem to have been (*a*) the want of an able organiser who could devote her whole time to the work ; (*b*) the unsteady membership of the girls, due to their inability, through poverty, to pay the union subscription, and to their fear of their employers dismissing them for becoming members of the union. The

objects of the union were set out to be : " To
maintain the rights and privileges of the trade, and
to grant relief to such members as may be out of
work or requiring legal advice." Out-of-work pay
was 5s. per week.

The National Amalgamated Union of Shop Assistants, Warehousemen, and Clerks, opened a branch in
Birmingham in 1898, and started with a membership
of thirty-eight, of whom three only were women.
For two years the members struggled on without
apparently making any progress; then in 1900 two
other branches were started, Aston with twenty-one
members, and Small Heath with thirteen members.
The Aston branch did not long survive, and in
1901 it was closed as all the members had either
lapsed or transferred to other districts. The same
year, however, saw two other branches opened, East
Birmingham with fourteen members, and Balsall
Heath with twelve members. In 1902 the Spark-
brook branch started with twenty-six members, and
Handsworth with thirty-one members.

The last complete returns show the present position
of membership as follows :—

Branch.			Total Membership.	No. of Women.
Birmingham Central	...	...	115	22
Small Heath	...	...	30	6
East Birmingham	...	...	32	1
Balsall Heath	...	...	31	7
Sparkbrook	...	...	21	—
Handsworth	...	...	36	4
Total	...	...	265	40

The number of organised women shop assistants is

pitifully small ; in fact they may be said to be
unorganised for any practical result. Throughout
the rest of the country the women membership is
one-sixth of the total membership, so from this point
of view the women of Birmingham do not compare
unfavourably with the men. In Cardiff, for example,
the total membership is 538, of whom eighty-seven
are women.

In considering the number of women in the union
in the country as a whole, we must remember that
prior to 1896 there were only a few isolated women
members, although the union started in 1891. Now
the women are entering the union in greater numbers
proportionately each year, and the officials are hopeful that there will be a revival even in Birmingham,
where so far it has been extremely uphill and
discouraging work.

This union appeals for membership on the following grounds[1] : The national membership is 16,500,
and the reserve fund is £15,000. " It is the only
organisation in existence which includes all the
workers in the distributive trade, and which is
managed and paid for by the workers themselves.
It is the only organisation which persistently attacks,
and is determined to get abolished, the iniquitous
system of living-in." Legal advice is given free to
members. It also protects its members " from the
one-sided and unjust system of references ; and the
union is the only society which is trying to secure
compulsory registered references." The money

[1] Official Publication No. 23 of N.A.U.S.A.

benefits are given in the table on the following page.

Generally the union aims at "uplifting the standard of life of the shop-workers by preventing injustice to individuals; by bringing the pressure of collective action to bear upon the problem of late hours, low wages, references, agreements, fines, the living-in system," &c. In a special appeal to the women the pamphlet says: "Women-workers should join because they specially need the protection the union offers." " Because special advantages are offered them in addition to all other benefits, *i.e.*, if a woman member gets married at the end of two years' membership, and has not, during the period of her membership, received either sick or unemployed benefit, 50 per cent. of her contributions are returned to her as a marriage portion." " Because women are admitted on equal terms." " Because unorganised women-workers act as a drag on the wheels of progress, and it is clearly in women's interest to co-operate for high wages rather than compete for low ones."

As we have stated above, the general attitude both of employers and workpeople is to take the conditions and wages of women's work for granted. The attitude of employers seems to be a relic of the time when employers considered that they found work and wages for their employees and that all the favours were received on one side, and that it is nothing less than impertinence for the women to desire any voice in regulating the conditions of their work or the remuneration they receive from the work. The girls

CONTRIBUTION AND BENEFIT TABLES.

Age of Entry.	Contribution. Weekly. (s. d.)	Benefit When Out of Employment or During Sickness.				Payment at Death to Members of		
		First 4 Weeks per Week. (£ s. d.)	Following 4 Weeks per Week. (£ s. d.)	Next 4 Weeks per Week. (£ s. d.)	Following 12 Weeks (per Week) In Sickness only. (£ s. d.)	2 Years and less than 5 Years. (£ s. d.)	5 Years and less than 10 Years. (£ s. d.)	10 Years and Upwards. (£ s. d.)
JUNIOR SCALE.								
*16 and under 18 ...	0 3	0 7 6	0 5 0	0 3 9	0 2 6			
MEN.								
18 and under 30	0 6	0 15 6	0 10 0	0 7 6	0 5 6	4 0 0	6 0 0	10 0 0
	0 9	1 2 0	0 15 0	0 12 6	0 7 6	6 0 0	9 0 0	15 0 0
	1 0	1 10 0	1 0 0	0 15 6	0 10 0	8 0 0	12 0 0	20 0 0
30 and under 40	0 7	0 15 6	0 10 0	0 7 6	0 5 6	4 0 0	6 0 0	10 0 0
	0 10½	1 2 0	0 15 0	0 12 6	0 7 6	6 0 0	9 0 0	15 0 0
	1 2	1 10 0	1 0 0	0 15 6	0 10 0	8 0 0	12 0 0	20 0 0
40 and under 50	0 8	0 15 6	0 10 0	0 7 6	0 5 6	4 0 0	6 0 0	10 0 0
	1 0	1 2 0	0 15 0	0 12 6	0 7 6	6 0 0	9 0 0	15 0 0
	1 4	1 10 0	1 0 0	0 15 6	0 10 0	8 0 0	12 0 0	20 0 0
WOMEN.								
18 and under 50 ...	0 3¼	0 10 0	0 7 6	0 5 0	0 3 6	3 0 0	4 10 0	6 10 0
	0 6	0 15 6	0 10 0	0 7 6	0 5 6	4 0 0	6 0 0	10 0 0
	0 9	1 2 0	0 15 0	0 12 6	0 7 6	6 0 0	9 0 0	15 0 0

Half-benefit only will be allowed to members of six months' standing and full benefit to members of twelve months' standing and upwards. The period of membership shall date from the Monday in the week in which the first contribution is paid.

* On reaching the age of 18, members paying on this scale must transfer to higher scale.

themselves look at the matter in the same way. Some of the opinions received from manufacturers and foremen in regard to unionism for women are interesting, if not always illuminating. One foreman in the Paper trade said, " Better leave well alone." A forewoman in Brass Caster Core Makers' trade said union " not needed." Another in the Custard Powder trade thought trade unions amongst the girls would be a mistake, as it would only cause irritation between employed and employers without resulting in any particular advantage to the girls, for it is not like a skilled trade and the workers could be readily replaced if necessary. Another foreman in Needle trade thinks it " not worth the trouble," and another in Tin-plate trade said any encouragement of union would " stir up the employers against the girls." A manager in Upholstery and Bedtrimming trade said " girls think more of getting married than of trade societies." A manufacturer in Brush trade did not see any need for unions in his shop : he encourages temperance and religious work amongst his employees ; he always interviews the parents of any applicants for a job ; he also looks for his employees in the choirs and other sections of religious bodies, because " if there *is* a difference in people, religion ought to turn out the best." He pays good wages and reserves the right to employ and dismiss whom he will.

One must commend the good work done for the welfare of the employees by men of this description, but at the same time there is much to be said for the spirit of independence on the part of the girls themselves, which would not leave them to the arbitrary will of an employer.

Foremen and forewomen in Camera Apparatus, Steel Hair Curlers, Cheap Jewellery, Lacquering, Tailoring, and Printing and Bookbinding trades were favourable to unions. A manager in a Silversmith's "knows nothing about it and has got no views at all."

In Gold and Silver Chain trade there is a kind of implicit combination, as the trade is kept very much in the hands of certain families, nearly every married woman having one or more daughters in the trade whom she is teaching or has already taught. This tends to make it difficult for an "outsider" to get employment at this work.

Generally men-workers are indifferent or opposed to women's unions. They fear them as competitors who inevitably cut wages, or, on the other hand, the work that the women do is so well marked off from that of the men that the latter have no concern as to the conditions and wages of the women's work. There were some exceptions, however, and some of the more enlightened working men were seriously concerned at the demoralising effect on the women of dirty and heavy work. In the Brass Trade, *e.g.*, strong exception was taken to women working either at polishing or stamping. It would be well both for men and women if the men would be less selfish and take a deeper and more enlightened interest in women and their work. With the help of the men, with capable organisers, and with an enlightened public opinion, more might be done even amongst the unskilled women-workers. Amongst the more skilled and better-class women-workers the possibilities of trade unionism are great, and the results already attained give promise of a great advance in the future.

CHAPTER XI

GIRLS' CLUBS, CLASSES, ETC.

A STUDY of the history of factory legislation shows that much has been done to better the conditions of industrial life, yet any acquaintance with the general or average conditions of labour at the present day leaves the impression that much remains to be done before

I. In the Factory.

the masses of our labouring population can have the possibility open to them of reaching a higher standard of life, a level which shall fulfil the elementary demands of decency and subsistence which are the right of every man and woman. It is given to leaders of men in all walks of life to rouse, stimulate, and educate public opinion, and so lead the way. This is nowhere more true than in industrial life, where the presence and example of "model factories," which are at the same time good investments from a business point of view, exert an undoubted influence over the conditions of work in neighbouring industries. Such model conditions need not be described here, as they are well known from many other sources. We are concerned now with the average factory and the average workers, and the problem before us is how the national average may best be raised, how it may be a progressive and not a stationary or a retrograde factor in the national life.

It is with great diffidence that we approach the matter where it deals with the interior organisation and arrangements of business houses. A small business is hampered by many impediments, and high rents and crowded buildings in a city often make it difficult for a business to expand and at the same time to ensure for the workers the legal minimum of space, ventilation, &c. There are, on the other hand, many minor difficulties which arise from want of thought on the part of the employer, and perhaps more from mutual ignorance and want of understanding between employer and employed.

We agree with those who advocate extension of the laws regulating factories and workshops, but while extension is necessary, much improvement could be effected if the present laws were more efficiently administered. At present the staff of inspectors [1] is inadequate to supervise all the factories in the

[1] " The number of factories and workshops under inspection in 1903 was as follows :—

Class of Works.					Number of Works.
Factories	...	...	...	...	100,444
„ (Laundries)	...	...	...	...	2,287
Workshops	...	...	...	...	139,691
„ (Laundries)		...	...	...	4,448
Docks, Wharves and Quays	...	...	...	...	2,472
Warehouses	...	...	...	...	4,524
					253,866

" At the present time the total has probably grown to about 255,000.

" The staff of inspectors and assistant inspectors in

country, and this applies especially to the women factory inspectors. Inspection can have no terrors to those who have nothing to conceal, but at present there are many places where girls work for months, or even years, without seeing an inspector, and thus the public can have no guarantee that the law is observed. Where it is broken an unfair element in competition is introduced, which gives the offender an advantage over his law-abiding neighbour, while the community inevitably suffers where there is waste of human material. Turning, however, to the average law-abiding employer, it seems that much more might be done to improve general conditions to the mutual advantage of employer and employed.

We have already advocated rules enforcing cleanliness and decency of language and behaviour, and it is in the power of every master to enforce such rules. He cannot enforce them except during working hours, but their observance in the factory has an inevitable influence on the lives of the employees, and the existence of such rules has been found to

August, 1904, was stated officially (Cd. 2324) to be of an authorised strength of 152 and of an actual strength of 151. If we imagine the 255,000 registered workplaces divided equally amongst the staff we see that each inspector has to deal, on the average, with 1,677 workplaces. If, then, each registered workplace were inspected only once in each year, each inspector would need to inspect 32 factories or workshops per week, or over five per day ! As this is a physical impossibility, it is clear that each registered workplace is not called upon even once in each year."—" Riches and Poverty,' Chiozza Money, pp. 114-15.

attract the best intelligence and capacity available for the work in question.   Adequate provision of washing conveniences is inseparable from such rules.

A definite break in any period of work more than four hours in length is another great advantage, especially where young girls are engaged in monotonous processes, and if these breaks give opportunity for the favourite lunch or cup of after-noon tea, the risk of over-fatigue and strain is con-siderably lessened.   Separate dining-rooms are now provided in many factories, but the accommodation is often very primitive, and we have known a cellar, a shed, and a cloak-room respectively do duty for this purpose.   Sometimes a clean table is provided in the workroom, or the girls adjourn to another workroom, but it is to be hoped that in the future employers will be forced by law to provide bright, airy dining-rooms in all workplaces where the employees have their meals on the premises.   Dining-rooms are occasionally provided with papers and magazines, and better-class work-girls often bring books or fancy work to occupy the second half of the dinner-hour.

The kindness of many employers has enabled the Girls' Friendly Society, the Factory Helpers' Union, and other agencies to start a work which might with advantage be considerably extended.   We refer to the "dinner-hour meetings," which are held weekly or fortnightly in many factories.   These meetings are of the simplest character, and usually take the form of a short service, including a Bible, temperance, or hygiene lesson.   The teachers in this way come into contact with many women and girls who cannot be reached outside the factory, and, modest as are the means employed, their visits have been found to make a distinct difference in the workrooms. Several employers have noticed an increase of refinement among the girls since a lady took interest in them, while the girls are often led to join the temperance societies, evening clubs, &c.

If there could be more co-operation between the philanthropic workers on the one hand and the masters on the other, more might be effected than is possible while there is such a singular lack of cohesion between the various social forces. Many employers justly fear the intrusion of well-meaning persons whose one-sided sympathy and ignorance of business are too apt to cause discontent and strife. It is always difficult to be a dinner-hour visitor, and the post can only be filled by those who will conform loyally to the rules of the employers whose hospitality they enjoy. Where this is done the visitor's scope might surely be extended, till she in some measure fills the place of the "welfare secretaries" who have been appointed with so much success by a few large firms in America and England. It is to be hoped that such appointments will in the future become general, two or three firms sharing the services of a lady where they are too small to need separate secretaries. Meanwhile, there are many who have an intimate knowledge of the lives and requirements of working girls who could with advantage suggest the little improvements needful for the health and happiness of the workers, and at the same time train the girls to make a proper use of the advantages conferred. There is at present a great lack of helpers for the dinner-hour work, a lack which is greatly to be deplored, as the openings for such work are increasing, and its usefulness is unquestioned and is capable of great extension.

So many agencies are at work outside the factory to better the conditions of working women that one **II. Outside the Factory.** is almost led to ask what more can be attempted. A closer study reveals the fact that a good deal of this work overlaps other efforts, and that a comparatively small proportion of the working girls are affected by it.

There are two classes of work. First, there are the agencies for rescuing girls who have wrecked their lives or their health. To this class belong homes and institutions which train girls and endeavour to give them a fresh start in life. The second and larger class includes what might well be called the preventive agencies, *i.e.*, all efforts which help girls to maintain or improve their standard of life, and to resist the evil influences of privation and environment. In short, the preventive work aims at extinguishing the need for the first or palliative agencies.

The chief " preventive work " is found in the girls' clubs and classes, and for convenience we use the **Girls' Clubs, &c.** word " club " to include all the different classes, evening homes, &c., which are open to girls on one or more evenings in the week. A great deal might be said on the various aspects of this subject, but space forbids us to do more than touch briefly on a few salient points.

The majority of these " clubs " are connected with one or other of the religious bodies, though church membership is rarely a condition of club membership for the girls. At the same time, religious training is generally an important part of the club work, whether it be given directly or indirectly. Some clubs are connected with a Bible class, and most close with prayer, while a few are also opened in the same way. Every kind of needlework is taught, and, if possible, some kind of drill is added for the more energetic spirits. Rules are few and simple. The **Rules.** minimum age of entrance varies between thirteen and fifteen years. Members pay for their work materials at cost price, and in addition there is generally a small subscription, amounting to $\frac{1}{2}$d. or 1d. per week. The enforcement of a subscription is increasing, as the girls are found to appreciate the club more when they have some share in its maintenance. In addition there is generally the useful rule that each member must have some definite occupation during the evening.

Members' payments and subscriptions rarely cover more than the working expenses, exclusive, as a rule, of rent, light, and firing. Very often these **Finance.** are supplied by the place of worship to which the club is attached, or an entertainment or rummage sale pays a share of the expenses. In such cases the actual outlay may amount to less than £5 per annum, but where all expenses have to be met, and the club is open four or more nights in the week, the expenses may be £70 or more a year, and these expenses are generally met by special subscriptions and donations. It is, however, easy to start a class on a simpler basis, if sufficient voluntary aid in teaching be forthcoming and a suitable room can be secured.

Every club aims at refining its members by offering opportunities for wholesome recreation and develop-
Aims. ment. In most cases the primary object is to provide a counter-attraction to the streets, where many a girl finds at present her sole relaxation. The clubs certainly exercise a wonderful influence over the members, an influence which seems to be largely independent of the subjects taught or the methods employed. After a year or two of club membership, most girls become quieter and more orderly in manner and dress, and it is gratifying to know that this outward change is often the sign of a real growth, in some cases an awakening, of inner refinement and progress.

Skilled and unskilled working girls represent, roughly, two broad divisions, and there must be some difference in the attempts to befriend them. The skilled girls suffer from a monotony of life and narrowness of outlook which need to be brightened and widened quite as much as the horizon of the rougher girl needs to be opened out to admit elements of which she has hardly dreamed. All alike want friends, and are pathetically grateful to any one who will take an interest in them.

There are many requests that ladies will come into neglected districts and start this work. As there seems to be a perennial lack of helpers in the clubs already existing it is difficult to see how the work can be extended. To those who have once entered into this sphere of work it is equally difficult to understand how any one with leisure can refuse to dedicate some of it to the working girls, so great is the reward when once an understanding has been established between teacher and pupils. The difficulties of evening journeys and the fear of infection deter many who would otherwise gladly give up one evening weekly. After extensive inquiries, we have been unable to discover a single instance of either of these supposed drawbacks being substantiated.

In Birmingham the narrowing effect of club isolation is combated by a union of clubs and classes, which holds yearly competitions in all the subjects taught, as well as a yearly _Union._ conference on club methods for the teachers. If the competitions give rise to some heart-burnings, they have indisputably much raised the level of the work. The materials, pattern, and cost of each subject are carefully and exactly prescribed, and thus rich and poor clubs stand on an equal footing in the competition, and excellence of execution becomes the sole object in the work. It has been interesting to find that the social status of the girls does not materially affect their chances, and the prize won for plain-sewing or musical drill by a class of skilled girls has been carried off with equal credit the next year by a party of press girls. The first prize in each subject is a shield, which is returned each year to the union, and only becomes the permanent property of the

winning club if won for three years in succession.
The best addition to the influence of the union would
be through more intervisitation between the different
clubs.   In the Priory Union of Women's Adult
Schools a regular scheme of intervisitation has been
found most efficacious in broadening the sympathies
and understanding of the members, and when a
teacher can take two or three girls to pay a friendly
call in a rival club the knowledge of other methods,
conditions, and difficulties is wonderfully helpful in
stimulating a broad and unselfish spirit among
the girls.

Temperance work forms another bond between
many differing sets of girls, by uniting them in
White Ribbon bands, which meet twice a year for
a united meeting.   The work is organised by a
central committee with the help of a secretary ; and
speakers and other workers are sent at regular
intervals to every meeting in which a White Ribbon
band has been formed, thus helping the regular
teachers to combat a serious evil and keeping the
subject before the girls.

Mothers' meetings often resemble adult clubs,
or, more often, Bible classes, but they are chiefly
attended by women who do not work,
though some home-workers with their
hooks and eyes or their buttons, may be
found in these meetings.

Mothers' Meetings.

It would be interesting to discover how many
of the 116,000 working women of Birmingham are
reached by these various meetings.   There are so
many isolated classes that it is impossible to give

the total number of members. Forty-five clubs, with a membership of nearly 4,000, are at present affiliated to the union, and among them are clubs belonging to the Church of England, the Congregationalists, Wesleyans, Friends, Unitarians and others, and the large Hebrew recreation classes.

The Girls' Friendly Society has thirty-five branches in the Birmingham diocese, of which only a small number are included in the union. There are at present about 5,500 members and candidates in these branches of the society. The Sunday School Union has fourteen Girls' Evening Homes, with a total membership of 800, but most of these belong to the central union. The White Ribbon branches are held in union and non-union clubs, Mothers' meetings, and Sunday schools (for girls over fourteen). This association has now seventy branches, of which sixteen are in women's and fifty-four in girls' meetings. The present membership is nearly 4,500, showing an increase of 660 in the past year. There are about 3,000 women and girls in attendance at the Evening Continuation schools and classes under the Education Department of the borough council. A large proportion of these girls work in shops, factories, &c., and a considerable number of those taking commercial subjects are engaged in offices, &c. These schools therefore occupy a few factory girls, but they are the exceptional ones who will apply themselves to a regular course of study after their working hours are over. The Priory Union of Adult Schools and Classes has at present twenty-one branches with a membership of 1,763, and

1,320 in average attendance. A great many of these women are mothers who do not go out to work, and many of the members have already been counted as members of clubs, &c., but we give these figures to show the scope and extent of yet another important organisation for the benefit of working women.

If all could be added together it is probable that the total number of members would fall considerably short of 10,000, or 8 per cent. of the total number of working women. The machinery for an organised system of extension exists both in the central committees of the Union and the White Ribbon bands, but nothing definite can be attempted till more helpers are forthcoming. There are several clubs which are mainly officered by working women who know the needs of the younger girls around them, but they have little time and strength to spare, and they are also the first to beg for the assistance of those who have had the advantages of culture and education. Machinery of another kind exists in the evening continuation schools, technical classes, &c., but without some direct and personal encouragement the girls have not sufficient initiative to avail themselves of these opportunities. Perhaps more might be achieved through the co-operation and help of the club teachers, but girls are too tired for sustained educational effort after nine or ten hours in the factory, and they need a combination of the educational and the social elements if they are to get the recreation as well as the widening of interests and intelligence which are so necessary to them.

One of the most remarkable features of club work in Birmingham is the co-operative holidays which many of these societies enjoy. The city possesses a Holiday Home at Conway, which is filled week after week by

Holidays and Homes.

parties of boys, girls, or adults during the summer months. Some clubs find their own quarters, but all the excursionists pay a contribution varying from 10s. to £1 1s. If they go to the Home they pay for their board, which amounts to about 7s. each per week. These holidays have made a wonderful difference to the girls. They are quick to appreciate the beauty of the surroundings, and the holiday is generally a delightful time to all concerned. Birmingham possesses another Holiday Home on the Lickey Hills, a few miles from the centre of the city. This house is open all the year round to receive small parties of the poorest girls free of charge for a fortnight at a time. The chief aim is to show them what home life and comfort should mean, and, while giving the benefit of country life, to give the girls some training in the home-making which should one day be their chief work. Another permanent boarding-house in the city tries to do the same work for some of the girls whose homes are no homes. At Shaftesbury House they board for about 7s. a week, under the charge of one of the Wesleyan sisters, and when a girl leaves to start a home of her own it is nearly always the acquired habits and not the earlier confusion and discomfort which prevail.

There comes a time in the experience of every

club worker when the question of employment comes strongly before her. Girls are out of work, under bad moral influence, suffering from unhealthy conditions, or bright young girls whose abilities warrant their learning a good trade drift into unskilled work for want of advice or help. Many clubs and some settlements have added the duties of an employment registry to their work, but it is difficult for the individual teacher to obtain all the commercial knowledge which is necessary if she is to give sound advice. London already possesses a central bureau which collects this information, but the idea is capable of expansion. Every city should have a central bureau of this kind, which might be a rallying-point for all the social work of the district and combine the best features of trade unionism with an attempt to decrease the trouble which many girls have in getting suitable employment. The girls who are unskilled by nature must in most cases remain so, but this is no reason why the general level both of work and worker should not be raised, and such a registry could help much by sifting the girls, training them in thrift and co-operation, and, above all, by helping them into good places ; and when this is achieved, by teaching them the law of give and take which is a part of all human relationships. The girls who are fitted for skilled trades need to be roused to a sense of the duty and necessity of efficiency. It is to be hoped that the system of apprenticeship or trades schools, which has been so successful on the Continent, may soon be extended to England. At present the London

County Council possesses one such school, and others are shortly to be opened. At the Borough Polytechnic girls can learn waistcoat-making, dressmaking, or upholstery, in a two years' course, and the trade subjects are combined with lessons in drawing, English, drill, &c. The trade teachers have had the best business experience, and the work is assisted by committees of trade experts, employers, and foremen, who are keenly interested and promise to give the girls a good chance when they leave the school. The effect of such education should be far-reaching, not only in regard to the girls helped individually, but also in its influence on the wages of unskilled girls in general. By the law of supply and demand the large numbers of women ready to take unskilled work of any kind must tend to depress the wages of unskilled labour in general, and anything that lessens this over supply of unskilled women would tend to raise wages. Therefore to educate girls who would otherwise swell the ranks of the unskilled, and so to direct them into skilled trades, would tend to raise the wages of unskilled women workers.[1]

Leaving this interesting line of thought, we venture to close with a hint to the teachers in the present clubs, &c. The spiritual training which they give to their girls is a wonderful boon to them, but we

[1] "So we are brought back to the old, old problem of how to restrict the numbers of the unskilled labourers. It is a question which has been apt to raise a storm of indignation whenever it has been asked. The promoters of the reformed Poor Law were even accused of a scheme for killing off the

cannot help thinking that the girls would realise
its meaning better if it were combined with more
teaching on civil matters, if the girls understood
more fully the possibilities of making the best of
life.   Many of them suffer unnecessarily through
ignorance of the laws of health and of the rights
conferred by the Factory Acts, the Compensation
Act, and the Sanitary Laws.   The girls need this
knowledge of their rights and duties as citizens,
and a sense of their responsibility as human beings,
in order to benefit by the safeguards which they
possess and make a better use of their gifts and
opportunities.   Above all they are helped by sympathetic and wise friendship, but the time has not
yet come when every working girl is within reach of
a friend who will help her to resist the difficulties
of her life and to make progress in her own class and
surroundings.

children of this class as the simplest way of keeping down
the numbers.   But it is a question which, to-day at any rate,
admits of a very simple and unobjectionable answer; one
which might well be written up large in every town without
provoking any hostility, *The way to restrict the numbers of the
unskilled workers is to turn more of them into skilled workers."—*
" The Strength of the People," p. 298, Helen Bosanquet.

CHAPTER XII

NATIONAL MINIMUM, WAGES BOARDS, CONCLUSION

A S we said above, when one turns to remedies
for raising the economic condition of women-
workers one's first thought is to suggest trade
unionism, but, as we have seen, the
conditions of the worst paid and un-   **Trades**
skilled women's work point out that   **Unions.**
little can be expected from this remedy in the near
future for the lower classes of women-workers.[1]
While accepting this conclusion in relation to this
particular class of workers, the results so far attained
show that much might be done amongst the better
class of women, and especially amongst such workers
as shop assistants, clerks, and teachers, where men

[1] The occasional success which has been obtained by
patient and efficient organisers amongst unskilled women-
workers does not invalidate this statement. Our point is,
that while such efforts are valuable and should be persisted
in, the rate of progress is so slow that we must look to other
means if reform is to come in the near future. Of course,
trade unionism, or some similar organisation, will probably
always be necessary, even under a collectivist form of industry. The recent friction between the Post Office employees
and the authorities shows this.

and women often do much the same quality and quantity of work. Experience seems to suggest that in these cases unionism would be much more to the advantage of both men and women if they could find some common basis of union and action. If the union of the Lancashire factory operatives tells for anything, it is that where men and women see that their interests are in common and form a joint union, the women's wages may become even equal to the men's level for equal work. By combining with the union the advantages of a provident and sick society, and by giving a bonus to a woman on marriage if she leaves the trade and the union, the woman might be attracted better than by a trade union organised merely to defend the wage levels of its members.

Thus unions which, in addition to the above, combine the functions of a labour bureau to help as far as is possible or desirable the mobility of the members, should be advocated, since in addition to the more obvious advantages, such organisations tend to develop foresight, independence, and common sympathy amongst the women. There is this educational influence of trade union propaganda even amongst the poorer workers.

But what has to be done for the lowest class of women-workers, those in the sweated trades who get

National minimum wage. less than a subsistence wage, and those who do work that needs practically no skill, and who do not seem capable of obtaining for themselves the benefits that trade unions would give? As pointed out above, there are many causes which make it almost impossible for these women to help themselves. The competition between the inefficient, unmarried girls, the wife whose husband is out of work or drunken and dissolute, and whose children must have food, and the widow who has also many little mouths to feed, plays into the hands of the unscrupulous employer.

In regard to those trades which employ women who are subsidised in various ways a few more remarks need to be made. These trades Mr. and Mrs. Sidney Webb call "Parasitic Trades."[1] Any advantage gained by employers in a particular trade by obtaining the use of labour not included in their wages bill is analogous to a subsidy or bounty, which under a Protectionist *régime* enables "the endowed manufacturers to bribe the public to consume their articles by ceding to them what they have not paid for."[2] This comes about in two distinct ways: "First, the case of labour partially subsisted from the incomes of persons unconnected with the industry in question."[3] Trades employing boy and girl labour often come under this heading. The employer of adult women is in the same case when he pays wages insufficient to sustain the efficiency of his workers, who are subsidised by others.

There is a more vicious form of parasitism in the case where employers use workers and pay them a wage insufficient to maintain health and vigour.

[1] "Industrial Democracy," Trades Unionists' edition, p. 749.

[2] Ibid.   [3] Ibid. p. 749.

" In thus deteriorating the physique, intelligence, and character of their operatives, they are drawing on the capital stock of the nation."[1]   Such a trade is a parasite on the present and the future. Nor is there anything peculiar in the products of the sweated trades to justify this parasitism. It merely means that the employers take the line of least resistance and instead of cheapening cost by the latest improved machinery and up-to-date business methods, look to low-paid labour for this end. Unfortunately there is no chance of the parasitic trades raising themselves by any sectional action of their own.

This means, then, since the workers are their own enemies and cannot protect themselves, we must bring in an enforced common minimum by legislation. " The remedy is to extend the conception of the common rule from the trade to the whole community, and by prescribing a national minimum, absolutely to prevent any industry being carried on under conditions detrimental to the public welfare."[2]   This proposal is merely a logical extension of the principle of providing a national minimum of hours and of sanitation, although even on these lines the law allows far too many exceptions in many trades.

Mr. and Mrs. Webb anticipate some of the objections offered to this proposal.[3]   Experience of public bodies shows that a legal minimum does

[1] " Industrial Democracy," p. 751.
[2] Ibid. p. 767.
[3] See Ibid. p. 776.

not necessarily become the actual maximum, as some critics assert.[1]

The objections to a national minimum from those making profit from the use of sweated labour take two main lines of argument. First, they assert that if compelled to raise wages their business would be ruined ; secondly, they ask what would become of the inefficient who are not worth this legalised minimum.

In regard to the first objection it is pointed out that when cheapness of cost is prevented on the lines of low wages, "it often happens that the industry falls back on another process which, less immediately profitable to the capitalists than the bounty-fed method, proves positively more advantageous to the industry in the long run."[2]

We must admit the inevitable hardships on individuals due to any change in trade or process. "Any deliberate improvement in the distribution of the nation's industry ought, therefore, to be brought about gradually, and with equitable consideration of the persons injuriously affected."[3] But there is no need to assume that all those now receiving less

---

[1] "I am pleased to report that, notwithstanding that several hands were receiving in one factory a higher rate of wages than prescribed by the Determination, the wages were unaltered."—Report of Mr. Duff (Ballarat), p. 11. Report of Chief Inspector of Factories, Victoria, 1904. Also see Report of Miss Thear, p. 13—"A good proportion of the girls in this trade are receiving more than the minimum wage of 20s. per week." Other inspectors report to the same effect, that wages above legal minimum are paid.

[2] "Industrial Democracy," p. 778.

[3] Ibid. p. 783.

than the national minimum would be displaced by
its enactment, and that trades brought under its
scope would be ruined.

This doctrine of a national minimum has been
much criticised. Mrs. Bosanquet, for instance, says
that large and increasing attention is now paid to
coercing the wills of the different parties concerned
in the production of wealth. "They assume that
employers can pay high wages if they like ; that
consumers can pay higher prices if they like ;
that workers can earn more if they like ; and they
aim at forcing the choice upon them. . . . 'They
can if they will, so they must be made to will,'
is the creed which finds its most complete expression
in the proposal of a National Minimum Wage to
be fixed by legislation."[1] Now one possible and
probable result of such a minimum, this writer
points out, since there is a limit to the shrinkage
of profits, would be to raise prices, and, moreover,
in most branches of production there is always the
danger that other employers who are not coerced
in the same way into raising prices will secure the
markets.

To take the last point first, in the long run it
would be to the advantage of consumers and wage-
earners alike for the work to be taken from the
inefficient masters and forced into the hands of
those who, *ex hypothesi*, are not paying unduly low
wages, and who therefore presumably reach low cost
of production through the most efficient and up-to-
date machinery and business methods.

[1] "Strength of the People," p. 270.

The next objection raised by this writer is more important, for she asserts that any increase of prices means that it is largely the wage-earners themselves who have to pay the increased prices; and therefore a national minimum would mean that the workers would only take out of one hand to pay into the other. Mrs. Bosanquet says: " The consumption of non-wage-earners consists largely of commodities and services with which the wage-earners have nothing to do. It would be physically impossible for them to increase their consumption of the products of the wage-earners to the extent here suggested. What they are spending their money on are such matters as expensive schooling for their children, preferential treatment in theatres and railways and building sites, highly paid services of professional men, highly paid products of artists and musicians; and in so far as these and many other luxuries are concerned, they are not touched by a rise in the price of the products of wage-earners. . . . *The great majority of wage-earners are engaged in producing for the benefit of other wage-earners*, and have no direct connection with the non-wage-earning classes. . . . More especially of the sweated trades is it literally true, almost without exception, that they are working for the wage-earners alone, and that a rise in the price of their products would be paid by the wage-earners alone. . . . It may, indeed, be worth their while to pay the price, especially if it should ultimately lead to their getting a better article; but we must frankly admit that if the effect of a National Minimum were to raise the price of the products of 'sweated' industries, then the cost of it must fall upon the wage-earners who buy those products." [1]

In regard to this, we point out again that it is a big assumption to assert that prices would rise; but even if this had to be at once admitted it would not invalidate the argument for a national minimum. In the first place, although it is difficult to fix the proportion, it is practically certain that the workers would not pay all the increase in price, and therefore they would be proportionately better off. Low prices do not compensate the workers for low wages. The idea that low-priced goods makes up to the worker for bad conditions of work and for low wages is one of the most fallacious of popular beliefs. Those who think like this must look upon the worker merely as a wealth-producing machine, and so mistake the whole end of economic effort. The community, and much less a private person, has no moral right to use a man or woman merely as a means of producing wealth. The end of work should be to develop and humanise the life of the worker. Of the two lines which the economic progress of the workers may take, *i.e.*, advancing wages or falling prices, there is no question which is preferable to the worker. When wages are raised, the worker alone gets the benefit in the first place, though, of course, so far as a higher wage develops the efficiency of the worker the community ultimately reaps the benefit as well. But when goods are reduced in price, those who consume them,

[1] "Strength of the People," p. 294.

namely the whole community, get the benefit. Thus low wages are never fully compensated by low prices. From the workers' point of view goods may be too cheap. The only question can be as to the proportion of benefit the workers get from an increase in wages.[1]

Again, it can hardly be correct that the great majority of wage-earners are engaged in producing for the benefit of other wage-earners, and have no direct connection with the non-wage-earning classes. In this connection we must remember that 5,000,000 people out of our population of 43,000,000 take half the national income each year. We can see what this means, for example, when we make a rough comparison of the demand for clothes by the rich and poor respectively. It is estimated by Booth and by Rowntree that about 12,000,000 people in this country are on or under the poverty line. Large numbers of these never get a new suit or new dress, their clothing requirements being satisfied as far as possible by gifts of clothes or by buying them second-hand. Any one who knows the conditions under which the poor live would at once admit that to estimate one new suit or dress a year on an average for each of this class of people would be an over-estimate. This would give for the very poor 12,000,000 suits and dresses. Then we get 26,000,000 people above the poverty line, but getting less than £3 per week for the family income. On an average these would not get more than two new suits or dresses each per year. This gives

[1] Prof. Smart, " Studies in Economics," p. 135.

52,000,000 suits and dresses; and the total for the
wage-earners equals 64,000,000 suits and dresses at
the outside. Next, we take the 3,750,000 whose
family incomes are between £150 and £700 per
year. Average these at five suits or dresses each
per year and we get 18,750,000. Lastly, we take
the 1,250,000 rich and very rich people, and for
these we can average at least ten suits or dresses
each per year, which gives a demand from them for
12,500,000 suits or dresses. For non-wage-earners
we thus get the total of 31,250,000 suits and dresses,
about half the number used by the wage-earners.
As the economists tell us, however, demand means
demand at a price, and so we must estimate not
merely the number of suits and dresses demanded
by each section, but the relative value. Now a very
poor man can get a suit for one sovereign or less,
while an artisan pays about £2 or £2 10s. But a
middle-class man pays £3 to £5 for a suit, and a
rich man more than that, so we see that we can
safely estimate that the 5,000,000 rich and middle-
class spend as much as, if not more, on suits and
dresses than the 38,000,000 wage-earners do. And
this would be equally true of underclothing, boots,
&c. Thus the comfortable and rich classes buy
as much as, if not more, of the labour of cloth
and cotton makers, button makers, tailors, &c., than
the wage-earners do. And the same with other
commodities which the workers produce for others
to use. As L. G. Chiozza Money points out[1]: "There
are certain well-defined servants of the rich wholly

[1] " Riches and Poverty," pp. 128-129.

devoted to their pleasure, such as menial servants, grooms, stablemen, gardeners, makers of expensive articles of food, clothing, furniture, &c., hotel servants, many of the inhabitants of the rich quarters of towns and of fashionable pleasure resorts, many trades-people and their shop-assistants, and other workers. Again, there are certain well-defined servants of the poor, such as petty trades-people, general storekeepers, the workmen and officials engaged in institutes, churches, free libraries, municipal tramways and other services, public gardens, and so forth. There is often, however, no clear distinction between those who serve the few rich and those who serve the many poor. Every trade, however useful nominally, has to give of its best to be poured into the cup of luxury and spilt in wanton extravagance. Our 1,300,000 builders, our 1,400,000 metal workers, engineers, and ship-wrights ; our 1,300,000 textile workers ; our 1,300,000 clothiers, and all our 'useful' industries, furnish their large quota of products for the rich and their small quota of products for the poor."

And again, a great deal of the "preferential treatment" that the middle-class and rich pay for in theatres, railway travelling, restaurants, hotels, &c., simply means paying for the personal services of proportionately more wage-earners, or for the right to use more of the products of wage-earners. A first-class railway carriage is the embodiment of utilities produced by wage-earners, and much greater value has been paid for the production of that carriage than for the production of a third-class carriage, while fewer people use it. And so in other cases.

Even granting that "more especially of the sweated trades is it literally true, almost without exception, that they are working for the wage-earners, and that a rise in the price of their products would be paid by the wage-earners alone," it would still be worth the while of workers to insist on this rise in wages. In the first place, the wage-earners already pay a good proportion of the subsidies that go in the form of help by parents and friends, charity, and poor relief, to make up the insufficient wage paid to the sweated worker. And in the second place, trade unionists have long recognised that it is worth while to pay members out-of-work pay for weeks and months rather than let them cut wages. And any increased cost due to a rise in wages that wage-earners paid as consumers of goods would be justified from their point of view on the same lines as out-of-work pay to members of the union. Therefore we quote with approval, as giving our views on the matter, what Charles Booth says [1] : "The same question—whether half a loaf is better than no bread—presents itself to the employer in another form. Granted that three girls at 10s. a week are worth the same as four girls at 7s. 6d. a week, is it not better to give employment to the four rather than to the three? If the employer decides that he will employ no one who is not worth 9s. a week, he really divides the work among a smaller number of fairly efficient girls. It

[1] "Life and Labour in London," vol. iv. p. 314.

may be true that no girl by herself can live respec-
tably on less than 9s. per week ; but it is also true
that there are many girls who would not be worth
employing at that rate. In other words, there are
girls who, as things are, are not worth decent
maintenance wages. The employer who only employs girls who are worth this may preserve the
even tenor of his way, and congratulate himself
that he at least is free from the guilt of employing
hands at starvation wages. But what about the
large numbers who are thus left unemployed? This
is the question asked by a large number of manufacturers, and their answer to those who demand that
a minimum wage should be fixed is that in that case
they will have to dismiss many of their hands. What
would be done with the great mass of unemployed
left to starve? I do not attempt to answer this
question. But two facts should be noticed. Fix a
minimum rate of wages, and an incentive is given
to those, whose working power has hitherto been
below par through indolence or lowness of standard,
to raise themselves to the required level. Those who
are left are the physically or mentally incapable or
the idle. Secondly, if these are left as the wholly
unemployed, they can be dealt with much more
easily than the half-paid or partly unemployed, who
drag down population to their level. They are not
left to starve. The parish rates and charitable contributions, which at present are spent in doing harm
to the many, and in lowering wages, could be wholly
devoted to the improvement of the condition of the
few, either in pleasure-houses or workhouses, accord-

ing to the circumstances of the case. The inefficient
are always irregularly employed. Irregular employment causes irregular demand, and irregular demand
causes irregularity of employment. Each force acts
with increased momentum."

To this we add one remark. The separation of
the "unemployable" from the others would be a
distinct step towards curing several social diseases.
It is not within our province in this book to discuss
at length the treatment of the "unemployable," but
we do not think that the institution of a national
minimum would necessarily mean that we should
"throw the problem out of the industrial world
into the world of Poor Law and charity," [1] in the
form that this exists at the present time. The
problem is already one of Poor Law and charity.
But public opinion is surely though slowly becoming
enlightened on this matter, and the problem of
finding a scientific and humane method of improving
the condition of the "rejected" amongst the poor
ought not to be too much for our social reformers
and statesmen. Needless to say we admit the
difficulties of this problem, yet assert that it is high
time they were faced. The difficulties in the way
of giving a national minimum are great, but the
economic loss, the waste and degradation of life
and character going on at the present time are also
great, and we are already paying a price, no less
heavy because hidden and little realised by the mass
of the community.

Those friends of the women-workers who are

[1] "Strength of the People"—Bosanquet, p. 291.

impressed by this view of the case are taking a more than theoretical interest in suggested schemes for legally fixing a minimum wage, at least in the sweated women's trades. A remedy is suggested on the lines of the Colonial system of Wages Boards. The memorandum to the Wages Boards Bill,[1] which was presented by Sir Charles Dilke, and supported by such well-known men as Mr. Alden, Mr. Bell, Mr. Crooks, Mr. Masterman, Mr. Shackleton, Mr. Harold Tennant, Mr. Trevelyan, and Mr. P. W. Wilson, runs as follows: " The object of this Bill is to provide for the establishment of Wages Boards with power to fix the minimum rate of wages to be paid to workers in particular trades. It is left to the Home Secretary to say for what trades Wages Boards are to be appointed, so that, at all events in the first instance, Wages Boards need be appointed only for what are known as the ' sweated industries,' that is, industries in which outworkers are largely employed, and in which the rate of remuneration is low. A Wages Board will have power to fix a minimum rate for any single kind of work or for any single class of workers in a particular trade. They will have the widest discretion as to fixing a time rate or a piece-work rate, and as to varying the minimum according to the kind of work and the class of persons employed. The Bill provides that a Wages Board shall be composed of representatives of employers and representatives of employed in equal numbers, with a chairman chosen by the members or nominated by the Home Secretary. It is pro-

[1] A copy of this Bill will be found in Appendix IV.

posed to entrust the enforcement of payment of the
minimum rate to factory inspectors."

In the Colonies the people concerned seem to
think these Wages Boards are on the whole a success,
and undoubtedly they have raised the level of wages.[1]
Various writers, however, in this country have criti-

[1] Report of Inspector of Factories, Victoria, for 1904,
p. 10 : "There are 38 Special Boards, affecting over 38,000
operatives, now in existence, namely :—

1. Aerated Water Trade Board.
2. Artificial Manure Board.
3. Bedsteadmakers' Board.
4. Boot Board.
5. Brassworkers' Board.
6. Bread Board.
7. Brewers' Board.
8. Brick Trade Board.
9. Brushmakers' Board.
10. Butchers' Board.
11. Cigar Trade Board.
12. Clothing Board.
13. Confectioners' Board.
14. Coopers' Board.
15. Dressmakers' Board.
16. Engravers' Board.
17. Fellmongers' Board.
18. Furniture Trade Board.
19. Ironmoulders' Board.
20. Jam Trade Board.
21. Jewellers' Board.
22. Leather Goods Board.
23. Malt Board.
24. Millet Broom Board.
25. Ovenmakers' Board.
26. Pastrycooks' Board.
27. Plate Glass Board.
28. Pottery Trade Board.
29. Printers' Board.
30. Saddlery Board.
31. Shirt Board.
32. Stonecutters' Board.
33. Tanners' Board.
34. Tinsmiths' Board.
35. Underclothing Board.
36. Wicker Board.
37. Woodworkers' Board.
38. Woollen Trade Board.

"Determinations made by the above Boards are now in
force, with the exception of the Tinsmiths' Board. The
Determinations appear to be well observed, and the Department has now comparatively little trouble in enforcing the
rates fixed by the Boards. An exception as regards the
general compliance above referred to must be made so far
as the Chinese employed in making furniture are concerned."

cised them adversely.   For example, a recent writer in the *Economic Journal* says:[1] " Though the number of Boards was largely increased under the Act of 1900, and for purposes of mere criticism some of the choicest material is provided by the new creations, enough has been said to indicate that the question of their efficacy is an open one.   Collusion is admitted, and there is no certainty as to its extent.   Old and slow workers suffered ; outworkers and workers in allied trades, to an unknown extent, lost their employment.   The adoption in all regulated industries of a task system has made the increase of wages nominal rather than real.   The wages have been earned in the usual way—by the sweat of the brow— not extorted from the employers merely by the operation of a legal device.   Such success as the system obtained was due to causes outside itself. It operated on trades in which some improvement was demanded by public opinion, and it was administered by a department which was intent on making this improvement."

We insert this adverse criticism for the benefit of the reader, although we think it is not altogether justified by the evidence offered.   It is to be noted that this writer admits the rise in wages, and so far as failure comes he does not show, nor do the official reports, that it was due to any inherent economic defect of the Boards as such, but to the evasion of the ruling of the Boards both by masters

[1] "Wages Boards of Victoria," G. W. Gough.—*Economic Journal*, September, 1905.   See also article by C. E. Collet.— *Economic Journal*, December, 1901.

and employees, and to the inefficiency of the machinery
for administering the law.   Again, it is no argument
against the Boards to suggest that they were successful because they "operated in trades in which
some improvement was demanded by public opinion."
This is surely an argument in their favour, and it
is because in this country public opinion is in favour
of reforming the conditions of sweated work that
the Wages Boards are suggested as a means of
attaining this end.

The fact that fixing a minimum wage would tend
to displace the inefficient workers is not an unmixed
evil, and to say that higher wages have to be earned
by more intense work hardly need frighten the
workers.   In most trades in this country, whether
wages are high or low, even now employers press
their workers and speed their machinery to the highest
limit.   And so far as a legal minimum wage and
limitation of overtime induced the employer to
adopt more efficient means of production, whether
that meant better organisation or labour-saving
machinery, in the long run it would be an economic
gain.

However, it is to the point to remember in this
discussion that, as Mr. Gough points out, the condition of things in this country and the Colonies
is "widely different."   Again he says: "While
offering some criticisms of particular parts of the
results achieved by the system, I am far from wishing
to suggest that there are materials at hand on which
a decided opinion may be based."

It seems, then, that as yet the evidence gained

from the Colonies is not conclusive as to the probable effect of such Boards in this country, but so far as a lead is given it seems to us to tell in favour of some such scheme, though we are aware that the administration of such an Act would meet many serious and practical difficulties, and at first legislation on these lines would have to be more or less tentative and experimental. In this country public opinion would be on the side of the sweated women-workers; the educational effect of such Boards would be very great both in regard to the women and to the public generally, and as a result trade unionism might be more successful amongst the workers. With the women more enlightened and with an increase in the number of factory inspectors, there seems to be no *a priori* reason why such Wages Boards should not be a success. To quote a well-known leader amongst women workers[1] : "So far as the sweated women's trades are concerned, some legal method of fixing a minimum wage, such as the Colonial system of 'Wages Boards,' the merits of which are already canvassed among trade unionists, appears to me to be a solution. I am stating here an individual opinion, not that of an official of the Women's Trade Union League, which has never pronounced on the matter. I feel all the difficulties so admirably put by Mr. Bowerman at the London Trade Union Congress two years ago, advocating as yet a general system of arbitration for this country. The colonial precedent for State Arbitra-

[1] "The Industrial Position of Women," by Gertrude Tuckwell, *Independent Review*, August, 1904.

tion on wages and other labour difficulties may answer well enough in countries where the trend of public opinion is on the side of Labour; but, as the compositors' secretary pointed out, the system will hardly have equal success in a country like ours, in which the sympathy of the average man is normally with the employers and against the employed, as, in view of recent legal decisions, we feel to be the case. But we are a country of inconsistencies; and the public attitude to the sweated woman worker is not the same as that of the average man or woman to the powerful trade unions and their members. Money is given and sympathy shown for the suffering of the former class, when the statement of the grievances of the latter class rouses only irritation and contradiction. Supposing that a Board of equal numbers of employed and employers, with an official chairman, could be formed in, say, the shirt-making trade, I believe that a levelling-up of the prices would be supported by public sympathy. The prices vary sometimes by as much as one-half, $1\frac{1}{2}$d. to 3d. being paid for the same work by different employers; and the sum of 5s. may be paid in a factory to workers who will receive only 2s. 6d. from a sub-contractor. Difficulties have been raised as to the possibility of finding competent representatives from the ranks of the workers to serve on such a Board. There should be no difficulty in finding, either from among the in-workers in the trade, or from some of the best of the out-workers, persons competent to argue out the worker's side."

We have now reached the end of the task we set

ourselves. We have passed in review the conditions of women's work in one of England's greatest cities. The monotony and hopelessness of the lives of the majority of our women-workers is unfortunately too evident, and detailed study of this complex problem made more insistent the thought that any far-reaching remedy must go to the root of things, and must be much more radical than many are prepared to admit. The proposed remedies that we have discussed—even the drastic one of a national minimum fixed by legislation—do not fill us with very great hopes that they will give a final and adequate solution of the problem, though we recognise and insist on their value as immediate palliatives, and as steps towards more radical remedies. More and more strongly it has been borne upon us that just because the problem of women's wages is part of the problem of remuneration of wage-earners generally, any adequate treatment of the subject must go much wider and deeper than we have gone. We have surveyed but a narrow part of the great problem of the distribution of our national income. Nor is it within the scope of our task here to follow out in detail this wider problem. But we claim the reader's indulgence while we state one or two facts bearing on the question, and venture to suggest a point of view from which the question may be approached. The national income of the 43 million people of the United Kingdom is estimated to be approximately £1,710,000,000. Out of this 1¼ million rich persons take £585,000,000; 3¾ million comfortable persons take £245,000,000; 38 million poor persons take £880,000,000. Again, of the total capital and wealth of this country more than half is owned by one-seventieth of the population. Of the land of our country more than half is owned by 2,500 persons. The factors of production are land, labour, and capital, yet of the joint products of these factors the owners of capital and land, though comparatively very few in number, take an enormous share. Even during the recent period of depression and bad trade, while want and misery has been the lot of large numbers of the workers, great profits have been earned by many companies and private firms. In Birmingham, *e.g.*, the following reports of some typical public joint stock companies have been published :—

First, the balance sheet of a large retail drapery stores. On a paid-up capital of £100,000 a dividend of 10 per cent. free of income tax is paid, and apparently this is deemed a poor dividend, for the report accompanying the balance sheet contains an apology to the shareholders that " taking into account the unsettled markets and the prevailing general depression of trade, the directors consider the result of the year's trading satisfactory." Other items of this balance sheet disclose that the Reserve Fund is nearly £50,000.

Turning to the report and balance sheet of a wholesale drapery company we find the same apology for small profits owing to depressed trade, and yet a dividend is paid of 10 per cent. free of income tax on the ordinary shares. The net profit for the year amounted to about £30,000 after deducting interest on debentures. This company have invested surplus profits to the extent of £50,000, and the reserve fund amounts to something like £30,000.

Our third balance sheet is that of a manufacturing firm, who also pay a dividend on their ordinary share capital of 10 per cent. free of tax, and carry forward to the next account £7,000, and to reserve £5,000, bringing up the total reserve fund to about £90,000. The goodwill of this company is estimated at £70,000.

We next take the accounts of a wholesale grocery firm, and find that a dividend of about 12 per cent. is paid on an ordinary share capital of £40,000. The reserve fund is £6,000.

Another company of Manchester warehousemen pays a dividend of 12½ per cent. on its ordinary capital, and the directors regret that the trade has been done at a less profit than usual. The reserve fund stands at more than £20,000.

By the large firms and combines in the trades and industries for which Birmingham is noted the same profitable dividends are shown:—

In the Cycle and Ammunition trades one very large concern shows high profits, and after paying 10 per cent. on its ordinary share capital, carried forward to next year's accounts a balance of profits of more than £50,000. On a share and debenture capital of about a million and a quarter, the reserve fund amounts to £150,000.

A similar trading concern also pays 10 per cent. on its ordinary shares, and a bonus in addition,

making the total dividend 15 per cent. for the year,
free of income tax.   £20,000 is carried to the
reserve fund, bringing it up to £60,000 on a capital
of about £510,000.

Of the Metal and allied trades the balance sheet
of one huge combine, with a debenture and share
capital of £4,500,000, shows a profit for the year
of nearly £408,000.   This company pays a dividend
on its ordinary shares of 10 per cent. free of tax, and
has a reserve fund of £750,000.

Fifteen per cent., free of tax, is the handsome
dividend paid by another company with a capital
of £460,000, and in addition £3,000 is carried to
reserve, the profit for the year amounting to about
£47,000.

On a capital of £290,000 another firm makes
a profit of £53,000, pays 6 per cent. on their preference shares, 12½ per cent. free of tax on their
ordinary shares, and adds £5,000 to reserve fund.
Even then nearly £10,000 of profits remain in hand
to be dealt with in the next year's accounts.

We have other balance sheets before us showing
the same ratio of profits.   None of the statements,
however, disclose the rate of wages paid, but it is
common knowledge that they are by no means
as handsome as the dividends.   Did shareholders
but think of the dreary, monotonous lives which are
so often the lot of the workers, 10 to 15 per cent.
dividend warrants might not, perhaps, be deemed
so " satisfactory " — to quote the word so much
beloved by the composers of company financial
reports.

These figures mean that the demand of the workers for a fairer and better life throws on the nation a moral responsibility. The nation can afford better conditions for those who win its wealth. The national income is increasing by leaps and bounds, and yet the mass of our people are in poverty. The problem of the future is the problem of distribution, and the trend of things seems to indicate that the hope of the future lies in a wise collectivism. The line of progress is suggested by the increase of voluntary co-operative undertakings on the part of the workers, and by the enormous development of municipal enterprise. As private enterprise fails to provide those common services that the community needs, the people in their collective capacity are taking the task upon themselves. There is a new idea behind imperial and local government activity. The community is collectively becoming more and more responsible for the health, education, and life of the individual, and he would be a daring man who attempted to fix the limits to the practical development of this new social ideal. What the people collectively need that they should collectively hold and use. The present system of production for profit is wasteful ; our nation, in spite of its increasing wealth, is cursed by poverty widespread, and the only way to mitigate the terrible results of the present inequalities of wealth and opportunity is through a social and industrial policy having for its end and aim a better and more equable distribution. We must set ourselves seriously to consider whether poverty is inevitable. Must the honour of our country be rooted in the dishonour and degradation of large numbers of the people. The fortunate ones amongst us can hardly be content to share in the refined, cultured, and even luxurious life of the comfortable and richer classes, when we remember that this enjoyment by the few means at the present time that millions of people are doomed from their birth to hard and monotonous work in order to provide the comfort, culture, luxury, and refinement in which they themselves never share.

APPENDICES

APPENDIX I

TABLE OF TRADES AND WEEKLY WAGES OF WOMEN WORKERS.[1]

METAL TRADES.

Trade and Processes.[2]	Minimum.	Maximum.[3]	Average[4] under 18 years.	Average[4] 18 years and over.	Average[4] Married Women.
	s. d.	s. d.	s. d.	s. d.	s. d.
AMMUNITION—					
Cartridge Case Maker	3 0	...	8 9	11 0	11 0
Cartridge Cutter-off...	3 0	18 0	...	8 6	...
Warehouse	8 0	13 4	6 10	9 0	...
Cartridge Metal Drawer	3 0	...	...	9 0	...
Cartridge Gauger......	6 0	18 0	7 0	12 6	...
Examiner	8 6	{13 0 to 14 2}	...	10 2	...
Filling Cartridges ...	7 0	18 0	...	...	...
Gun-stock	7 0	14 0	...	11 0	...
Piercing..................	2 0	18 0	...	...	...

[1] This is a full table of trades and wages investigated for the purpose of this book, but in all cases where our evidence as to wages was insufficient to form a basis we have left wages blank, although for the benefit of the reader the full list of trades is given.

[2] The names of these processes were given by the workers, and it is possible that in some cases more than one title is given for the same kind of work.

[3] The maximum wages are in many cases exceptional, as they are sometimes stated as a maximum by only one of the women working in the process.

[4] The averages are obtained by taking the total amount earned by the employees in each class for a full week's work, and dividing it by the number of such employees. The table takes no account of short time, holidays, or overtime. It is estimated that, in considering the yearly wages, on an average at least four weeks must be reckoned for short time due to various causes. In periods of depression of trade this is, of course, greater still. For example, one woman (aged 29) whose full week's wage was 10s., has for the last twelve months averaged 6s.

METAL TRADES (continued)—

Trade and Processes.	Mini-mum.	Maximum.	Average under 18 years.	Average 18 years and over.	Average Married Women.
	s. d.	s. d.	s. d.	s. d.	s. d.
AMMUNITION (continued)					
Japanning	2 0	18 0	7 0	...	...
Polishing	...	...	...	...	...
BEDSTEAD [1]—					
Cutter-off	...	...	...	10 0	...
Lacquering	4 0	19 0	5 4	11 6	12 0
Painter	3 6	15 0	7 6	12 0	12 0
Ornamenting	4 0	15 0	6 6	9 0	12 0
Wrappers-up	3 0	16 0	...	11 6	...
Wire Mattress Weaver	5 0	14 0	...	12 2	...
Tube Charger	5 0	...	...	12 0	...
Knob Solderer	5 0	12 0	...	10 8	11 0
Stover	...	15 0	...	10 0	...
Warehouse	5 0	12 0	7 3	8 0	...
Press Work	5 0	14 0	8 6	11 0	11 0
Polishers	4 0	15 0	...	13 0	...
Brass Casters	...	...	...	...	...
Burnishers	...	...	...	12 0	12 0
Enamellers	3 0	20 0	...	...	...
Wire Mattress Pounders	4 0	...	6 3	...	...
Wire Mattress Grinding	5 0	8 6	8 6	...	...
Knob Rounding	6 4	9 0	...	...	...
BELTS AND BUCKLES—					
Press Work	6 0	12 0	...	8 6	8 6
Fancy Belts	...	...	8 6	...	...
Polisher	...	15 0	...	...	...
Filer	5 0	10 0	...	...	...
Lacquerer	4 6	...	...	...	...

[1] In women's work in the Bedstead Trade the system known as the "piece-master's system" is still in vogue in some firms. One woman contracts to do the work at a certain piece rate, and then she engages girls or women to help her and pays them what she thinks fit. In one factory we found a woman "painter" who averaged 35s. per week after paying two under hands at 9s. and 6s. per week respectively. There was also a married woman engaged as "wrapper-up," and she averaged 35s. per week piece-work after paying four under hands each 16s. per week day-work. At "ornamenting" one married woman earns 30s. per week piece-work, after paying one married woman 13s. per week and one girl of fifteen 7s. per week day-work. The paymistress fulfils the function of forewoman, but even recognising this fact the distribution of the total money earned seems unfair.

METAL TRADES (*continued*)—

Trade and Processes.	Minimum.		Maximum.		Average under 18 years.		Average 18 years and over.		Average Married Women.	
	s.	d.	s.	d.	s.	d.	s.	d.	s.	d.
BOLT MAKER...............	...		16	0	...		...		...	
BRASS TRADE—										
Lacquerer	3	6	20	0	6	2	10	6	11	6
Polisher	5	0	18	0	6	11	13	6	14	9
Burnisher	5	0	12	0	...		11	2	12	0
Scratch Brusher	5	0	14	0	...		12	0	11	0
Press Worker	3	6	17	0	7	0	9	8	9	2½
Driller.....................	4	0	13	0	6	4	10	9	...	
Nail Stamper............	...		...		...		10	0	10	0
Nail Turner	4	0	11	0	...		9	0	9	0
Turner	4	0	13	0	...		11	9	...	
Riveter	4	0	14	0	7	0	9	0	...	
Stamper	3	6	11	0	5	10	10	8	...	
Solderer	4	6	12	0	5	9	11	0	...	
Tube Charger	4	0	17	6	9	4½	...		...	
Piercing Knobs.........	4	0	10	0	...		...		...	
Dipping Knobs	4	0	10	0	5	0	...		...	
Polishing Knobs	5	0	15	0	...		...		...	
Small Hinges	4	0	16	0	...		...		...	
Buttons	...		12	0	5	0	...		...	
Chains.....................	4	6	10	0	8	0	...		...	
Small Taps	...		12	0	...		...		...	
Brass Rules	5	0	10	0	8	0	...		...	
Safety Pins	5	6	14	0	7	6	...		...	
Small Pins	6	0	14	0	...		...		...	
Warehouse	3	6	14	0	6	5	9	8	...	
Wrappers-up............	3	6	12	0	6	6	9	4	...	
Packing	...		12	0	7	0	...		...	
Sorting	5	0	12	0	...		...		...	
Weighing	4	6	8	0	7	0	...		...	
Core Makers	6	0	30	0	...		17	5½	17	7
Dipping	3	6	...		...		...		...	
BUTTON MAKING—										
Covering	2	2	17	0	5	10	10	0	...	
Japanning	8	0	18	0	...		11	6	...	
Turning	4	6	11	0	6	6	...		...	
Sorting	5	0	8	0	6	9	...		...	
Warehouse	2	6	14	0	6	0	10	2	...	
Cutter	4	6	14	0	...		11	0	12	0

METAL TRADES (*continued*)—

Trade and Processes.	Mini-mum.		Maximum.		Average under 18 years.		Average 18 years and over.		Average Married Women.	
	s.	d.	s.	d.	s.	d.	s.	d.	s.	d.
BUTTON MAKING (*continued*)—										
Press Work	5	0	14	0	...		10	4	10	6
Stampers	7	0	18	0	...		...		...	
Polishing	4	0	15	0	...		...		...	
Skimming	2	1	11	9	...		...		...	
CAGE MAKING	4	6	...		...		...		...	
CHAIN MAKING—										
Press Work	5	6	12	0	6	3	...		...	
Linking	3	6	13	6	6	0	...		...	
Polishing	...		...		...		...		...	
General	3	0	20	0	7	8	12	1½	...	
CHANDELIERS—										
Press Work	...		16	0	7	6	10	8	...	
Lathe Work	5	0	14	0	7	6	10	3	...	
Lacquering	3	6	10	0	7	3	...		...	
Scratch Brushing	7	0	12	0	...		...		...	
Warehouse	5	0	10	0	...		...		...	
Linking	...		12	0	7	0	...		...	
Burnishing..............	...		...		5	9	...		...	
Stamping	...		12	0	...		...		...	
COPPER TRADE—										
Press	...		...		...		...		...	
Turners	...		...		...		...		...	
Polishers	...		14	0	...		...		...	
CYCLE ACCESSORIES—										
Lamp Solderer	7	0	18	0	6	9	...		...	
Fitting Burners.........	6	0	10	0	...		...		...	
Fitting Backs...........	6	0	16	0	...		...		...	
Saddle Machinist	4	0	16	0	6	0	...		...	
Saddle Stitcher	5	0	12	0	...		...		...	
Saddle Frame Maker	...		10	0	...		...		...	
Bells	6	0	16	0	...		...		...	
Chains...................	9	0	16	0	...		...		...	
Nickel Plating	6	0	20	0	...		...		...	

METAL TRADES (continued)—

Trade and Processes.	Minimum.	Maximum.	Average under 18 years.	Average 18 years and over.	Average Married Women.
	s. d.	s. d.	s. d.	s. d.	s. d.
CYCLE TRADE—					
Press Work	4 6	16 10	8 3	10 0	...
Polishing	5 0	16 0	8 0	10 0	10 8
Enameller and Japanner	4 6	16 0	5 6	10 4	11 0
Lacquerer	7 0	{ 12 6 to 14 0 }	...	12 0	12 0
Chains	6 0	...	6 0	10 0	...
Valves	9 0	16 0	...	...	...
Screws	4 6	15 0	8 6	12 0	...
Testing	8 6	12 0	...	...	...
Rims	5 3	9 6	...	...	...
Hub Turner	...	...	...	...	...
Wheel Webbing	9 0	12 0	...	...	...
Machine Packing	...	...	...	...	...
Cleaner and Packer	6 0	...	...	...	...
Warehouse	5 0	14 0	...	...	...
Office	5 0	...	...	...	...
Wrapper-up	6 0	10 0	...	...	...
Sorting Screws	4 0	14 0	6 4	...	...
Spanners	...	...	...	...	...
Lathe Workers	5 0	12 0	9 2	10 3	...
Rubber Section	...	15 0	...	...	...
Drilling	9 0	19 9	...	...	...
Plating Shop	9 0	11 3	...	...	...
ELECTRIC FITTINGS—					
Switch Makers	4 0	25 0	8 3	16 4½	...
Turner	7 0	14 0	...	...	...
Wires	5 0	...	...	...	...
Bridges	...	10 0	...	...	...
Dollies	...	13 0	7 6	...	...
Lacquering	...	...	...	...	...
Warehouse	4 0	15 0	...	...	...
Batteries	...	...	...	...	...
ENAMEL WORKS—					
Iron Enamel	...	20 0	6 1	12 5	...
Brushing on Colours	...	...	...	...	...

METAL TRADES (*continued*)—

Trade and Processes.	Mini-mum.	Maximum.	Average under 18 years.	Average 18 years and over.	Average Married Women.
	s. d.	s. d.	s. d.	s. d.	s. d.
FENDERS—					
Painting	6 0	14 0	6 0	...	...
Varnishing	4 6	10 0	6 0	...	...
Blackers	...	...	...	...	...
GAS FITTINGS—					
Polishers.................	4 0	12 0	...	11 0	...
Press	6 3	11 6	...	...	...
Incandescent............	...	15 0	...	...	...
GERMAN SILVER—					
Burnishing...............	3 0	18 9	...	...	...
GUN WORK—					
Boring	...	15 0	...	...	...
HAIR CURLERS—					
Fitting and Riveting	4 0	12 0	7 4	10 0	...
Warehouse...............	4 0	10 0	...	9 0	...
Press	4 0	11 0	7 0	10 0	...
Boxing	4 0	12 0	7 6	...	...
HAIR-PINS—					
Plaining	...	...	...	9 0	...
Wrapper-up	2 0	{ 6 0 to 7 0 }	...	5 6	...
Warehouse	...	...	8 0	...	...
Making pins of wire	3 0	10 0	8 0	...	...
HINGES—					
Lacquering	5 0	12 0	...	10 0	...
Dressers.................	...	...	...	...	...
Warehouse	...	10 0	...	9 0	...
HOOKS—					
Curtain	...	...	...	...	...
Hooks and Eyes	...	...	...	...	...
HORSE COMB AND CLIP-PERS.....................	5 0	13 0	...	12 0	...

METAL TRADES (*continued*)—

Trade and Processes.	Mini-mum.		Maximum.		Average under 18 years.		Average 18 years and over.		Average Married Women.	
	s.	d.	s.	d.	s.	d.	s.	d.	s.	d.
JAPANNING	5	0	18	0	5	3	10	0	...	
LAMP WORKS—										
Solderers	4	0	15	0	...		10	0	...	
Press	4	6	14	0	8	1½	10	0	12	0
Brass Polishers.........	4	0	16	0	6	0	13	0	...	
Burnishers	...		...		...		...		...	
Lamp Cleaners.........	3	6	12	0	5	7	9	0	10	0
Lacquerers..............	5	0	12	0	...		10	0	11	0
Japanners	4	0	18	0	7	0	12	4	...	
Preparing for Casters	...		...		...		8	0	...	
Stampers	5	0	11 0 to 12 0		...		10	0	11	0
Cutters	...		14	0	...		...		...	
Piercers	6	0	12	0	...		10	6	...	
Electric Fitters.........	7	6	9	0	8	6	...		...	
Screw Lathe Workers	4	0	...		9	0	...		...	
Wrappers-up............	5	0	12	0	8	0	10	6	...	
Warehouse...............	3	0	12	0	6	6	11	0	...	
Finisher	5	0	14	0	5	6	...		...	
Wires for Dippers ...	5	6	6	6	5	6	...		...	
Shade Making	...		...		...		...		...	
METAL PLATES—										
Galvanised Buckets ...	6	0	...		6	0	10	3	12	0
Fancy Bucket Painter	6	0	...		...		9	0	...	
Warehouse	3	0	15	0	7	4½	10	6	...	
Kettles	3	4	12	0	8	3	10	0	11	0
Polishers	4	0	15 0 to 16 0		...		12	0	8	0
Iron Washer	...		12	0	...		...		...	
Tin Soldering	3	0	15	0	7	9	9	3½	9	10
Press	2	5	14	0	6	0	8	6	8	9
Polishing Tin	...		...		4	6	9	6	...	
Tin Stamping	5	0	14	0	7	1½	11	1½	...	
Tin Cleaners	3	6	16	0	5	8	10	9	12	8
Guillotine Workers...	...		20	0	...		...		...	
Iron Trunk Painter...	...		...		...		...		...	
Small Iron Hooks, &c.	5	0	10	0	7	2	9	0	...	

METAL TRADES (continued)—

Trade and Processes.	Minimum.		Maximum.		Average under 18 years.		Average 18 years and over.		Average Married Women.	
	s.	d.	s.	d.	s.	d.	s.	d.	s.	d.
METAL PLATES (cont.)—										
Lathe Workers	4	0	...		...		...		...	
Wrapper-up	4	0	11	0	7	0	...		...	
Tin Enamel Warehouse	3	6	9	0	...		...		...	
METAL WORKS—										
Polishing	6	0	15	0	...		...		...	
Press	...		10	0	6	0	9	0	...	
Turning	5	0	...		...		...		...	
Fuses	5	0	16	6	...		...		...	
Shoe Rivets	8	0	11	0	...		...		...	
Metal Hilts	5	0	10 0 to 11 0		8	0	...		...	
Threading Centres	...		15	0	...		...		...	
Machinists	8	0	12	0	...		...		...	
Cutting	3	6	10	0	...		...		...	
Metal Ornaments	3	6	11	0	7	0	...		...	
Clasps, Rims, &c.	5	0	12	0	...		...		...	
Soldering	5	6	11	0	...		9	6	...	
Warehouse	4	0	11	0	...		...		...	
Magnetising Brass Dust	3	6	10	0	...		...		...	
Examining	4	9	17	0	...		...		...	
NAILS—										
Cutters	4	0	15	0	...		9	8½	9	8
Casters	...		14	0	...		...		...	
Press	7	0	10	0	...		9	0	...	
Stampers	4	3	14	0	...		...		...	
Warehouse	-5	0	...		...		...		...	
NEEDLES—										
Packeting and Labelling	4	0	10	0	...		8	6	...	
Cutting Labels	3	0	...		...		...		...	
PENS—										
Press	3	0	14	0	6	4½	9	3	...	
Slitters	4	0	16	0	7	0	11	3	11	6
Grinders	3	0	16	0	8	10½	11	6	12	6

METAL TRADES (continued)—

Trade and Processes.	Mini-mum.	Maximum.	Average under 18 years.	Average 18 years and over.	Average Married Women.
	s. d.	s. d.	s. d.	s. d.	s. d.
PENS (continued)—					
Raisers	2 0	14 0	8 0	11 0	...
Piercers	5 0	15 0	8 1½	10 2	...
Stampers	3 9	12 0	...	9 6	...
Marking	5 6	10 0	6 6	8 9	9 0
Labelling	4 0	14 0	6 0	9 0	...
Sifter of Pens	...	...	...	...	...
Warehouse	3 6	15 0	6 5	10 0	...
Cleaners	5 0	...	...	8 0	...
Wiring up	4 0	...	5 6	...	...
Cutters-out	3 0	16 0	...	...	...
PINS—					
Press	4 0	12 0	...	8 6	...
Sheeting Pins	3 6	9 0	5 4	...	...
Warehouse	4 0	...	...	9 11	...
Brushing	4 0	...	4 6	...	...
PERAMBULATORS—					
Wheel Maker	4 0	14 0	6 6	11 0	12 0
Upholsterer	2 6	14 0	...	13 0	...
RULE-MAKING—					
Sawing Machine	5 6	...	...	...	...
Gauging	4 0	11 0	...	10 0	...
Jointing	4 6	15 0	...	...	...
SAFETY PINS—					
Press	3 6	12 0	6 0	10 3	11 0
Turning	...	...	...	10 0	10 0
Shield Makers and Fixers	8 0	15 0	...	...	...
SCREWS—					
Wormers	5 0	17 0	9 0	11 0	10 6
Machinists	6 0	17 9	7 6	9 6	...
Press	...	...	4 6	10 0	10 0
Lathe	4 6	15 0	8 7	10 0	...
Turning	7 0	16 0	...	11 6	...
Tapping	2 9	15 0	9 10	12 0	12 0
Minding Self-feeders	...	14 0	...	10 3	...
Warehouse	5 0	15 0	6 10	10 0	...

METAL TRADES (*continued*)—

Trade and Processes.	Minimum.	Maximum.	Average under 18 years.	Average 18 years and over.	Average Married Women.
	s. d.	s. d.	s. d.	s. d.	s. d.
SCREWS (*continued*)—					
Cutters	7 0	12 0	8 0	9 0	...
Sorters	...	...	6 6	...	...
SPOONS AND FORKS—					
Buffer Work	6 0	21 0	...	16 0	17 6
Polishing	3 6	20 0	5 0	12 6	13 6
Warehouse	5 0	...	...	9 0	...
Edging	4 6	...	...	10 0	...
Cutting-out on Machine	7 0	...	...	10 0	...
STEEL TRADE—					
Swivels	...	12 0	...	10 0	12 0
Polishing	...	...	...	...	...
Press	3 4	12 0	8 3	...	...
TACKS—					
Weighing	3 6	8 0	...	...	...
THIMBLES—					
Roller	...	10 0	...	...	...
Stamper	5 0	10 0	...	...	...
TOYS—					
Press	4 0	11 6	6 9	...	...
Fixing Ferrules	4 0	...	5 0	...	...
Painting	...	...	6 0	...	...
Steel Toys	6 0	11 0	...	9 6	...
Polishers	5 0	12 0	...	10 0	...
Tool Boxes	5 0	13 0	...	...	...
Lathe Workers	...	...	...	...	...
UMBRELLA TRADE—					
Cutting-out	...	...	...	...	...
Machinist	6 0	14 0	8 0	11 6	...
Rib Stampers	5 0	14 0	...	11 6	12 6
Rib Riveter	5 6	14 0	7 0	10 6	...
Press	...	...	...	11 0	11 6
Umbrella Furniture	5 0	12 0	...	...	...
Warehouse	4 0	13 0	...	10 6	...
Japanning Frames	...	...	...	...	...

METAL TRADES (*continued*)—

Trade and Processes.	Mini-mum.	Maximum.	Average under 18 years.	Average 18 years and over.	Average Married Women.
	s. d.	s. d.	s. d.	s. d.	s. d.
WIRE WORKS—					
Wire Bird Cages	...	...	...	...	...
Wire Flower Stands	4 0	12 0	...	10 0	...
Warehouse	...	...	...	10 0	...
Cutters	5 0	...	...	9 0	...
Winders	3 0	12 0	...	10 0	...

CLOTHING AND SEWING TRADES.

CORSET-MAKING—					
Machinist	3 0	13 0	7 0	9 0	...
Covering Busks	...	...	...	8 0	...
Marking	...	...	7 6	...	...
Trimming	4 0	...	...	...	...
Warehouse	3 0	...	7 0	...	...
Press	4 0	10 0	8 0	9 0	...
DRESSMAKING—					
General	...	25 0	4 9	11 6	...
Machinist	...	16 0	6 0	14 6	...
Bodice Hands	2 6	12 0	5 0	10 0	...
Skirt Hands	0 6	14 0	...	14 0	...
Errand Girls	0 9	...	4 6	...	...
MILLINERY—					
Hats, Caps, Bonnets...	2 6	25 0	...	12 0	...
Babies' Millinery	...	...	...	10 0	...
General	1 0	22 0	...	12 0	...
NEEDLEWORK—					
Seamstresses............	...	20 0	...	...	...
Pinafores and Baby Linen	1 0	20 0	6 0	10 0	10 8
Under-linen	2 0	15 0	...	10 0	...
Shirts	3 0	15 0	6 9	10 0	10 0
Skirts	3 0	18 0	...	12 6	...
Button-holes	5 0	12 0	7 0	...	...
Smocking	3 0	14 0	...	12 0	...
Aprons	...	...	...	12 0	...
PALLIASSE MAKER	...	...	...	...	...

CLOTHING AND SEWING TRADES (*continued*)—

Trade and Processes.	Mini-mum.	Maximum.	Average under 18 years.	Average 18 years and over.	Average Married Women.
	s. d.	s. d.	s. d.	s. d.	s. d.
SHROUD MAKERS—					
Cutter	3 6	12 0	...	10 6	...
Frillers	3 6	12 0	...	10 10	...
TAILORING—					
Trousers	1 0	16 0	6 0	12 6	13 0
Coats	1 6	18 0	6 9	14 10	16 0
Waistcoats	0 6	21 0	9 8	11 0	...
Button-holes	3 0	24 0	7 6	13 6	...
Errand Girls	3 6	...	3 10	...	...
Cleaning Clothes	...	...	...	10 0	...
Skirts	3 6	30 0	...	11 6	...
Ladies' Coats	...	...	...	...	...
UPHOLSTERING—					
Bed and Mattress Covers	3 0	25 0	6 9	13 7	...
Curtain Makers	5 0	12 0	...	11 3	...
Carpet Sewers	5 0	15 0	...	13 3	...
Bed Trimmers	3 6	20 0	...	...	...
WEAVING—					
Braids	...	...	5 0	...	...

FOOD TRADES.

BORAX PACKERS	...	16 0	...	...	...
BOTTLING—					
Bottling Wine	...	...	...	...	...
Bottling Beer	...	...	...	...	...
Capping	6 0	...	6 0	...	...
Trucking away	5 0	12 0	5 6	...	...
Bottle Labellers	4 0	11 6	5 0	10 0	...
Mineral Waters	8 0	11 0	...	9 0	9 0
Perfumes	8 0	17 0	...	10 0	...
CONFECTIONERY—					
Warehouse	3 0	...	5 4	7 6	...
Wrapper-up	4 0	10 0	5 5	9 0	...
Packing	5 0	...	5 6	...	...
Making Jujubes	6 0	...	...	...	...

FOOD TRADES (*continued*)—

Trade and Processes.	Mini-mum.	Maximum.	Average under 18 years.	Average 18 years and over.	Average Married Women.
	s. d.	s. d.	s. d.	s. d.	s. d.
CONFECTIONERY (*cont.*)—					
Juice	...	...	...	...	...
Chocolate Moulding...	5 0	20 0	6 4	...	...
Biscuit Creamer	6 0	12 0	...	11 0	...
FISH CURING...............	6 0	20 0	...	12 6	12 6
POWDERS—					
Warehouse	1 10	18 0	7 9	10 6	...
PICKLE WORKS—					
Bottling	...	...	5 6	...	...
VINEGAR—					
Finisher	...	12 0	...	10 0	...

JEWELLERY, &c., TRADES.

Trade and Processes.	Mini-mum.	Maximum.	Average under 18 years.	Average 18 years and over.	Average Married Women.
JEWELLERY—					
Gold Polisher	5 0	20 0	6 0	12 8	...
Gold Cutter	3 0	16 0	...	12 0	...
Press	4 0	15 0	8 6	10 5	10 9
Polishing	3 6	20 0	6 9	12 2	...
Soldering	6 6	...	7 0	12 0	...
Finishing	4 0	20 0	...	9 10	...
Brooch Gilder	4 0	18 0	7 0	11 6	...
Charging and Solder-ing	3 6	...	6 0	...	...
Studs	...	17 0	...	10 0	...
Burnishing Studs	5 0	14 0	...	9 0	...
Polishing Rings	3 0	18 0	...	12 0	...
Gold Beads	4 0	12 0	...	10 0	...
Masonic	...	14 0	...	10 0	...
Medals, Press Work	5 0	12 0	5 0	8 6	...
Warehouse	3 6	25 0	7 2	17 3	...
Pearl Stringer	5 0	12 0	...	...	...
Scratch Brusher	...	12 0	8 0	...	...
Burnishing...............	2 6	17 0	3 6	...	...
Gold Froster	5 0	12 0	...	...	...
SILVERSMITHS—					
Pencil Cases	...	...	4 0	...	...

JEWELLERY, &c., TRADES (*continued*)—

Trade and Processes.	Minimum.	Maximum.	Average under 18 years.	Average 18 years and over.	Average Married Women.
	s. d.	s. d.	s. d.	s. d.	s. d.
SILVERSMITHS (*cont.*)—					
Photo Frames	...	...	...	10 0	...
Press .:....................	6 0	14 0	...	9 0	10 0
Stampers	3 0	16 0	...	10 0	12 0
Polishers	3 9	16 0	5 4	10 0	...
Burnishers..............	6 0	17 0	9 9	13 6	...
Scratch Brushers	5 6	...	...	9 0	...
Finishers	5 0	...	5 0	...	...
Warehouse	5 0	20 0	...	12 0	...
WATCHES—					
Turning and Polishing Jewels..................	3 0	16 0	...	12 0	...
Watch Swivels	4 0	14 0	...	10 0	...
Watch Keys	6 0	12 6	...	10 0	...
Watch Cases............	2 0	16 0	...	10 0	...
ELECTRO-PLATE—					
Burnishing..............	2 0	20 0	7 10	12 4	11 3
Polishing	2 0	15 0	7 6	11 0	12 3
Press	...	...	5 0	8 0	...
Warehouse	4 6	12 0	5 6	10 9	...
Scratch Brushing	8 0	11 0	9 0	...	...
GOLD AND SILVER CHAINS—					
Gold Chains	2 0	20 0	6 9	14 6	16 0
Silver Chains............	2 6	20 0	4 0	11 0	...
Various Chains	2 6	20 0	9 9	12 0	13 0
GOLD LEAF CUTTER ...	...	...	...	...	...

PAPER, CARDBOARD, AND PRINTING TRADES.

Trade and Processes.	Minimum.	Maximum.	Average under 18 years.	Average 18 years and over.	Average Married Women.
BOOKBINDING—					
Sewing	4 0	15 0	7 0	12 0	...
Printing	3 0	...	...	...	...
Lining.....................	4 0	...	5 0	...	...
Ruling.....................	4 0	20 0	4 0	...	...
Folding	4 0	12 0	8 0	9 9	...
Paging	4 0	15 0	8 0	13 6	...

PAPER, CARDBOARD, AND PRINTING TRADES (*cont.*)—

Trade and Processes.	Minimum.		Maximum.		Average under 18 years.		Average 18 years and over.		Average Married Women.	
	s.	d.	s.	d.	s.	d.	s.	d.	s.	d.
BOOKBINDING (*cont.*)—										
Gumming	4	0	11	0	8	0	10	0	...	
Perforating	4	0	12	0	7	0	10	6	...	
Wire Stitcher	4	0	11	0	...		10	0	...	
BOXES (VARIOUS)	2	0	15	0	7	0	10	0	...	
PAPER MANUFACTURING—										
Paper and Rag Sorting	2	6	12	0	5	10	9	0	8	6
Paper Varnishing......	4	6	...		...		9	0	...	
Warehouse	4	0	13	0	5	5	7	8	10	0
Sand-paper	4	6	...		...		...		...	
Knocking-up	5	0	11	6	...		...		...	
Hot Press	3	6	10	0	...		...		...	
Glazing	4	0	10	0	...		...		...	
PAPER BAGS	3	0	16	0	7	0	10	6	10	3
PAPER BOXES	0	6	15	0	6	11	9	6	8	6
PRINTING—										
Machine Work	5	0	10	0	8	2	9	8	...	
Machine Ruler	3	0	18	0	6	0	...		...	
Liners	12	0	25	0	...		...		...	
Lithographers	10	0	...		...		12	0	...	
Laying-on	3	6	11	0	5	10	9	7	10	0
Label Cutters	5	0	...		...		...		...	
Folding and Stitching	4	6	12	6	5	4	9	0	...	
Takers-off	4	0	10	0	6	0	...		...	
STATIONERY—										
Rulers	4	0	20	0	5	0	...		...	
Warehouse	3	6	...		...		...		...	
Envelopes	4	0	15	0	7	0	12	0	...	
Paying Books	3	6	18	0	6	6	...		...	

LEATHER TRADES.

Trade and Processes.	Minimum.		Maximum.		Average under 18 years.		Average 18 years and over.		Average Married Women.	
BOOTS—										
Boot Upper Machinist	1	0	14	0	8	0	11	3	...	
Tips for Boots (Stamp)	5	0	12	0	...		10	0	...	

LEATHER TRADES (continued)—

Trade and Processes.	Minimum.		Maximum.		Average under 18 years.		Average 18 years and over.		Average Married Women.	
	s.	d.	s.	d.	s.	d.	s.	d.	s.	d.
BOOTS (*continued*)—										
Tips for Boots (Pressing)	...		...		...		10	0	...	
Tips for Boots (Polishing)	...		...		...		11	0	...	
Tips for Boots (Riveting)	7	0	13	0	...		...		...	
Bottoms	...		...		...		10	0	10	0
Boot Finisher	3	6	12	0	...		10	0	...	
Warehouse	5	0	15	0	...		...		...	
Fitter	2	0	12	0	...		12	0	...	
Eyeletting	5	0	...		7	0	...		...	
CASE MAKERS—										
Jewel Cases	3	0	18	0	7	5	12	0	...	
Banjo Cases	4	0	16	0	7	0	11	0	...	
Pencil Cases	5	0	15	0	...		10	9	...	
HARNESS-MAKING—										
Harness Stitcher	3	0	18	0	8	0	10	6	...	
Dresser	...		...		...		...		...	
Saddle Stitching	2	6	20	0	6	0	15	0	...	
LEATHER GOODS—										
Stitchers....................	0	9	20	0	7	4	10	3	...	
Preparing for Stitchers	4	0	12	0	...		9	0	...	
Linking	4	0	...		...		...		...	
Marking	4	0	...		...		...		...	
Purses, Pocket-books, Belts	3	0	20	0	5	6	11	3	...	
Braces.....................	4	0	18	6	5	0	12	0	...	
Warehouse...............	2	6	12	0	...		10	0	...	
Leather Goods	4	0	...		6	9	...		...	
Leather Boot Laces...	4	0	10	0	6	6	10	0	...	
MILITARY WORK—										
Leather Stitchers	3	0	20	0	...		10	0	...	
Ornaments...............	5	0	15	0	...		11	0	...	
Buttons	3	6	16	0	6	0	10	3	...	
Badges	9	0	...		...		...		...	
SLIPPER MAKERS—										
Uppers	2	6	14	0	...		10	0	...	

WOOD TRADES.

Trade and Processes.	Minimum.		Maximum.		Average under 18 years.		Average 18 years and over.		Average Married Women.	
	s.	d.	s.	d.	s.	d.	s.	d.	s.	d.
BOXES	2	6	15	0	8	0	9	11	10	0
FRENCH POLISHERS	1	6	30	0	6	0	13	0	14	6
FURNITURE AND CABINET—										
Lacquering	4	0	14	0		...	12	0		...
Warehouse		...		...		...	10	0		...
Press		...	12	0		...	10	0		...
PICTURE FRAMES—										
Gilder	6	0		...		...	10	0		...
Errand Girls		...		...	5	0		...		...
Warehouse	4	0		...		...	10	0		...

MISCELLANEOUS TRADES.

Trade and Processes.	Minimum.		Maximum.		Average under 18 years.		Average 18 years and over.		Average Married Women.	
BONE WORKS—										
Driller (Teat Maker)	5	3		...		...		...		...
Turner ,,	5	0		...		...		...		...
Warehouse ,,		...		...		...	10	0		...
BOTTLE WASHERS	5	0	10	0	6	8	9	2	9	8
BRICKMAKER—										
Carrier-off		...	20	0		...	14	0	14	0
BROOM MAKER—										
Bass Brooms		...	18	0		...	12	0		...
BRUSH-MAKING—										
Wire Drawing	3	0	17	0	6	9	9	7		...
Dressing	4	0	12	0	5	0	10	0		...
Warehouse	5	0	10	0	6	8	10	0		...
CARDING—										
Hooks and Eyes		...		...		...	5	11	5	11
Studs		...		...		...	6	0		...
Pearl Buttons		...		...		...	8	0		...
Needles	8	0	15	0		...	10	0		...
Boot Protectors	5	0	12	0	7	0	9	6		...

MISCELLANEOUS TRADES (*continued*)—

Trade and Processes.	Minimum.		Maximum.		Average under 18 years.		Average 18 years and over.		Average Married Women.	
	s.	d.	s.	d.	s.	d.	s.	d.	s.	d.
CHEMIST—										
Warehouse	...		...		8	0	10	2	...	
Mixing Chemicals	5	0	12	0	7	0	...		...	
Labels	5	0	10	0	6	6	...		...	
CIGAR-MAKING—										
Cigars	2	6	24	0	...		...		...	
Cigarettes	2	6	20	0	3	9	...		...	
COFFIN FURNITURE—										
Blackers	5	0	18	0	...		12	0	...	
Warehouse	4	0	15	0	4	0	9	0	10	0
Bronzing	3	0	15	0	5	0	10	0	...	
Polishers	5	0	15	0	...		11	0	...	
CORK TRADE—										
Cutter	...		...		...		...		...	
DESIGNERS—										
Carpets	...		...		...		...		...	
FIREWORKS	5	6	12	0	...		...		...	
GLASS WORKS—										
Plate Glass Finisher	...		...		...		...		...	
Glass Nipper	...		...		...		...		...	
Glass Polisher	3	6	17	0	6	0	12	0	...	
Painting on Glass	8	0	15	0	8	0	12	0	...	
Gilding and Emboss-ing	6	0	...		7	0	...		...	
Globes	9	0	11	0	...		...		...	
Press Workers	...		...		6	6	...		...	
Stenciller	3	0	11	0	...		...		...	
Brushing Letters on	4	0	12	0	7	6	10	0	...	
HAIR PREPARER	...		...		...		...		...	
LACE—										
Wrapping	...		...		...		...		...	
LAUNDRY WORK—										
Washers	...		12	0	...		8	6	9	4

MISCELLANEOUS TRADES (*continued*)—

Trade and Processes.	Minimum.	Maximum.	Average under 18 years.	Average 18 years and over.	Average Married Women.
	s. d.	s. d.	s. d.	s. d.	s. d.
LAUNDRY WORK (*cont.*)—					
Ironers	3 0	20 0	7 3	9 11	...
Starching	4 6	10 0	6 0	...	...
Collars......................	2 0	17 0	4 6	11 9	12 0
Shirts	6 0	18 0	...	...	...
Packers and Sorters...	3 6	10 0	6 9	9 0	...
Calenderers	4 0	10 0	5 8	...	...
General	3 0	15 0	...	7 4	12 0
MEDICAL AND SURGICAL APPLIANCES—					
Machinists	...	...	6 0	...	...
Belts	...	...	...	...	...
Sanitary Towels	1 6	...	...	10 0	...
Warehouse..............	...	...	6 0	10 0	...
Pad Makers	3 0	...	...	...	...
MOP-MAKING	...	...	...	...	...
OPTICIANS—					
Spectacle Glazing.......	4 0	24 0	...	...	...
PEARL MANUFACTURE—					
Pearl Button Turning	...	...	...	10 0	...
Grinding	4 6	11 0	...	...	...
Polishing	5 0	...	...	...	...
Lever	4 0	13 0	...	...	...
PERFUMES—					
Warehouse..............	...	14 0	...	10 0	...
PHOTOGRAPHIC APPARATUS—					
Cameras	3 6	15 0	...	11 9	...
PHOTOGRAPHY—					
General	...	...	7 6	...	...
Warehouse	6 0	12 0	...	10 0	...
POTTERY—					
Painters	2 6	16 0	6 0	...	...

MISCELLANEOUS TRADES (*continued*)—

Trade and Processes.	Minimum.	Maximum.	Average under 18 years.	Average 18 years and over.	Average Married Women.
ROPE AND TWINE MAKERS—	s. d.	s. d.	s. d.	s. d.	s. d.
Twisters	...	...	...	9 0	9 0
Rollers	...	...	...	9 0	...
String Balls	...	...	...	9 0	...
Warehouse	...	...	...	9 0	...
Winders	5 6	...	5 6	...	...
RUBBER WORKS—					
Stamper	...	...	...	...	...
Football Bladders	...	15 0	...	...	...
Stripping Tubes	6 3	17 0	8 0	...	...
SHIPPING FURNITURE—					
Hammocks	6 0	...	...	...	...
SLATE—					
Polishing	6 0	...	...	...	...
STOPPERS (PATENT)—					
Warehouse	6 9	...	...	...	...
Lathe	...	15 0	...	...	...
TICKET WRITERS	4 0	...	6 0	...	...
TYRES—					
Tyre Sewing	...	15 0	7 0	...	...
Rolling Tyres	8 6	...	9 2	...	...
Solution for Punctures	4 0	10 0	6 0	9 0	...
Tubes	...	...	7 6	...	...
Tyre Wrapping	6 6	...	8 0	...	...
Warehouse	5 0	...	9 0	10 0	...
Covering Tyres	5 0	17 0	...	12 0	...
WHIP-MAKING—					
Braiding	3 6	13 0	7 9	10 0	...
Soldering	4 0	...	...	...	...
Stitching Handles	3 0	...	4 0	...	...
Varnishing	4 0	10 0	5 0	...	...
WICKER CANE—					
Caning Chairs	5 0	30 0	...	16 0	...
Mail Carts, &c.	8 0	...	...	9 0	...

MISCELLANEOUS TRADES (*continued*)—

Trade and Processes.	Minimum.	Maximum.	Average under 18 years.	Average 18 years and over.	Average Married Women.
	s. d.	s. d.	s. d.	s. d.	s. d.
WINDOW BLIND AND FITTINGS—					
Press	3 6	10 0	...	...	...

OCCUPATIONS NOT REGULATED BY FACTORY AND WORKSHOP ACTS.

Trade and Processes.	Minimum.	Maximum.	Average under 18 years.	Average 18 years and over.	Average Married Women.
ATTENDANTS—					
Bath	8 0	16 0	...	14 0	14 0
Medical	...	...	...	...	...
Door	...	10 0	...	10 0	...
CARETAKER—					
School.....................	...	...	...	15 0	15 0
CHARWOMEN	1 6 per day	2 0 per day	...	7 9 per week	7 9 per week
CLERKS—					
General	2 6	25 0	6 9	13 2	18 0
Cash Desk	5 0	16 0	6 6	...	...
Invoice	...	...	...	...	...
Addressing Envelopes	5 0	...	6 0	...	...
Typists	10 6	30 0	...	...	...
Metal Trade	5 0	...	...	10 0	...
Jewellery	4 6	18 0	9 0	13 6	...
COLLECTORS AND CANVASSERS—					
Assurance	10 0	30 0	...	...	...
Club......................	10 0	...	...	...	...
Miscellaneous	10 0	30 0	7 0	...	...
COOKS AND CATERERS...	2 6 per day	30 0	...	...	...
ERRAND GIRLS............	5 6	...	6 9	...	...
FIREWOOD—					
Chopping	4 0	12 0	4 0	9 10	9 9
Bundling	3 0	...	...	...	...

OCCUPATIONS NOT REGULATED BY FACTORY AND WORKSHOP ACTS (continued)—

Trade and Processes.	Mini-mum.	Maximum.	Average under 18 years.	Average 18 years and over.	Average Married Women.
	s. d.	s. d.	s. d.	s. d.	s. d.
HAWKERS—					
Flowers	5 0	20 0	10. 0	10 5	10 5
Ferns	...	...	6 0	...	...
Fruit and Vegetables	7 6	20 0	...	...	...
Paper Flowers	3 0	10 0	...	...	...
Wood	...	10 0	5 0	...	...
Fish	...	...	...	...	...
Matches	...	...	...	...	...
HOUSEKEEPERS	...	...	...	17 6	...
MINDING BABIES	...	...	...	3 3	3 3
POST OFFICE EM-PLOYEES—					
Manageress	...	...	...	...	...
Telegraphists	12 0	35 0	...	...	...
PUBLIC-HOUSE—					
Manageress	21 0	...	...	26 6	27 3
Barmaids	4 0	18 0	...	8 8	12 0
TELEPHONE GIRLS	...	...	...	...	...
THEATRE EMPLOYEES—					
Pantomime	...	30 0	...	...	...

APPENDIX II

TABLE SHOWING THE AGE OF MARRIAGE OF WOMEN IN DIFFERENT OCCUPATIONS.

Occupation.	Service.	Press Work.	Polishing.	Warehouse.	French Polishers.	Lacquerers.	Screw Workers.	Solderers.
Average Weekly Wage.	...	10/-	12/-	10/6	13/-	10/-	10/8	9/9
Age of Marriage.	Per cent.	Per cent.	Per cent.	Per cent.	Per cent.	Per cent.	Per cent.	Per cent.
17 and under	3·37	...	1·33	...	...	...	...	...
18	·56	4·00	5·33	...	...	...	9·68	3·57
19	3·37	11·20	10·67	5·36	7·50	11·43	22·58	25·00
20	5·62	20·80	17·33	8·93	15·00	14·29	22·58	10·72
21	18·54	20·00	12·00	7·14	30·00	11·43	16·13	10·71
22	14·05	15·20	18·67	16·07	22·50	25·71	3·23	3·57
23	16·29	19·20	14·67	21·43	5·00	20·00	12·90	21·43
24	16·29	4·00	10·67	19·64	7·50	5·71	6·45	17·86
25	11·80	1·60	2·67	14·29	7·50	8·57	...	3·57
26	3·93	·80	1·33	3·57	5·00	2·86	6·45	3·57
27	...	1·60	2·67	...	...	...	...	...
28	2·25	·80	1·33	3·57	...	...	...	...
29	1·12	...	...	...	...	...	...	...
30	1·69	...	...	...	...	...	...	...
Over 30	1·12	·80	1·33	...	...	...	...	...
	100·00	100·00	100·00	100·00	100·00	100·00	100·00	100·00

TABLE SHOWING AGE OF MARRIAGE OF 1,000 WORKING WOMEN.

Age of Marriage.		Per cent.
Women who married at 17 or under		1·20
„ „ „ 18		2·40
„ „ „ 19		9·70
„ „ „ 20		13·00
„ „ „ 21		16·30
„ „ „ 22		13·80
„ „ „ 23		17·20
„ „ „ 24		10·50
„ „ „ 25		8·80
„ „ „ 26		3·10
„ „ „ 27		·70
„ „ „ 28		1·20
„ „ „ 29		·40
„ „ „ 30		·50
„ „ „ over 30		1·20
		100·00

APPENDIX III

WEIGHTS AND MEASUREMENTS OF GIRLS AFTER ATHLETIC TRAINING.

Acr. Chest, U. = Across Chest, Uninflated.
Acr. Back, U. = Across Back, Uninflated.
Rnd. Ribs, U. = Round Ribs, Uninflated.
I. = Inflated.

No. 1. Entered Class Sept., 1905. Age 13 years 10 months.

MEASUREMENTS.

Date.	Acr. Chest, U.	I.	Acr. Back, U.	I.	Rnd. Ribs, U.	I.	Height.	Weight.
5/ 9/05	11	12	9½	10	25½	27½	5 ft. 3¼	7 st. 6
15/12/05	9	11	10	11	23	30	5 ft. 3¾	7 st. 9
9/ 3/06	10¾	11¾	12	12¾	24½	29	5 ft. 3⅜	7 st. 13

REMARKS.

Tendency to Scoliosis.
Left Shoulder higher.
9/3/06 Shoulders normal.

No. 2. Entered Class Sept., 1905. Age 12 years 10 months.

MEASUREMENTS.

Date.	Acr. Chest, U.	I.	Acr. Back, U.	I.	Rnd. Ribs, U.	I.	Height.	Weight.
6/ 9/05	10	10¼	10	10¾	24	25½	4 ft. 7¼	5 st. 2
15/12/05	10	11¼	8	9	23	26	4 ft. 7¾	5 st. 4
9/ 3/06	11½	12¼	12	12¾	23½	27½	4 ft. 8¼	5 st. 11½

No. 3. Entered Class Sept., 1905. Age 13 years 10 months.

MEASUREMENTS.

Date.	Acr. Chest, U.	I.	Acr. Back, U.	I.	Rnd. Ribs, U.	I.	Height.	Weight.
5/ 9/05	10½	11¼	9	10	23¾	25¾	4 ft. 9	5 st. 8
12/12/05	10½	11⅜	10¼	11	23¾	26¼	4 ft. 9⅜	6 st. 3
9/ 3/06	11½	12⅛	10¼	11⅝	23	27	4 ft. 9⅛	6 st. 10½

No. 4. Entered Class Sept., 1905. Age 14 years 1 month.

MEASUREMENTS.

Date.	Acr. Chest, U.	I.	Acr. Back, U.	I.	Rnd. Ribs, U.	I.	Height.	Weight.
5/ 9/05	11¾	12½	9¼	9¾	24	27¼	4 ft. 11½	6 st. 6
16/12/05	11½	13	9	9½	24	28	5 ft. 0½	6 st. 3
9/ 3/06	11¾	13	10½	11½	22½	26½	5 ft. 0½	6 st. 7

No. 5. Entered Class Sept., 1905. Age 13 years 7 months.

MEASUREMENTS.

Date.	Acr. Chest, U.	I.	Acr. Back, U.	I.	Rnd. Ribs, U.	I.	Height.	Weight.
5/ 9/05	10	10½	8¾	9¼	23	25½	5 ft. 0½	5 st. 12
15/12/05	11	12½	9	10	24	28	5 ft. 1	6 st. 2
9/ 3/06	11¼	12¼	11⅛	12⅝	23	27¾	5 ft. 1⅞	6 st. 6½

No. 6. Entered Class Sept., 1905. Age 12 years 11 months.

MEASUREMENTS.

Date.	Acr. Chest, U.	I.	Acr. Back, U.	I.	Rnd. Ribs, U.	I.	Height.	Weight.
6/ 9/05	10¼	11	9¼	9¾	23	25½	4 ft. 9½	5 st. 3
12/12/05	11¼	11¾	10	10⅝	24	26	4 ft. 10½	5 st. 8
8/ 3/06	10	11	9	10	22½	27	4 ft. 11¼	5 st. 9

REMARKS.

Lordosis.
Left shoulder higher.

No. 7. Entered Class Sept., 1905. Age 12 years 10 months.

MEASUREMENTS.

Date.	Acr. Chest, U.	I.	Acr. Back, U.	I.	Rnd. Ribs, U.	I.	Height.	Weight.
4/ 9/05	9¾	10¼	10¼	11¼	24½	25¾	4 ft. 10¾	6 st. 1
12/12/05	11	12	9¾	10¾	24½	27	4 ft. 11½	6 st. 2¼
9/ 3/06	12	13	10¾	11¼	24½	28¼	4 ft. 11⅝	6 st. 10

REMARKS.

Right shoulder considerably lower, and both very round. Deviation to left in upper dorsal region.
12/12/05 Curve slighter and shoulders much improved. Right shoulder still dropped.
9/ 3/06 Spine straight. Right shoulder slightly dropped.

No. 8. Entered Class Sept., 1905. Age 13 years 9 months.

MEASUREMENTS.

Date.	Acr. Chest, U.	I.	Acr. Back, U.	I.	Rnd. Ribs, U.	I.	Height.	Weight.
5/ 9/05	11	12	9¼	10¼	25½	27½	5 ft. 3½	7 st. 6
12/12/05	12¼	13½	10¾	11⅝	25	26½	5 ft. 3⅞	7 st. 6
8/ 3/06	12	13½	9½	10½	24	29	5 ft. 3½	8 st. 0

REMARKS.

Round shoulders.
12/12/05 Shoulders much improved.

No. 9. Entered Class Sept., 1905. Age 13 years 6 months.

MEASUREMENTS.

Date.	Acr. Chest, U.	I.	Acr. Back, U.	I.	Rnd. Ribs, U.	I.	Height.	Weight.
5/ 9/05	11	12	10	10½	23½	26	4 ft. 10½	5 st. 13
12/12/05	11	11⅜	10¾	11½	23	25⅞	4 ft. 10⅜	6 st. 1½
9/ 3/06	11⅛	12	10	10½	23½	26¼	4 ft. 11	6 st. 4½

No. 10. Entered Class Sept., 1905. Age 14 years 4 months.

MEASUREMENTS.

Date.	Acr. Chest, U.	I.	Acr. Back, U.	I.	Rnd. Ribs, U.	I.	Height.	Weight.
4/ 9/05	12½	12¾	10¾	11½	26	28½	4 ft. 11½	6 st. 12½
12/12/05	12¼	13½	10½	11½	26½	29½	5 ft. 0½	7 st. 9
9/ 3/06	13¼	14¼	10¾	11½	25	29½	5 ft. 0½	8 st. 4

No. 11. Entered Class Sept., 1905. Age 13 years 2 months.

MEASUREMENTS.

Date.	Acr. Chest, U.	I.	Acr. Back, U.	I.	Rnd. Ribs, U.	I.	Height.	Weight.
6/ 9/05	11¼	11¾	10½	10¾	26	28	4 ft. 11¾	6 st. 4
11/12/05	10	11¼	8	9	26	29	5 ft. 0	7 st. 0
8/ 3/06	10½	12¼	9	10	23	27	5 ft. 0½	7 st. 3

REMARKS.
Right shoulder slightly drooped.

No. 12. Entered Class Sept., 1905. Age 14 years 4 months.

MEASUREMENTS.

Date.	Acr. Chest, U.	I.	Acr. Back, U.	I.	Rnd. Ribs, U.	I.	Height.	Weight.
9/ 9/05	10¾	10¾	11½	12¼	25	26½	5 ft. 0½	6 st. 8
11/12/05	11½	12½	9½	10¾	26½	30	5 ft. 2½	7 st. 5
8/ 3/06	10½	12½	8	9	24	28½	5 ft. 2½	7 st. 5

No. 13. Entered Class Sept., 1905. Age 13 years.

MEASUREMENTS.

Date.	Acr. Chest, U.	I.	Acr. Back, U.	I.	Rnd. Ribs, U.	I.	Height.	Weight.
25/ 9/05	10¾	11	10½	11	23½	25	4 ft. 9¾	5 st. 4
15/12/05	10	11½	9½	10¾	21½	26	4 ft. 10¾	5 st. 5
9/ 3/06	10¼	11½	10¾	11½	21¼	26½	4 ft. 11½	5 st. 13½

No. 14. Entered Class Sept., 1905. Age 13 years 7 months.

MEASUREMENTS.

Date.	Acr. Chest, U.	I.	Acr. Back, U.	I.	Rnd. Ribs, U.	I.	Height.	Weight.
5/ 9/05	11½	12	10	10¾	27½	29½	5 ft. 0½	7 st. 1
12/12/05	11¼	12	12½	13½	26½	29	5 ft. 0½	7 st. 5½
8/ 3/06	9½	11½	8½	9½	24½	30	5 ft. c¾	7 st. 7

REMARKS.
Left shoulder higher.

No. 15. Entered Class Sept., 1905. Age 14 years 8 months.

MEASUREMENTS.

Date.	Acr. Chest, U.	I.	Acr. Back, U.	I.	Rnd. Ribs, U.	I.	Height.	Weight.
5/ 9/05	10½	11¾	10½	10¾	25½	29	5 ft. 0½	6 st. 6
12/12/05	12¼	12¼	10½	10⅝	24	27½	5 ft. 0½	6 st. 10
8/ 3/06	11	13	9	10	24	30	5 ft. 1	6 st. 13

REMARKS.
Tendency to Scoliosis. Right shoulder higher.
12/12/05 Still a tendency, but right shoulder improved.

No. 16. Entered Class Sept., 1905. Age 13 years 9 months.

MEASUREMENTS.

Date.	Acr. Chest, U.	I.	Acr. Back, U.	I.	Rnd. Ribs, U.	I.	Height.	Weight.
5/ 9/05	10	10½	9	9½	24½	26½	4 ft. 9	6 st. 2
15/12/05	9½	11	8	9	23	28½	4 ft. 9¼	6 st. 11
8/ 3/06	9½	11	9	10	24	28	4 ft. 9½	6 st. 11

REMARKS.

Lordosis.

No. 17. Entered Class Sept., 1905. Age 13 years 7 months.

MEASUREMENTS.

Date.	Acr. Chest, U.	I.	Acr. Back, U.	I.	Rnd. Ribs, U.	I.	Height.	Weight.
4/ 9/05	10	10½	9½	10	23	24¾	4 ft. 9½	5 st. 1
12/12/05	10¾	11¼	9	9½	22	25	4 ft. 10⅛	5 st. 9
8/ 3/06	11	13	9	10	21½	26½	4 ft. 11	6 st. 0

No. 18. Entered Class Sept., 1905. Age 15 years 8 months.

MEASUREMENTS.

Date.	Acr. Chest, U.	I.	Acr. Back, U.	I.	Rnd. Ribs, U.	I.	Height.	Weight.
25/ 9/05	10	10½	11¼	11½	23	25	4 ft. 11¼	5 st. 12
13/12/05	10	11	9	9½	22½	26	4 ft. 11½	6 st. 7
8/ 3/06	11	12¼	8½	9½	22	28	5 ft. 0	6 st. 12

No. 19. Entered Class Sept., 1905. Age 13 years 7 months.

MEASUREMENTS.

Date.	Acr. Chest, U.	I.	Acr. Back, U.	I.	Rnd. Ribs, U.	I.	Height.	Weight.
4/ 9/05	10¾	11¼	11¾	12	24	26½	4 ft. 8½	5 st. 3
12/12/05	10½	11⅛	10½	11	24	27	4 ft. 9¾	5 st. 11½
8/ 3/06	11	13	8	9	23	28	4 ft. 10½	6 st. 2

REMARKS.

Left hip higher (stands on left leg habitually).

No. 20. Entered Class Sept., 1905. Age 13 years 8 months.

MEASUREMENTS.

Date.	Acr. Chest, U.	I.	Acr. Back, U.	I.	Rnd. Ribs, U.	I.	Height.	Weight.
6/ 9/05	10	10¼	12	12½	24	25	4 ft. 10	6 st. 2
12/12/05	10½	12¼	8	9	25	28½	4 ft. 10¾	6 st. 6
8/ 3/06	10¾	12¼	8	9	25	29	4 ft. 11	7 st. 0

No. 21. Entered Class Sept., 1905. Age 12 years 10 months.

MEASUREMENTS.

Date.	Acr. Chest, U.	I.	Acr. Back, U.	I.	Rnd. Ribs, U.	I.	Height.	Weight.
4/ 9/05	11¼	11¾	9½	10¼	24	26½	4 ft. 8	5 st. 5
12/12/05	10¾	11½	9½	10¼	23½	26½	4 ft. 9½	5 st. 9
8/ 3/06	11½	13¼	8	9½	22	28	4 ft. 10	6 st. 0

No. 22. Entered Class Sept., 1905. Age 13 years 3 months.
MEASUREMENTS.

Date.	Acr. Chest, U.	I.	Acr. Back, U.	I.	Rnd. Ribs, U.	I.	Height.	Weight.
5/ 9/05	11	12¼	9¾	10¼	24½	27½	4 ft. 10¼	6 st. 1
15/12/05	12	13	9	10	24	30	4 ft. 11	6 st. 8
9/ 3/06	13½	14½	11	11¾	22¼	28	4 ft. 11¾	6 st. 13

No. 23. Entered Class Sept., 1905. Age 14 years.
MEASUREMENTS.

Date.	Acr. Chest, U.	I.	Acr. Back, U.	I.	Rnd. Ribs, U.	I.	Height.	Weight.
29/ 9/05	10	10½	11⅜	12½	23	25½	4 ft. 8	5 st. 0
16/12/05	10	12	10	11	23	26	4 ft. 8½	5 st. 5½
7/ 3/06	11	12¼	12	12¾	23½	26	4 ft. 9	5 st. 10¼

No. 24. Entered Class Sept., 1905. Age 13 years 1 month.
MEASUREMENTS.

Date.	Acr. Chest, U.	I.	Acr. Back, U.	I.	Rnd. Ribs, U.	I.	Height.	Weight.
5/ 9/05	11	12	9¾	10½	26	28	5 ft. 0¾	6 st. 10
16/12/05	11½	13	9	10	22	26	5 ft. 1½	7 st. 11
9/ 3/06	12¼	13½	10	11	23¼	28½	5 ft. 1¼	8 st. 0

REMARKS.
Right shoulder higher.

No. 25. Entered Class Sept., 1905. Age 13 years 3 months.
MEASUREMENTS.

Date.	Acr. Chest, U.	I.	Acr. Back, U.	I.	Rnd. Ribs, U.	I.	Height.	Weight.
5/ 9/05	10	11½	10	10½	25	29	4 ft. 10½	5 st. 13
15/12/05	12	13½	9½	10½	25	31	4 ft. 11	6 st. 0
8/ 3/06	10½	12½	10	11	24½	30	4 ft. 11	6 st. 6

No. 26. Entered Class Sept., 1905. Age 14 years 3 months.
MEASUREMENTS.

Date.	Acr. Chest, U.	I.	Acr. Back, U.	I.	Rnd. Ribs, U.	I.	Height.	Weight.
4/ 9/05	9¼	9½	12¼	12½	25	25¾	4 ft. 8½	5 st. 2½
12/12/05	10¼	11⅛	10	10½	25	27	4 ft. 8¼	5 st. 4
9/ 3/06	10¼	11	11½	11⅛	24¾	27½	4 ft. 9¼	5 st. 11

REMARKS.
Left shoulder slightly higher, ½ in. nearer spine at angle.
12/12/05 Left shoulder still higher, but angles more equal.

No. 27. Entered Class Sept., 1905. Age 13 years 11 months.
MEASUREMENTS.

Date.	Acr. Chest, U.	I.	Acr. Back, U.	I.	Rnd. Ribs, U.	I.	Height.	Weight.
6/ 9/05	10¼	10¾	10½	10¾	25	25½	4 ft. 5½	4 st. 12
16/12/05	9½	11¼	8	9	22	26	4 ft. 6	5 st. 0
9/ 3/06	11¼	11⅛	10	10⅜	21½	26¼	4 ft. 6¾	5 st. 0¼

No. 28. Entered Class Sept., 1905. Age 13 years.

MEASUREMENTS.

Date.	Acr. Chest, U.	I.	Acr. Back, U.	I.	Rnd. Ribs, U.	I.	Height.	Weight.
25/ 9/05	10¾	11	10¼	10½	25¾	26½	4 ft. 8½	5 st. 8½
15/12/05	9½	11	9	9½	23	26	4 ft. 9½	6 st. 3½
9/ 3/06	12¼	13	10	11⅛	24	27½	4 ft. 10	6 st. 12½

No. 29. Entered Class Sept., 1905. Age 13 years 6 months.

MEASUREMENTS.

Date.	Acr. Chest, U.	I.	Acr. Back, U.	I.	Rnd. Ribs, U.	I.	Height.	Weight.
6/ 9/05	10	10¾	10¾	11¼	25⅛	28	5 ft. 1¾	6 st. 10
16/12/05	10½	12	8½	9½	23½	30	5 ft. 2½	7 st. 5
8/ 3/06	11	13	9½	10½	24	30	5 ft. 2½	7 st. 13

No. 30. Entered Class Sept., 1905. Age 13 years 8 months.

MEASUREMENTS.

Date.	Acr. Chest, U.	I.	Acr. Back, U.	I.	Rnd. Ribs, U.	I.	Height.	Weight.
6/ 9/05	10¼	10½	8¼	9¼	23¾	25	4 ft. 7½	5 st. 3
15/12/05	10½	12	8	9	24½	27	4 ft. 8½	5 st. 8
9/ 3/06	11½	12¾	9¼	10⅛	23	27⅛	4 ft. 9	5 st. 12

No. 31. Entered Class Sept., 1905. Age 13 years 10 months.

MEASUREMENTS.

Date.	Acr. Chest, U.	I.	Acr. Back, U.	I.	Rnd. Ribs, U.	I.	Height.	Weight.
25/ 9/05	10½	10½	9	10	24¾	26	4 ft. 5	4 st. 10
11/12/05	10	10¾	9	10½	25¼	28	4 ft. 5½	5 st. 2
9/ 3/06	11	12⅛	10½	11⅛	23	26¾	4 ft. 5⅞	5 st. 0½

No. 32. Entered Class Sept., 1905. Age 14 years 1 month.

MEASUREMENTS.

Date.	Acr. Chest, U.	I.	Acr. Back, U.	I.	Rnd. Ribs, U.	I.	Height.	Weight.
25/ 9/05	10¼	10½	11¼	11¾	24¼	26	5 ft. 0	5 st. 9
13/12/05	11	12½	10	11⅞	22	26	5 ft. 0½	6 st. 0
9/ 3/06	12	13½	10¾	11⅞	22½	27½	5 ft. 1	6 st. 5½

No. 33. Entered Class Sept., 1905. Age 13 years 10 months.

MEASUREMENTS.

Date.	Acr. Chest, U.	I.	Acr. Back, U.	I.	Rnd. Ribs, U.	I.	Height.	Weight.
5/ 9/05	10½	11¼	9¾	10¼	24½	27	5 ft. 2	6 st. 7
13/12/05	12½	14	8	9	21½	26	5 ft. 2	7 st. 1
8/ 3/06	11	13	8	9	24	29	5 ft. 2½	7 st. 6

No. 34. Entered Class Sept., 1905. Age 14 years 4 months.

MEASUREMENTS.

Date.	Acr. Chest, U.	I.	Acr. Back, U.	I.	Rnd. Ribs, U.	I.	Height.	Weight.
4/ 9/05	10¼	10½	10¼	10¼	23	26	4 ft. 10¾	6 st. 7
12/12/05	11¼	12	10¾	11⅞	25	28	4 ft. 11¾	6 st. 11
7/ 3/06	12	13	10	10⅞	24½	28⅛	5 ft. 0	6 st. 9½

No. 35. Entered Class Sept., 1905. Age 13 years 4 months.

MEASUREMENTS.

Date.	Acr. Chest, U.	I.	Acr. Back, U.	I.	Rnd. Ribs, U.	I.	Height.	Weight.
4/ 9/05	11	11¾	11¾	12¼	25	28	5 ft. 0⅛	6 st. 8
12/12/05	11⅛	12¼	10¾	11½	24½	28½	5 ft. 1⅜	7 st. 0
7/ 3/06	11½	12¼	10⅞	11⅞	23½	27½	5 ft. 2¼	7 st. 3½

REMARKS.

Very slight deviation to right in upper dorsal. Shoulder blades prominent. 12/12/05 Improved.

No. 36. Entered Class Sept., 1905. Age 13 years 4 months.

MEASUREMENTS.

Date.	Acr. Chest, U.	I.	Acr. Back, U.	I.	Rnd. Ribs, U.	I.	Height.	Weight.
6/ 9/05	11	12¼	11	12	23	26	5 ft. 1¾	6 st. 10
15/12/05	10	11½	9	10	24⅛	28	5 ft. 2	6 st. 9
7/ 3/06	13	13½	10	11½	23⅜	26¾	5 ft. 2¾	7 st. 1

REMARKS.

Lordosis.

No. 37. Entered Class Sept., 1905. Age 13 years 3 months.

MEASUREMENTS.

Date.	Acr. Chest, U.	I.	Acr. Back. U.	I.	Rnd. Ribs, U.	I.	Height.	Weight.
25/ 9/05	10	10⅜	11¼	11¾	24½	26	4 ft. 8¼	5 st. 4
11/12/05	10¾	11¾	9½	10¾	26	29½	4 ft. 9	5 st. 7
7/ 3/06	11	11⅞	11½	12	24¼	28	4 ft. 9½	5 st. 9

REMARKS.

Round shoulders

No. 38. Entered Class Sept., 1905. Age 14 years 3 months.

MEASUREMENTS

Date.	Acr. Chest, U.	I.	Acr. Back, U.	I.	Rnd. Ribs, U.	I.	Height.	Weight
4/ 9/05	11	11¾	11	11¼	26	27½	4 ft. 9¾	6 st. 4
12/12/05	11	11½	11¼	11½	25½	27½	4 ft. 10	6 st. 9
7/ 3/06	11⅛	11¾	11½	12⅜	24⅛	27⅛	4 ft. 10¾	6 st. 11

No. 39. Entered Class Sept., 1905. Age 13 years 3 months.

MEASUREMENTS.

Date.	Acr. Chest, U.	I.	Acr. Back, U.	I.	Rnd. Ribs, U.	I.	Height.	Weight.
6/ 9/05	9	9½	9¼	9¾	22½	24½	4 ft. 7¼	4 st. 10
16/12/05	9⅜	11	8	9	24	27	4 ft. 8	5 st. 8
7/ 3/06	10⅛	11½	10	11½	23½	26½	4 ft. 8½	6 st. 0

No. 40. Entered Class Sept., 1905. Age 14 years 2 months.

MEASUREMENTS.

Date.	Acr. Chest, U.	I.	Acr. Back, U.	I.	Rnd. Ribs, U.	I.	Height.	Weight.
4/ 9/05	11	11½	10⅜	11½	25	26½	5 ft. 3	7 st. 0½
2/12/05	11	12	10	11	24	26	5 ft. 3¼	7 st. 6½
8/ 3/06	11	13½	8	9	24	30	5 ft. 4	8 st. 1

No. 41. Entered Class Sept., 1905. Age 14 years 8 months.

MEASUREMENTS.

Date.	Acr. Chest, U.	I.	Acr. Back, U.	I.	Rnd. Ribs, U.	I.	Height.	Weight.
25/ 9/05	10	10½	11	11½	23	24	4 ft. 10	5 st. 0
13/12/05	11	12	10	11	22	25	4 ft. 10¾	5 st. 1
8/ 3/06	11	12½	8	8½	22½	26	4 ft. 11⅛	5 st. 6

REMARKS.

Round shoulders. Adenoids.

No. 42. Entered Class Sept., 1905. Age 14 years 7 months.

MEASUREMENTS.

Date.	Acr. Chest, U.	I.	Acr. Back, U.	I.	Rnd. Ribs, U.	I.	Height.	Weight.
6/ 9/05	10	11	11½	11¾	26	29	4 ft. 10⅛	6 st. 6
16/12/05	11⅛	13½	8	9	22	29	4 ft. 11¼	7 st. 0½
8/ 3/06	11	13	9	10	23	29	4 ft. 11½	7 st. 6

REMARKS.

Round shoulders.

No. 43. Entered Class Sept., 1905. Age 14 years 4 months.

MEASUREMENTS.

Date.	Acr. Chest, U.	I.	Acr. Back, U.	I.	Rnd. Ribs, U.	I.	Height.	Weight.
5/ 9/05	9¾	10½	10½	10¾	25	28	5 ft.	6 st. 2
15/12/05	9¾	11	9	10	23	29	5 ft.	6 st. 6
10/ 3/06	11½	12½	10¾	11½	24	29	5 ft. 0¾	6 st. 13

No. 44. Entered Class Sept., 1905. Age 14 years 8 months.

MEASUREMENTS.

Date.	Acr. Chest, U.	I.	Acr. Back, U.	I.	Rnd. Ribs, U.	I.	Height.	Weight.
4/ 9/05	10	10⅞	10	10⅞	24½	25¾	4 ft. 10½	6 st. 0
10/ 3/06	11	11⅝	10⅝	10⅛	24½	27½	4 ft. 10⅞	6 st. 10

REMARKS.

Round shoulders. Poking head.
10/3/06 Shoulders improved ; head improving.

No. 45. Entered Class Sept., 1905. Age 14 years 1 month.

MEASUREMENTS.

Date.	Acr. Chest, U.	I.	Acr. Back, U.	I.	Rnd. Ribs, U.	I.	Height.	Weight.
4/ 9/05	10	10½	11¾	12¾	24	26	4 ft. 11	5 st. 7
12/12/05	10½	11	10¾	11½	25	27	5 ft.	6 st. 0
10/ 3/06	11	12	11¾	12⅛	24	27	5 ft. 0¾	6 st. 4

REMARKS.

Round shoulders, left shoulder higher.
10/3/06 Shoulders improved, but left still higher.

No. 46. Entered Class Sept., 1905. Age 14 years 3 months.

MEASUREMENTS.

Date.	Acr. Chest, U.	I.	Acr. Back, U.	I.	Rnd. Ribs, U.	I.	Height.	Weight.
5/ 9/05	9½	10	8¾	9	25	28	4 ft. 10¾	6 st. 4
15/12/05	10	12	8	9	24	28	4 ft. 11⅛	6 st. 5
10/ 3/06	11⅛	12⅛	10	11⅛	23	27½	4 ft. 11⅛	6 st. 7½

No. 47. Entered Class Sept., 1905. Age 13 years 3 months.

MEASUREMENTS.

Date.	Acr. Chest, U.	I.	Acr. Back, U.	I.	Rnd. Ribs, U.	I.	Height.	Weight.
25/ 9/05	11¼	11½	12	12½	25	26½	5 ft. 0¼	7 st. 8
12/12/05	11½	13	9¾	10	24	28	5 ft. 1	7 st. 9
7/ 3/06	11¼	11⅞	11¼	12¾	24	28½	5 ft. 1¼	7 st. 13

No. 48. Entered Class Sept., 1905. Age 13 years 7 months.

MEASUREMENTS.

Date.	Acr. Chest, U.	I.	Acr. Back, U.	I.	Rnd. Ribs, U.	I.	Height.	Weight.
4/ 9/05	10½	11	8¾	9¼	22½	24½	4 ft. 10	5 st. 2½
12/12/05	12	12¾	9⅛	10	25	26¼	4 ft. 10¾	5 st. 7½
8/ 3/06	10¾	12¼	8	9	21½	27	4 ft. 11⅛	5 st. 13

No. 49. Entered Class Sept., 1905. Age 13 years 2 months.

MEASUREMENTS.

Date.	Acr. Chest, U.	I.	Acr. Back, U.	I.	Rnd. Ribs, U.	I.	Height.	Weight.
6/ 9/05	11¼	11½	9	9½	23½	26	4 ft. 8¼	5 st. 10
11/12/05	12	13¼	7¾	9	24	28	4 ft. 9½	6 st. 8
8/ 3/06	12	14¼	9	10	23½	30	4 ft. 10⅛	7 st. 2

No. 50. Entered Class Sept., 1905. Age 14 years 6 months.

MEASUREMENTS.

Date.	Acr. Chest, U.	I.	Acr. Back, U.	I.	Rnd. Ribs, U.	I.	Height.	Weight.
5/ 9/05	10¼	11	9	9¾	24	27	5 ft. 3¾	6 st. 10
15/12/05	11	12½	9½	10½	24	29	5 ft. 4	6 st. 13½
9/ 3/06	12	13	10⅛	11¼	25	29	5 ft. 4	7 st. 0

No. 51. Entered Class Sept., 1905. Age 14 years 1 month.

MEASUREMENTS.

Date.	Acr. Chest, U.	I.	Acr. Back, U.	I.	Rnd. Ribs, U.	I.	Height.	Weight.
6/ 9/05	10¾	11¼	11½	12	26½	29	5 ft. 0¼	6 st. 13
14/12/05	11¼	12½	8½	10	27	30	5 ft. 1	7 st. 6
8/ 3/06	10¾	12¼	9½	10½	25	30	5 ft. 1¼	7 st. 2

No. 52. Entered Class Sept., 1905. Age 13 years 9 months.

MEASUREMENTS.

Date.	Acr. Chest, U.	I.	Acr. Back, U.	I.	Rnd. Ribs, U.	I.	Height.	Weight.
6/ 9/05	12¼	12½	11	11½	23	26	5 ft. 3¾	7 st. 7
11/12/05	13	14¼	8¾	11½	25	29	5 ft. 3¾	8 st. 6
9/ 3/06	13¼	14½	12	13¼	22½	28	5 ft. 3⅝	8 st. 9

APPENDIX IV

WAGES BOARDS BILL.

MEMORANDUM.

The object of this Bill is to provide for the establishment of Wages Boards with power to fix the minimum rate of wages to be paid to workers in particular trades. It is left to the Home Secretary to say for what trades Wages Boards are to be appointed, so that, at all events in the first instance, Wages Boards need be appointed only for what are known as the "sweated industries," that is, industries in which outworkers are largely employed, and in which the rate of remuneration is low. A Wages Board will have power to fix a minimum rate for any single kind of work or for any single class of workers in a particular trade. They will have the widest discretion as to fixing a time rate or a piece-work rate, and as to varying the minimum according to the kind of work and the class of persons employed. The Bill provides that a Wages Board shall be composed of representatives of employers and representatives of employed in equal numbers, with a chairman chosen by the members or nominated by the Home Secretary. It is proposed to entrust the enforcement of payment of the minimum rate to factory inspectors.

WAGES BOARDS BILL.

ARRANGEMENT OF CLAUSES.

A

BILL

TO

Provide for the Establishment of Wages Boards.

A.D. 1906.

Be it enacted by the King's most Excellent Majesty, by and with the advice and consent of the Lords Spiritual and Temporal, and Commons, in this present Parliament assembled, and by the authority of the same, as follows :—

1.—(1) The Secretary of State may, if he thinks fit, on application being made and an inquiry being held as herein-after provided, direct that a wages board shall be appointed in the manner herein-after provided for any trade in any district.

Appointment and powers of wages board.

(2) A wages board shall have power to make regulations fixing the minimum rate of wages to be paid to persons employed in their district in or about their trade.

2.—(1) Application for the appointment of a wages board for any trade in any district may be made to the Secretary of State by any trade union or trades council which represents persons employed in the trade in the district, or by any six persons who are either employers of labour or employed in the trade in the district.

Applications and inquiries.

(2) On application being made as provided in this section, the Secretary of State shall cause an inquiry to be held into the desirability of appointing a wages board in accordance

with the application, and the provisions of sections forty-five and forty-six of the Coal Mines Regulation Act, 1887, shall apply to the inquiry with the necessary modifications.

Composition and mode of appointment of wages board.

3.—(1) A wages board shall consist of a chairman and such number of other members, not less than four and not more than ten, as the Secretary of State in each case may determine.

(2) One half of the number of members other than the chairman shall be representatives of employers and one half representatives of persons employed in the trade in the district.

(3) The representatives of employers and of persons employed shall be chosen by the employers and the persons employed respectively in such manner as the Secretary of State may on each occasion determine, or in default of such choice being made shall be nominated by the Secretary of State.

(4) The chairman shall be chosen by the other members within *fourteen days* from their appointment, or in default shall be nominated by the Secretary of State.

Term of office, resignation, and casual vacancies.

4.—(1) The term of office of a wages board shall be *five years*, or such shorter time not being less than *two years* as the Secretary of State may in any case at any time determine, and at the end of such term of office all the members of the board shall go out of office.

(2) The chairman or any other member of a wages board may resign on giving to the board one month's previous notice in writing of his intention to do so.

(3) A casual vacancy on a wages board among the representatives of employers, or among the representatives of persons employed, shall be filled by the remaining representatives of employers or of persons employed, as the case may be within *fourteen days* after the vacancy occurs, or in default the Secretary of State shall nominate a new representative of employers or of persons employed.

Manner of calculating minimum rate of wages.

5.—(1) The minimum rate of wages fixed by a wages board may be calculated either by time or by piece-work, or so as to give an employer the option of paying either by time or by piece-work, except that in case of work given out from factory or workshop or other place to be done elsewhere it shall be calculated by piece-work only.

(2) The minimum rate of wages may be fixed for any kind or kinds of work in a trade, and may be different for different kinds of work, as the board think fit.

(3) The minimum rate of wages may be fixed for any class or classes of persons employed in a trade, and may be different for different classes of persons employed, as the board think fit.

6.—(1) Regulations made by a wages board fixing a minimum rate or rates of wages for a trade in their district shall state the date from which the minimum rate or rates of wages shall be established, and the minimum rate or rates of wages shall be established for that trade in that district as from that date, and shall continue established until they are cancelled by the wages board or their successors.

Establishment, publication, and evidence of minimum rate of wages

(2) Such regulations shall be published as soon as they are made, in such manner as the Secretary of State may direct.

(3) Section eighty-six of the Factory and Workshop Act, 1901, so far as it relates to the publication of regulations under that Act in factories and workshops, shall apply to the publication of regulations under this Act as if they were regulations under that Act.

(4) A document purporting to be a copy of regulations under this Act, and to be signed by an inspector appointed under the Factory and Workshop Act, 1901, shall be evidence (but not to the exclusion of other proof) of the regulations and of the minimum rate or rates of wages fixed by them, and of the fact of the due establishment of the minimum rate or rates under this Act.

7.—(1) Any determination of a wages board under this Act may be made by a majority of the members present.

Proceedings of wages boards

(2) On all questions which come before a wages board the chairman, besides his ordinary vote, shall have an additional or casting vote.

(3) The Secretary of State when determining the number of members of a wages board, shall determine what number of members, not being more than one half of the total number members, shall form a quorum, but the formation of a

A.D. 1906.

quorum shall not depend on the presence of any number or proportion of representatives either of employers or of persons employed.

Offences and penalties.

8.—(1) Where a minimum rate of wages is established in any district for any class of persons employed in any kind of work in any trade, any person carrying on business in the district who pays or offers wages, or on whose behalf wages are paid or offered, at a lower rate than the minimum, to any person of that class employed by him in that kind of work in that trade, shall be guilty of an offence against this Act.

(2) If wages are paid or offered by time where the minimum rate established is calculated by piece-work, or if wages are paid or offered by piece-work where the minimum rate established is calculated by time, the wages shall be deemed to be paid or offered at a lower rate than the minimum.

(3) Any person guilty of an offence against this Act shall be liable on summary conviction in case of a first conviction to a fine of not less than *one pound* or more than *five pounds* for each offence, and in case of a second or subsequent conviction within *two years* from the last conviction to a fine of not less than *two pounds* and not more than *twenty pounds* for each offence.

Enforcement of Act by factory inspectors.

9. It shall be the duty of inspectors appointed under the Factory and Workshop Act, 1901, to enforce the provisions of this Act within their districts, and for this purpose they shall have the same powers and authorities as they have for the purpose of enforcing the provisions of that Act, *and all expenses incurred by them under this Act shall be deemed to be expenses incurred by them under that Act.*

Interpretation.

10. In this Act, unless the context otherwise requires,—

The expression " trade " means any manufacture, process, trade, or business ;

The expression " district " means any local area, whether county, borough, part of a county, or part of a borough within the discretion of the Secretary of State.

Commencement of Act. Short title.

11. This Act shall come into operation on the *first day of January one thousand nine hundred and seven.*

12. This Act may be cited as the Wages Board Act, 1906.

APPENDIX V

Specimens of Investigation Cards used for the Purposes of Inquiry into Individual Cases.

June 15.04   SPECIAL INDIVIDUAL'S CARD.   Investigator....*F.W.W.*.....

Trade *Printer* . Sub. Div.*Layer on* M.S. Name *M.B.* Age *22* Emplr. *A.B.* *Bee here 5 years*

Wages:—Min. *4/.*   Increase 6 *10/.*   Max *10/.*

Time Rate per hr.:—Day — O'time *none now* Home work. —

Deductions *if late, stop time? ? this for 1st half* Average weekly wage *10/.* *no 2 is*

know, 2 hrs after p.m. Sat'dy   *1*   Overtime *limited & T.*

Hours:—a.m. *8*   Din.   *7*   Tea *½ hour* Where taken *same room* *has stopped all overtime*

Meals:—Bkfst. *none*   *1-2*   Where taken *same room*

Promotions *none possible*

Wages compared to Men's same trade *boys get more*   If lower, why? *Can't say — paid class same work ?*

Is it dirty, dangerous or unhealthy? *Yes (see over)* Strgth. or Intel. needed. *Both.*

Prop. of married and single *none married*   Age of marriage —

Weekly payts. to H'hold Exs. at home *6/.*   In lodgings —

Amt. saved yearly *none*   Amt. paid to sick clubs *to Hospital*

Training:—Age *13*   Method —   Prem. —   Wages during —

Organisation —   Any attempted —   Attitude towards —

Trade flourishing, or decreasing *Busy*   Season trade? *Before Christmas.*

How many short weeks in a year *Holidays and 1 week Stocktaking.* *Very busy now.*

Is separate Sanitary convenience provided for Men and Women? *Yes. new.*   *P.T.O.*

Wages raised every six months by 6

Pays 1/6 a week into Money Club to clear rent £1.

* Dirty when washing machine.
Dangerous. They get hands cut off if careless.
Unhealthy. But smells bad, & spoils appetite, as
hanging is very unhealthy – milk allowed.

WOMEN'S WORK and the HOME.   Investigator...*G.D*...........

Trade *Surgical Belt* Sub. Div. *Sewing.* Name *Mrs L.*

Occupation & wage of Husband *Baker* 24/.   No. of rooms in house *3*

Habits of Husband *Industrious now*   Rent *5/.*

Amt. given by Woman to H'hold Exs *10/.*   Emplt. of W'n prev. to M'ge *Sewing*

Any other income *2 daughters work*   Wages " " " *10/.*

Cost of care of Children during day —   Age of Marriage *18*

Health and attendance at School of Children *Good health*   *Fairly regular*

Number and age of Children *18, 11, 8, 5, 4, 2, (4 at school)*   Comfort of Home *Father untidy*

Are Children well cared for? *Fairly well*   What "Class"? *Fairly respectable.*

Left work at all during married life? *No*   How is leisure spent? *Sewing*

If so, why started work again? —

(over)

My husband used to drink; more industrious the last twelve months.

Jan. 19. 04. SPECIAL INDIVIDUAL'S CARD. Investigator....M.C.M......

Trade *Jewellery* Sub. Div. *Polisher* M.S. Name *L.R.* Age 20 Emplr. *C.D.* 3 years here

Wages:—Min. 6/. Increase to 12/. Max £1 possible at best work

Time Rate per hr.:—Day — O'time *same rate as day* Home work. —

Deductions *Pay cost if late* Average weekly wage 12/.

Hours:—a.m. 8 p.m. 7 Sat'dy 12 Overtime occasionally

Meals:—Bkfst. *Lunch while* Din. 1—2.10 Tea 15 minutes Where taken work room.
work Longer if they like

Promotions *hardly any chance*

Wages compared to Men's same trade *Men make* If lower, why? *Different work.*

Is it dirty, dangerous or unhealthy? *Rather dirty* ⇒ Strgth. or Intel. needed. *Intelligence*
unhealthy (see over) (see over)

Prop. of married and single *Only 4 gvals* — *None married* Age of marriage —

Weekly payts. to H'hold Exs. at home 6/6 In lodgings —

Amt. saved yearly *Could save. but* Amt. paid to sick clubs 1 week to Hospital
does it save much. Saturday 2d ⇒ optional

Training:—Age — Method *7 yrs full* Prem. *earned* Wages during 6/. to start

Organisation — Any attempted — Attitude towards —

Trade flourishing, or decreasing *Decreasing* *now* but Season trade? Oct. & Xmas busy.
now *Please note bad.*

How many short weeks in a year — Generally short in summer.

Is separate Sanitary convenience provided for Men and Women? Yes, & own wash.
R.T.O.

Not extra clean work. Rouge said to be bad for
chest, but she does not think it enough to hurt.
Work very trying to the eyes.

Very nice place. She likes it. *Master very kind.*

Only the best work done (Rings &c set with diamonds &c)

Stages of polishing {
1. Thread the rings, &c. rub them with emery. *Rubbed.*
2. rouge them to brighten the colour.
3. Gilding

Stones can be set   before)   polishing, but usually set
                              after.

INDEX

___

INDEX

Factory influence, effects of, 48, 193, 200, 267

Factory inspectors, 26, 34, 36, 43

Factory inspectors, insufficient number of, 266

Factory legislation, 19 *et seq.*

Factory work, opinion of workers on, 113, 114, 115, 116

"Facts for Socialists," 144*n*

Family income, 151, 153, 154, 155, 157, 160, 164, 173, 179, 227

Family income, inadequacy of, 217, 228, 230, 235

Fancy leather goods, 82, 85, 324

Felling, 100, 101

Fines, 93, 107, 193, 200, 204, 208, 257

Finishing, 91

Fire-iron making, 41

Fish-curing, 27, 321

Fittings, 77

Flat chain-making, 50

Food and tobacco workers, 45

Food workers, 105, 320

Folding, 91

Forming, 55, 57

Frame-making, 85

Free apprenticeship, suggested necessity for, 229

French polishing as a temptation to drunkenness, 81

French polishing, process of, 78

French polishing trade, 38, 46, 77, 166, 219, 244, 325, 331

Fruit preserving, 27

Furniture trades, 45, 77, 325

Gas, contribution towards cost of, 95

Gas fumes, 70

General attitude with regard to women's work and wages, 89, 132, 260, 262, 263

Germany, 104*n*, 123*n*

Ginger-beer making, 149

Gipsy party, 239*n*

Girls taking place of boys, 40

Girls' clubs, classes, &c., 265 *et seq. See also* "Social Clubs," "Technical Classes," "Dinner-hour Meetings," &c.

Girls' Friendly Society, 268, 275

Girth stitching, 168

Glasgow, 106, 135, 169

Glasgow Council for Women's Trades, *see* Scottish Council for Women's Trades.

Glass work, 105, 326

Gold and silver chain trade, 263, 322

Gold and silver cheap jewellery, 40

Gold-cutting, 74

Gold-frosting, 74

Gold-leaf cutting, process of, 74

Gough, G. W., 297 *quoted*

Government work, 83, 120*n*

Grinding (pen trade), 55, 316

Grouping, methods of, 44

Gun and sword making, 33

Gun-bag making, 168

Gun-stock polishing, 149, 166

Habits of husbands, 214, 215, 216, 218, 220, 228

Hair curlers, 263, 314

Halesowen, 23

Half-time system, 99

Hand burnishing, 46, 66

Hand lacquering, 46, 66, 68

Hand stitching, 42, 83, 84

Harness-making, 40, 42, 82, 83, 84, 130, 163, 324

Hawkers: hawking, 113, 162, 179, 210, 219, 330

Health of children, comparison of those of occupied and unoccupied married women, 221

Heavy work, 48, 62, 63, 81

Hinge-making, 41, 314

"History of Factory Legislation," 23*n*, 25*n*, 26*n*

Holiday home, influence of, 277

"Home Industries in Birmingham," 145*n*

Home life, necessity for a better, 247

Home work, *see* Outwork

"Home work amongst women," 135*n*

Home work, definition of, 145

Home work, help of children in 150, 151, 153, 160

UNWIN BROTHERS, LIMITED, PRINTERS, WOKING AND LONDON.

The List of Titles
in the Garland Series

9. Edward Cadbury, M. Cécile Matheson and George Shann. **Women's Work and Wages.** London, 1906.

10. Arnold Freeman. **Boy Life and Labour. The Manufacture of Inefficiency.** London, 1914.

11. Edward G. Howarth and Mona Wilson. **West Ham. A Study in Social and Industrial Problems.** London, 1907.

12. B.L. Hutchins. **Women in Modern Industry.** London, 1915.

13. M. Loane. **From Their Point of View.** London, 1908.

14. J. Ramsay Macdonald. **Women in the Printing Trades. A Sociological Study.** London, 1904.

15. C.F.G. Masterman. **From the Abyss. Of Its Inhabitants by One of Them.** London, 1902.

16. L.C. Chiozza Money. **Riches and Poverty.** London, 1906.

17. Richard Mudie-Smith, Ed. **Handbook of the "Daily News" Sweated Industries' Exhibition.** London, 1906.

18. Edward Abbott Parry. **The Law and the Poor.** London, 1914.

19. Alexander Paterson. **Across the Bridges. Or Life by the South London River-side.** London, 1911.

20. M.S. Pember-Reeves. **Round About a Pound a Week.** London, 1913.

21. B. Seebohm Rowntree. **Poverty. A Study of Town Life.** London, 1910 (2nd ed.).

22. B. Seebohm Rowntree and Bruno Lasker. **Unemployment. A Social Study.** London, 1911.

23. B. Seebohm Rowntree and A.C. Pigou. **Lectures on Housing.** Manchester, 1914.

24. C.E.B. Russell. **Social Problems of the North.** London and Oxford, 1913.

25. Henry Solly. **Working Men's Social Clubs and Educational Institutes.** London, 1904.

26. E.J. Urwick, Ed. **Studies of Boy Life in Our Cities.** London, 1904.

27. Alfred Williams. **Life in a Railway Factory.** London, 1915.

28. [Women's Co-operative Guild]. **Maternity. Letters from Working-Women, Collected by the Women's Co-operative Guild with a preface by the Right Hon. Herbert Samuel, M.P.** London, 1915.

29. Women's Co-operative Guild. **Working Women and Divorce. An Account of Evidence Given on Behalf of the Women's Co-operative Guild before the Royal Commission on Divorce.** London, 1911.

    bound with Anna Martin. **The Married Working Woman. A Study.** London, 1911.